Bartleby in Manhattan

Elizabeth Hardwick

Bartleby
in Manhattan
and Other Essays

VINTAGE BOOKS
A DIVISION OF RANDOM HOUSE
NEW YORK

First Vintage Books Edition, May 1984
Copyright © 1962, 1963, 1964, 1965, 1966, 1967, 1968,
1970, 1974, 1975, 1976, 1978, 1979, 1980, 1981, 1982, 1983
by Elizabeth Hardwick
All rights reserved under International and Pan-American Copyright
Conventions. Published in the United States by Random House, Inc.,
New York, and simultaneously in Canada by Random House of Canada
Limited, Toronto. Originally published by Random House Inc. in 1983.

Some of these essays had been previously published in *Daedalus, The
New York Review of Books,* and *The New York Times Book Review.*

Grateful acknowledgment is made to The New York Times Company for
permission to reprint "Simone Weil" and "Nabokov: Master Class."
Copyright © 1977, 1980 by The New York Times Company. Reprinted
by permission.

Library of Congress Cataloging in Publication Data
Hardwick, Elizabeth.
Bartleby in Manhattan, and other essays.
I. Title.
[PS3515.A5672B3 1984]   814'.52   83-40315
ISBN 0-394-72374-0 (pbk.)

Manufactured in the United States of America

To Robert Silvers

Acknowledgments

Minor changes have been made in most of these essays. "Sad Brazil" has been considerably altered and expanded. "Simone Weil," "Thomas Mann at 100," and "Nabokov: Master Class" appeared in *The New York Times Book Review*. "Domestic Manners" was first published in *Daedalus*. The rest of the essays were printed in *The New York Review of Books*. I am grateful to the editors of these publications for the opportunity to write them and for permission to reprint them.

Contents

part one: OUT IN THE COUNTRY

The Charms of Goodness   3

The Apotheosis of Martin Luther King   9

The Oswald Family   20

Militant Nudes   29

The Portable Canterbury   41

part two: LIVES AND LOCAL SCENERY

Ring Lardner   59

Robert Frost in His Letters   64

Sex and the Single Man   73

Domestic Manners   79

A Bunch of Reds   98

part three: AFTER GOING TO THE THEATER

A Death at Lincoln Center   121

The Theater of Grotowski   127

Auschwitz in New York   140

Timon of Paris   146

part four: MEMORIES

Simone Weil   157

Svetlana   166

Thomas Mann at 100   174

Wives and Mistresses   183

Nabokov: Master Class   207

part five: READINGS

Bartleby in Manhattan   217

Sue and Arabella   232

Sad Brazil   244

The Sense of the Present   260

English Visitors in America   273

part one

⬥⟨⟨

Out in the Country

The Charms of Goodness

What a sad countryside it is, the home of the pain of the Confederacy, the birthplace of the White Citizens Council. The khaki-colored earth, the tense air, the vanquished feeding on their permanent Civil War—all of it inevitably brings to mind flamboyant adjectives and images from Faulkner. Immemorial, doomed streets, policed by the Snopeses and Peter Grimms, alleys worn thin in the sleepless pursuit of a thousand Joe Christmases, and Miss Coldfield and Quentin behind the dusty lattices, in the "empty hall echoing with sonorous, defeated names." And as you pass Big Swamp Creek, you imagine you hear the yelp of movie bloodhounds. The cabins, pitifully beautiful, set back from the road, with a trail of wood smoke fringing the sky; the melancholy frogs unmindful of the highway and the cars slipping by; the tufts of moss, like piles of housedust, that hang trembling on the bare winter trees; the road that leads at last to just the dead Sunday afternoon Main Streets you knew were there. We've read it all, again and again. We've seen it in the movies, in the Farm Security Administration photographs of almost thirty years ago: the voteless blacks, waiting tentatively on the courthouse steps, the angry jowls of the racists, the washed-out children, the enduring Negroes, the police, the same old sheriff: the entire region is fiction, art, dated, something out of a second-hand bookstore. And this, to be sure, is the "Southern way of life," or part of it—these photographs of a shack standing under a brilliant sky, the blackest of faces, the whitest mansions with front-porch columns, the impacted dirt of the bus station, the little, cottagey, non-denominational churches, standing in the dust, leaning a bit, and the big Methodist and Baptist with yellow brick turrets and fat belfries. If this that meets the eye as an expectation as familiar as the New York City skyline is not the South, what can the word mean? The rest might be anywhere, everywhere—mobile homes, dead cars in the yard, ranch houses shading their eyes with plastic awnings.

Life arranges itself for you here in Selma in the most conventional tableaux. Juxtapositions and paradoxes fit only for the most superficial art present themselves again and again. The "crisis" reduces the landscape to genre. At their best the people who rule over Selma, Alabama, seem to suffer from a preternatural foolishness and at their worst just now from a schizophrenic meanness. Just as they use the Confederate flag, so they use themselves, without embarrassment, in the old pageantry. A tableau which might have been thought up decades ago by one of the Hollywood Ten: the eary morning fog is lifting and a band of civil rights demonstrators stands at its post at the end of a dusty street. At just that moment a State Highway truck appears and lets out three desolate Negro convicts wearing black and white striped convict uniforms, uniforms still in use but appearing to the contemporary eye to be a selection from a costume warehouse. The convicts take up their brooms and, heads down, jailhouse and penitentiary hopelessness clinging to them, begin their morose sweeping up. The brooms meet the very shoelaces of the demonstrators, brush against the hem of a nun's black skirts. Soon the soft melodies fall on the heads of the convicts: We will overcome or else go home to our Lord and be free.

Great, great, we say of the arrangement, the curious, fortuitous performance. Then off the convicts shuffle in their black and white trousers, part of Alabama's humble devotion to symbolism.

How do they see themselves, these posse-men, Sheriff Clark's volunteers, nearly always squat, fair-faced, middle-aged, now wearing helmets and carrying guns and sticks? The state troopers seem one ghostly step ahead on the social ladder. The troopers ride around in cars, their coats hanging primly in the back seat. They might be salesmen, covering the territory, on to the evening's motel. The posse-men do not appear contented or prideful so much as merely obsessive and meager, joyless, unconsoled. The ignoble posture one observes so frequently in them is a puzzle. This cramped, hunched distance from bodily, even from masculine, grace makes them indeed among the saddest-looking people in the world. Even the hungry, bone-thin poor of Recife do not present such a picture of deep, almost hereditary, depression.

This group of Southerners has only the nothingness of racist preoccupation, the burning incoherence. Their bereft, static existence seems to go back many generations and has its counter-part in the violent, deranged hopelessness of the deprived youth in the cities. Here in the ameliorating sunlight of the Civil Rights Movement, the volunteer posse-men lead one to thoughts of remedial assistance. Who will open the doors of the University of Alabama or Clemson or Tulane to the children of Klansmen?

A poor young man, a native of Alabama, in a hot, cheap black suit, and the most insistent of false teeth clinging to gums not over twenty-one years old, back-country accent, pale, with that furry whiteness of a caterpillar, rimless glasses, stiff shoes, all misery and weakness and character armor, said to me, "When I saw those white folks mixed in with the colored it made me right sick." And what could one answer: Go to see your social worker, find an agency that can help you, some family counsellor, or perhaps an out-patient clinic? I did say, softly, "Pull yourself together." And he too shuffled off, like the convicts, his head bent down in some deep perturbation of spirit.

What charity can lift up the young man? There are no students welcomed to sleep on the floor of the racist home, no guitars and folk lyrics transposed to the key of the moment. It is true that these outcasts, men who are not in the state legislature and who do not belong to "nice" white Southern society because they are back-country and ignorant of style, make certain claims. They carry guns and whips and vote for the senators and governors. They try to have influence over who buys the books in the window in Montgomery (*Herzog, Les Mots* in translation) and subscribes to *The New Republic*. They keep in line, or try to, those Southern queers who are "mad about Negroes" and who collect jazz records. Their main "influence" is over the black population, an influence their very existence assures. And yet they are a degraded and despised people, even if their ferrety kinsman, Lester Maddox, can get on the ballot in Georgia.

The intellectual life in New York and the radical tone of the Thirties are the worst possible preparation for Alabama at this stage of the Civil Rights Movement. In truth it must be said that the demonstrators are an embarrassment of love and brotherhood and hymns offered up in Jesus' name and evening services after that. Intellectual pride is out of place, theory is simple and practical, action is exuberant and communal, the battlefield is out-of-doors and demands of one a certain youthful athleticism that would, in a morning's work, rip the veins of the old Stalinists and Trotskyites.

The political genius of Martin Luther King is, by any theory, quite unexpected. The nature of his protest, the quality and extent of his success sprang from the soil of religion and practicality most liberals had thought to be barren. Looking back, it is curious to remember how small a part the Negro's existence played in the earlier left-wing movements. The concentration on industrial labor, white sharecroppers, the Soviet Union and the Nazis left the Negro as only a footnote. That it should with King have come to this was unthinkable: this cloud of witnesses, this confrontation of hymn singers and local authorities. Martyred clergymen, Negro children killed at their Sunday School prayers, the ideas of Gandhi imposed upon restless blacks and belligerent whites—these appear as some sort of mutation of a national strain. "God will take care of you," they sing, Billy Eckstine style.

In the demonstrations and marches in Alabama you are watching—good people. The foundation is the Civil Rights Movement built by Southern Negroes and into this plot, like so many extras, these fantastic white people have come. On that "hallowed spot," Sylvan Street in Selma, you feel you are witness to a new Appomattox played out with the help of exceedingly refined, somewhat feminine Yankee clerics, upright people, marching in their prudent overshoes, some of them wearing Chesterfield coats with velvet collars.

The deputy sheriff spoke of these "so-called ministers," but that indeed was a joke. Even a deputy can see that these are preacher faces. On a Sunday after the white churches had turned away the groups of "mixed worshippers" who had knocked at the doors, a Church of Christ found a verse in the Gospel of Matthew that seemed to explain the refusal of the morning. The verse was put up outside in the announcement box and it read: "When you pray, be not as hypocrites are, standing in the street."

But of course hypocrisy is as foreign to these people as vice and that, perhaps, is their story. There is no doubt that they have been, before this opportunity to be a witness, suffering from considerable frustration, aching with the shame of a Christian who is busy most of the time ridding the church of the doctrine of the past as he waits for some meaning in the present. The moral justice of the Civil Rights Movement, the responsible program of the leaders, the murderous rage of the white people: this was the occasion at last. For the late-comers perhaps the immediate instrument had to be the death of a young white idealistic Protestant minister.

So, in Alabama the cause is right, the need is great, but there is more to it than that. There is the positive attraction between the people. The racists, with their fear of touch, their savage superstition, their reading of portents, see before them something more than voting rights. They sense the elation, the unexpected release. Few of us have shared any life as close as those "on location" in the Civil Rights Movement. Shared beds and sofas, hands caressing the shoulders of little children, smiles and a spreading comradeship, absorption: this is, as the pilgrims say again and again, a great experience. The police, protected by their helmets, are frightened and confused by these seizures of happiness. The odd thing is that it should not be beatniks and hipsters and bohemians who are sending out the message, but good, clean, downright folk in glasses and wearing tie clasps.

The Apotheosis of
Martin Luther King

The decaying, downtown shopping section of Memphis—still another Main Street—lay, the weekend before Martin Luther King's funeral, under a siege. The deranging curfew and that state of civic existence called "tension" made the town seem to be sinister, again very much like a film set, perhaps for a television drama, of breakdown, catastrophe. Since films and television have staged everything imaginable before it happens, a true event, taking place in the real world, brings to mind the landscape of films. There is no meaning in this beyond description and real life only looks like a fabrication and does not feel so.

The streets are completely empty of traffic and persons and yet the emptiness is the signal of dire and dramatic possibilities. In the silence, the horn of a tug gliding up the dark Mississippi is background. The hotel, downtown, overlooking the city park, is a tomb and perhaps that is usual since it is downtown where nobody wants to go in middle-sized cities. It is a shabby place, poorly staffed by aged persons, not grown old in their duties, but newly hired, untrained, depressed, worn-out old people.

The march was called for the next day, a march originally called by King as a renewal of his efforts in the Memphis garbage strike, efforts interrupted by a riot in the poor, black sections the week before. Now he was murdered and the march was called to honor him. Fear of riots, rage, had brought the curfew and the National Guard. Perhaps there was fear, but in civic crises there is always something exciting and even a sort of humidity of smugness seemed to hang over the town. Children kept home from school, bank and ten-cent store closed. If one was not in clear danger, there seemed to be a complacent pleasure in thinking, We have been brought to this by Them.

Beyond and beneath the glassy beige curtains of the hotel room, the courthouse square was spread out like a target, the destination of the next day's march and ceremony. All night long little hammer blows, a ghostly percussion, rang out as the structure for the "event" was being put together. The stage, slowly forming, plank by plank, seemed in the deluding curfew emptiness and silence like a scaffolding being prepared for a beheading. These overwrought and exaggerated images came to me from the actual scene and from a crush of childhood memories. Memphis was a Southern town in which a murder had taken place. The killer might be over yonder in that deep blue thicket, or holed up in the woods on the edge of town, ready to come back at night. Of course this was altogether different. The assassin's work was completed. Here in Memphis it was not the killer, whoever he might be, who was feared, but the killed one and what his death might bring.

Not far from the downtown was the leprous little hovel where, from a squalid toilet window, the assassin had been able to look across and target the new and hopeful Lorraine Motel. Now the motel was being visited by mourners. The black people of Memphis, dressed in their best, filed silently up and down the ramp, glancing shyly into the room which King had occupied. At the ramp before the door of the room where he fell there were flowers, glads and potted azaleas.

All over the Negro section, rickety little stores, emptied in the "consumer rebellion," were boarded up, burned out, or simply empty, with the windows broken. The stores were for the most part of great modesty. Who owned that one? I asked the taxi driver.

"Well, that happened to be Chinee," he said.

Shops are a dwelling and their goods and stuffs, counters and cash registers are a form of interior decoration. Sacked and disordered, these Memphis boxes were amazingly small and only an active sense of possibility could conceive of them as the site of commercial enterprise. It did not seem possible that by stocking a few shelves these squares of rotting timber could merit ownership, license, investment and produce a profitable exchange. They are lean-tos, chicken coops—measly and optimistic. Looters had sought the consolations of television sets and whiskey. The intrepid dramas of refrigerators and living room suites, deftly transported from store to home, were beyond the range of this poor section of the romantic city on the river.

The day of the march came to the gray, empty streets. The march was solemn and impressive, but on the other hand perhaps somewhat disappointing. A compulsive exaggeration dogs most of the expectations of ideological gatherings and thereby turns success to failure. The forty to sixty thousand predicted belittled the eighteen thousand present. The National Guard, alert with gun and bayonet as if for some important marine landing, made the quiet, orderly march appear a bit of a sell.

The numbers of the National Guard, the body count, spoke almost of a sort of psychotic imagining. They were on every street, blocking every intersection, cutting off each highway. There, in their large brown trucks, crawling out from under the olive-brown canvas, were men in full battle dress, in helmets and chin straps which concealed most of their pale, red-flecked and rather alarmed Southern faces. They guarded the alleys and the horizon, the river and the muddy playground, thoroughfare and esplanade, newspaper store and bank. It was as if by some cancerous multiplication the sensible and necessary had been turned into a monstrous glut.

The march, after all, was mostly made up of Memphis blacks. Was this a victory or a defeat? There were also some local white students from Southwestern, a few young ministers, and from New York members of the teachers' union with a free day off and a lunch box. Mrs. King came from Atlanta for the gathering, a tribute to her husband and also a tribute to the poor sanitation workers for whom it had all begun.

The people gathered early and waited long in the streets. They stood in neat lines to indicate the absence of unruly feelings. Part of the ritual of every public show of opinion and solidarity is the presence of a name or, preferably, the body of a Notable ("Notable" for a routine occasion, and "Dignitary" for a more solemn and affecting event such as the funeral to be held in Atlanta the next day). Notables are often from the entertainment world and the rest are usually to be known for political activities. Like a foundation of stone moved from site to site, only on the notables can the petition for funds be based, the protest developed, the idea constructed.

The marchers waited without restlessness for the chartered airplane to arrive and to announce that it could then truly begin. A limousine will be waiting to take the noted ones to the front of the line, or to leave them off at the stage door. The motors are kept running. After an appearance, a speech, a mere presence, out they go by the back doors used by the celebrated, out to the waiting limousine, off to the waiting plane, and then off.

These persons are symbols of a larger consensus that can be

transferred to the mass of the unknown faithful. They are priests giving sanction to idea, struggle, defiance. It is believed that only the famous, the busy, the talented have the power to solicit funds from the rich, notice from the press, and envy from the opposition. Also they are a sunshine, warming. They have the appeal of the lucky.

The march of Memphis was quiet; it was designed as a silent memorial, like a personal prayer. Hold your head high, the instructions read. No gum chewing. For protection in case of trouble, no smoking, no umbrellas, no earrings in pierced ears, no fountain pens in jacket pockets. One woman said, "If they make me take off my shades, I'm quitting the march." Among those who had come from some distance a decision had been made in favor of the small gathering in Memphis over the "national" funeral in Atlanta the following day. "I feel this is more important," they would say.

In the march and at the funeral of Martin Luther King, the mood of the earlier Civil Rights days in Alabama and Mississippi returned, a reunion at the grave of squabbling, competitive family members. And no one could doubt that there had been a longing for reunion among the white ministers and students and the liberals from the large cities. The "love"—locked arms, hymns, good feeling—all of that was remembered with feeling.

This love, if not always refused, was now seldom forthcoming in relations with new black militants, who were set against dependency upon the checkbooks and cooperation of the guilty, longing, loving whites. Everything separated the old Civil Rights people from the new black militants; it could be said, and for once truly, that they did not speak the same language. A harsh, obscene style, unforgiving stares, posturings, insulting accusations and refusal to make distinctions among those of the white world—this was humbling and perplexing. Many of the white people had created their very self-identity out of issues and distinctions and they felt cast off, ill at ease, with the new street rhetoric of "self-defense" and "self-determination."

Comradeship, yes, and being in the South again gave one a remembrance of the meaning of the merely legislative, the newly visible. Back at the hotel in the late afternoon the marchers were breaking up. The dining room was suddenly filled with not-too-pleasing young black boys—not black notables with cameras and briefcases, or in the company of intimidating, busy-looking persons from afar—no, just poor boys from Memphis. The aged waitresses padded about on aching feet and finally approached with the questions of function. Menu? Yes. Cream in the coffee? A little.

So, at last business was business, not friendship. The old white waitresses themselves were deeply wrinkled by the stains of plebeianism. Manner, accent marked them as "disadvantaged"; they were diffident, ignorant, and poor and would themselves cast a blight on the cheerful claims of many dining places. They seemed to be the enduring remnants of many an old retired trailer camp couple, the men with tattooed arms and the women in bright colored stretch pants; those who wander the warm roads and whose traveling kitchenettes and motorized toilets are a distress to the genteel and tasteful.

In any case, joy and flush-cheeked nuns were past history, a folk epic, full of poetry, simplicity and piety. The pastoral period of the Civil Rights Movement had gone by.

At the funeral in Atlanta, rising above the crowd, the *nez pointu* of Richard Nixon . . . Lester Maddox, short-toothed little marmoset, peeking from behind the draperies of the Georgia State House . . . Many Christians have died without the scruples of Christian principles being to the point. The *belief* of Martin Luther King—what an unexpected curiosity it was, the strength of it. His natural mode of address was the sermon. "So I say to you, seek God and discover Him and make Him a power in your life. Without Him all our efforts turn to ashes and our sunrises into darkest nights."

At the end of his life, King seemed in some transfigured state, even though politically he had become more radical and there were traces of disillusionment—with what? messianic hope perhaps. He had observed that America was sicker, more intransigent than he had realized when he began his work. The last, ringing, "I have been to the mountaintop!" gave voice to a transcendent experience. It is this visionary strain that makes him a man elusive in the extreme, difficult to understand as a character.

How was it possible for one so young as King to seem to contain, in himself, so much of the American past? At the very least, the impression he gave was of an experience of life coterminous with the years of his father. The depression, the dust bowl, the sharecropper, the old back-country churches, and even the militance of the earlier IWW—he suggested all of this. He did not appear to belong to the time of Billy Graham (God bless you real good) but to a previous and more spiritual evangelism, to a time of solitude and refined simplicity. In *Adam Bede*, Dinah preaches that Jesus came down from Heaven to tell the good news about God to the poor. "Why, you and me, dear friends, are poor. We have been brought up in poor cottages, and have been reared on oatcake and lived coarse. . . . It doesn't cost Him much to give us our little handful of victual and bit of clothing, but how do we know He cares for us any more than we care for the worms . . . so long as we rear our carrots and onions?" There remains this old, pure tradition in King. Rare elements of the godly and the political come together, with an affecting naturalness. His political work was indeed a Mission, as well as a political cause.

In spite of the heat of his sermon oratory, King seems lofty and often removed by the singleness of his concentration—an evangelical aristocrat. There is even a coldness in his public character, an impenetrability and solidity often seen in those who have given their entire lives to ideas and causes. The racism in America acts finally as an exhaustion to all except the strongest of black leaders. It leads to the urban, manic frenzy, the sleeplessness, hurry, and edginess that are a contrast to King's steadiness and endurance.

Small-town Christianity, staged in some sense as it was, made King's funeral supremely moving. Its themes were root American, bathed in memory, in forgotten prayers and hymns and dreams. Mule carts, sharecroppers, dusty poverty, sleepy Sunday morning services, and late Wednesday night prayer meetings *after work*. There in the reserved pews it was something else—candidates, former candidates, and hopeful candidates, illuminated, as it were, on prime viewing time, free of charge, you might say, free of past contributions to the collection plate, free of the envelopes of future pledges.

The rare young man was mourned and, without him, the world was fearful indeed. The other side of the funeral, Act Two ready in the wings, was the looting and anger of a black population inconsolable for its many losses.

"Jesus is a trick on niggers," a character in Flannery O'Connor's *Wise Blood* says. The strength of belief revealed in King and in such associates as the Reverend Abernathy was a chastening irregularity, not a regionalism absorbed. It stands apart from our perfunctory addresses to "this nation under God." In a later statement Abernathy has said that God, not Lester Maddox or George Wallace, rules over the South. So, Negro justice is God's work and God's will.

The popular Wesleyan hymns have always urged decent, sober behavior, or that is part of the sense of the urgings. As you sing, "I can hear my Savior calling," you are invited to accept the community of the church and also, quite insistently, to behave yourself, stop drinking, gambling and running around. Non-violence of a sort, but personal, thinking of the home and the family, and looking back to an agricultural or small-town life, far from the uprooted, inchoate, *communal* explosions in the ghettos of the cities. The political non-violence of Martin Luther King was an act of brilliant intellectual conviction, very sophisticated and yet perfectly consistent with evangelical religion, but not a necessary condition as we know from the white believers.

One of the cruelties of the South and part of the pathos of Martin Luther King's funeral and the sadness that edges his rhetoric is that the same popular religion is shared by many bellicose white communicants. The religion seems to have sent few peaceful messages to them in so far as their brothers in Christ, the Negroes, are concerned. Experience leads one to suppose there was more respect for King among Jews, atheists, and comfortable Episcopalians, more sympathy and astonishment, than among the white congregations who use, with a different cadence, the same religious tone and the same hymns heard in the Ebenezer Church. Under the robes of the Klan there is an evangelical skin; its dogmatism is touched with the Scriptural, however perverse the reading of the text.

At one of the memorial services in Central Park after the murder, a radical speaker shouted, "You have killed the last good nigger!" This posturing exclamation was not meant to dishonor King, but to speak of his kind as something gone by, its season over. And perhaps so. The inclination of white leaders to characterize everything unpleasant to themselves in black response to American conditions as a desecration of King's memory was a sordid footnote to what they had named the "redemptive moment." But it told in a self-serving way of the peculiarity of the man, of the survival in him of habits of mind from an earlier time.

King's language in the pulpit and in his speeches was effective but not remarkably interesting. His style compares well, however, with the speeches of recent Presidents and even with those of Adlai Stevenson, most of them bland and flat in print. In many ways, King was not Southern and rural in his address, although he had a melting Georgia accent and his discourse was saturated in the Bible. His was a practical, not a frenzied exhortation, inspiring the Southern Negroes to the sacrifices and dangers of protest and yet reassuring them by its clarity and humanity.

His speech was most beautiful in the less oracular cadences, as when he summed up the meaning of the Poor People's March on Washington with, "We have come for our checks!" The language of the younger generation is another thing altogether. It has the brutality of the city and an assertion of threatening power at hand, not to come. It is military, theatrical, and at its most coherent probably a lasting repudiation of empty courtesy and bureaucratic euphemism.

The murder of Martin Luther King was a "national disgrace." That we said again and again and it would be cynical to hint at fraudulent feelings in the scramble for suitable acts of penance. Levittowns would henceforth not abide by local rulings, but would practice open housing; Walter Reuther offered $50,000 to the beleaguered sanitation workers of Memphis; the Field Foundation gave a million to the Southern Christian Leadership movement; Congress acted on the open housing bill. Nevertheless, the mundane continued to nudge the eternal. In 125 cities there was burning and looting. Smoke rose over Washington, D.C.

The Reverend Abernathy spoke of a plate of salad shared with Dr. King at the Lorraine Motel, creating a grief-laden scenery of the Last Supper. How odd it was after all, this exalted Black Liberation, played out at the holy table and at Gethsemane, "in the Garden," as the hymns have it. A moment in history, each instance filled with symbolism and the aura of Christian memory. Perhaps what was celebrated in Atlanta was an end, not a beginning—the waning of the slow, sweet dream of Salvation, through Christ, for the Negro masses.

The Oswald Family

The Warren Report appears, as if it were the last chorus of a tragedy by Euripides: "Many things the gods achieve beyond our judgement. What we thought is not confirmed, what we thought not, the gods contrive. And so it happens in this story." In the fading light, the Report sums up: "Out of these and many other factors which may have molded the character of Lee Harvey Oswald there emerged a man capable of assassinating President Kennedy."

From the shades of their anxious, detested obscurity, the calamity brought forth to view some of the most disquieting people we have ever encountered. We are given lives and desires we would not willingly have confronted, and we have seen a sort of nakedness we were not eager to acknowledge.

Oswald: There is about him a special invisibility, a peculiar opacity. Those few persons who remain in doubt about his guilt are perhaps reinforced by the impenetrability of this disturbing figure. He does not seem equal in mania or in tenacity of Idea to the catastrophic deed. He had made the most dramatic and awful effort at self-definition but even so he remains buried, unyielding. He is pale, rancorous, with a special sullen yearning whose dimensions are impossible to measure. Odd words occur to those who remember him: he is all smirks and mutterings, silences and unsociable shrugs. We see him nearly always in some mood of strained, self-conscious chagrin. Not laughter or joking; only sulky refusals or arguments.

Oswald is a ghostly anachronism in a cast of characters completely caught up in the lusts of the 1960s. How hard it is to believe he was born in 1939, that he had just barely turned twenty-four when he died. Most of all he is a Depression figure; unemployment, despair, scarcity follow him about. The tone of his aspirations, the very notes of his formulations ring out dimly from another decade. He says he thinks of his mother and brother only as "workers." The boom, the Eisenhower era, do not seem to have touched him. The arguments of the Thirties interest him much more deeply than Civil Rights, that great cause of his generation. He is hostile to society but the beatnik "revolt," centering as it does on personal relations, has nothing to say to him. His sensibility is metallic, he walks about, borne down by the iron of his backward-looking temperament. He arises as if from a troubled sleep of a decade or two. He lived in Texas, an open highway, and could not drive a car. Only his interest in Cuba connects him with the present, and even there, as always, we find obfuscation, peculiarity, invisibility.

In many ways, Oswald's early years are the most easily understood because they come to us through our seers who foretell the future and interpret the past: the social workers and psychiatrists. Oswald with their help takes shape; he is like many another whose biography we read in the daily press. He is fatherless, underprivileged, neglected. His circumstances were bleak, especially during the New York period when he and his mother seemed to have been friendless, isolated, and confused. The seers are quick to put the blame on the mother. She is self-concerned, neglectful.

Oswald's hopes for himself are intellectual rather than practical. He is not concerned with acquiring skills or a trade but rather with an effort to solve his problems by ideas. The striking aspect of this is Oswald's paralysis with words. The "Historic Diary" published in *Life* magazine is just barely on the border of literacy. Books are taken out from libraries, but there is every evidence that Oswald was incapable of systematic, careful reading about Communism or anything else. When he applied for admission to the Albert Schweitzer School in Switzerland he gave as his favorite authors, Jack London, Charles Darwin, and Norman Vincent Peale. The incongruity of the list points to his ignorance of all three. Yet it is pretension, the projection of his ambitions and hopes in ideological terms that stay in one's mind as a puzzle. He seems a good deal like those *lumpen* intellectuals of the early Thirties in Germany and Austria, empty, ignorant, rootless men, without any gifts or skills but still with a certain conceit that made them want to make from the negative of their personalities some sort of programmatic certainty. There is nothing in Oswald's letters or in his papers that shows any comprehension of radical polemics. His interest in Communism and the Soviet Union is of the sketchiest kind. "I am a Marxist, but not a Leninist-Marxist," he says, whatever that may mean. His pathetic "Historic Diary" is completely free of generalizing power or political observation. He seems to know nothing about Russia; his discomforts there are not intellectual or moral but mundane, day to day.

Just as he listed Darwin and Norman Vincent Peale, so he holds up in his fascinating photograph—that profoundly interesting self-portrait he has left to posterity—two guns and two newspapers, the Communist *Daily Worker* and the Trotskyist *Militant*. There he stands in the midst of his iconography, his composition of himself surrounded by his weapons and his emblems of Idea.

Along with his ignorance, his failure with words, Oswald

does not seem to have had any general capabilities. His tragic achievements—including the sure marksmanship that killed President Kennedy—can be explained only as accidental, statistical. He was fired from his job in a photographic shop, but he had learned just enough to forge, by tricks of photography, a Selective Service card for his alias, A. Hidell.

So far as we can tell, it was not so much laziness that made Oswald such a poor worker as a lack of capability and no doubt the same impatience and shallowness that appear in his intellectual efforts. His nature is secretive, but if the Report is telling us all it knows his secretiveness is more disabling than efficient. (Insofar as any detective-story aspects of the case still remain after the Warren Report, the most mysterious questions about Oswald's activities are the visit to Mexico, his letter to the Soviet Embassy in Washington, and the awful choice of President Kennedy as his victim.) He made the extreme commitment when he asked for Soviet citizenship, but he could not carry this to completion. Even his most daring decision, before he began to shoot, could not give form to his formlessness. He tried Russia for a while and then changed his mind.

Oswald seemed to feel his defection could be erased, when it suited him, washed off with a sponge. No doubt he felt this because he had been so little changed by it. Indeed he was soon back where he had started. In a letter to Governor Connolly he gives a startling indication of the way his mind worked. The letter was written from Russia, protesting the change of his Marine discharge from honorable to dishonorable. He speaks of himself and his situation as though they belonged to someone else. He calls himself "a case," and then makes the impenetrable suggestion: "this person [himself] had gone to the Soviet Union to reside for a short time (much in the same way E. Hemingway resided in Paris)." In some sense Oswald, even after he returned, wanted to be "this person" who had been to the Soviet

Union. But of course he stopped short of Soviet citizenship and even residence and came back home with nothing accomplished except that a Russian girl had married him.

We are told that he was arrogant, but he could make little use of this because in the end there was always the problem of his great ignorance. His arrogance was only a part of his striking puritanism. The positives he might have built upon were really negatives: he did not care, apparently, for luxury or possessions and his indifference to these is another way in which he was out of touch with the 1960s. He spent a good deal of his slim earnings paying back the State Department and a loan from his brother. These were genuine acts of sacrifice and planning, a little unexpected in a drifter like Oswald and again more like the poor man of the Thirties than the giddy installment buyer of today. No matter from what angle we view him, Oswald remains narrow and shrunken. And we are not surprised when, upon the release of the Report, sex makes an entrance into his drama. We are told he was a poor performer there, too.

Above all, Oswald was a pre-television spirit. Perhaps only a person somehow immunized to TV by the iron of his nature *could* actually kill Kennedy. The President and his wife were magical beings, spectacularly favored, and engraved like a tattoo on a national psyche because of their position and their natural pre-eminence as television personalities. By assassinating President Kennedy, the embodiment of the 1960s at its most attractive, Oswald suddenly cast light upon the Sixties at its most distressing.

Out of the darkness there appeared Marina Oswald, a revelation we can hardly interpret. But who can doubt the coming "pop" Americanization of Russia after he has studied this young girl from Minsk? History, or events, exposed her to us in a series of frames: first, shabby, reserved, a proletarian with a tooth missing in front; in the end, on the day the Report was made public, a "famous" person, with eyelids darkened over in "Cleopatra" fashion, hair teased high, the gap in the smile filled, a people's capitalist, a success. From the nettle, danger, Marina had deftly plucked the flower, safety. Adaptability so accomplished is perhaps singular. She is like some convert, freshly lifted up; she knows us better than we know ourselves. Marina seems to have been born for the American Southwest. But what an unpropitious coupling with Oswald—the boring, disintegrating zealot. This young woman, as current as today's weather, must have been fortified in her decision by the whisperings of destiny. She herself gave voice to the whisperings when she said somewhere that she would not have married Oswald if he hadn't been an American. In him, she seems to have seen her chance to live in fact what she was in spirit. And no sooner was she in America than she apparently began to feel about Oswald much as those contemporaries of his in high school had felt—a complete distaste for the "loner," the turtle-like Oswald who didn't "mix," and who "kept to himself." And Marina, modern girl, demanded her right to sexual satisfaction we are told; it was what she had expected, like a washing machine.

Marina Oswald has not only shown a readiness to tell the truth about her husband, but a talent for the exploitation of sub-plots. Hardly a week passes without some bit in the tabloids. She busies herself and divides with her helpers the profits of recollection. One of the most interesting actions of Marina's— equal to Oswald's sudden inspiration of his likeness to Hemingway—was her invitation to a television crew to cover the baptism of her daughter, Rachel. Father, what shall I do to be saved? The television baptism is one of those instinctive transcendental unions with the over-soul. But, indeed, what other course was left? Rejection, indignation, a bleak, Russian, lower-depths suffering would otherwise have been the lot of the Soviet wife of a presidential assassin. Marina salivates when the bells ring; the country is reassured. Her story must mean something. How to decipher the code? A news account carries her further: a collaborating writer resigned from her employ saying, "I quit because Marina has come to believe she is as important as the President of the United States."

Oswald's mother comes to us in the most desolating light. One can only pity her. About her, too, there is the hint of Queen for a Day, the hand waving outside the television studio in the early morning, the testimonial to percentages gained by judicious purchase; but if her son is somehow pre-television, she is, for all her readiness, a television failure and comes off as a villain. The psychiatric chorus had damned her in any case: aggressive, self-centered, neglectful, ineffectual. "We warn you, Clytemnestra, Orestes will return from exile. You will die by the hand of your son."

Mrs. Oswald tends to mount a defense at just the moment a prudent person would withdraw or acquiesce. She defended her son against the doctors and social workers and she refused "treatment." Now, after his "conviction" as the assassin of President Kennedy she, previously neglectful as we have been told, stands almost alone in her insistence upon his innocence. But she sees her son, not as a young man like others and likewise free of guilt, but as a counterintelligence agent, a historical personage—by which she means, no doubt, a "celebrity." Her son has jumped out of the mass of the looking into the company of the looked at. And call her as they will The Terrible Mother, the catastrophe, still she too has her story, the Marguerite Oswald story. She has the great disposition to "appear," so common in this case. She realized that it was her turn now to rise up from the audience.

Jack Ruby and his sister, Eva, held a sort of instant wake as they sat sobbing before the television set at the time of President Kennedy's death. In his book, *Dallas Justice*, Melvin Belli tells us that Ruby, turning away from his usual struggle to diet, rushed out and bought ten dollars' worth of kosher delicatessen food. "We cried but we ate," he said. Ruby, like Oswald, had had a miserable youth, observed and recorded by the angels of the state. He had been in foster homes, and was the damaged son of damaged parents. But he is the opposite of Oswald. Ruby cannot keep out of the way. He is hyperactive, chaotic, talkative. He spends and he owes; he is stingy here and prodigal there: he is sentimental and sadistic. In a rage he nearly beats to death a troublesome visitor to his nightclub, but he cries easily. He seems to be held together by bravado and there are no brakes on his feelings. One doctor spoke of Ruby as "in love" with Kennedy. The ravening lust for publicity *would* make Ruby "love" those to whom publicity was a natural result of function and position. And Ruby's identification is nearly complete. He is drawn by the magnet of his hunger. There is the "Commie rat," Oswald, and here is the ferocious patriot, Ruby. The confrontation is too lucky for Ruby to resist. In truth he did it, as he humbly said, "for Jackie and the children," and what folly it was for Belli to ignore this truth in favor of electro-encephalograms, fugue states, blackouts and the "psychomotor pool," as the prosecution called his experts. With an appalling trust, Ruby actually believed in cops and famous people, in news reporters and network men. With all his ardor, he rushed in to fill the hole and murdered Oswald. Doing away with the Commie rat was his tribute to the cops, the reporters, the TV gods, and the beloved Kennedys. Even after he was given a death sentence he could think of himself only as a celebrated person, a figure in a wax museum. "Burn my clothes," he begged his lawyer, fearful lest they be put upon his eternal waxen image.

The Warren Report tells a sordid story of greeds too fierce to measure. The greatly favored and the greatly crippled suffer out their destinies. You feel they have been together on the stage for a long time. It was only that the light had not shone in the dingy corners before. There these impatient people, longing for immortality, were waiting to tell us something.

Militant Nudes

Gimme Shelter
DIRECTED BY DAVID MAYSLES, ALBERT MAYSLES,
CHARLOTTE ZWERIN

Ice
DIRECTED BY ROBERT KRAMER

Dance the Eagle to Sleep
BY MARGE PIERCY

Trash
PRODUCED BY ANDY WARHOL,
DIRECTED BY PAUL MORRISSEY

The Groupies
DIRECTED BY RON DORFMAN AND PETER NEVARD

Troubling Images: 1.) Professor Theodor W. Adorno, at the University of Frankfurt, was, not long before his death, the audience for—or the object of—a striking bit of symbolic action. Adorno, a distinguished philosopher and the teacher of many leftist students, had come to be worried about student zeal for immediate action, about spontaneity, random rebellion, and, of course, the possibility of repressive actions by the government. And how was the sacred old father rebuked? A girl got up in the classroom and took off her clothes.

A bit of *The Blue Angel* here? No, perhaps the key is found in the famous scene in *Swann's Way*. Mlle. Vinteuil, making love to her girl friend, puts the photograph of her doting, gifted father on the table next to the sofa so that the girl can spit on it. Proust says about the scene: "When we find in real life a desire for melodramatic effect, it is generally the 'sadic' instinct that is responsible for it."

"Sexuality"—the word has become a sort of unfleshed abstraction as it trails along with liberty, fraternity, and equality in the youth revolution—is suddenly political. The body, the young one at least, is a class moving into the forefront of history.

In *Gimme Shelter*, a brilliant documentary film about the Rolling Stones and their concert outside San Francisco that ended in murder, several accidental deaths, and an outburst of desolation, anger, and danger that is thought to have signaled the end of something in the rock and roll scene—in this film a number of people, mostly girls, take off their clothes. Each has an expression both blank and yet sure that something is being done, accomplished, signified. They stand there in the crowd, enclosed in their sad flesh, as lonely as scarecrows among the angry, milling thousands. The gestures did not cause a head to turn and all one could feel was that the body, the feet, the breasts were foolishly vulnerable, not because of any attractions they might have for the crowd, but merely due to the lack of protecting clothing. The nude bodies were no match in dramatic interest to the fabulously dressed performers, whose tight pants, scarves, snakeskin boots, spangled boleros, red silk ruffled shirts, represented what is meant in the entertainment world by a "personal statement."

2.) Huey Newton in New Haven, visiting Bobby Seale in jail. "If Ericka and Bobby are not set free, if the people can't set them free, then we'll hold back the night, there won't be day—there'll be no light." The eschatological mode has in modern times wearied the Christian world, but it served them well enough for centuries and so perhaps militant leaders naturally feel there is some life left in this style. At the Black Panther convention recently—a small and dispirited gathering, according to journalists—Huey Newton outlined the program: "First, focus on closing down Howard University, second on liberating Washington, and third the seizure of the White House." Liberating Washington. For a little group of the faithful these words perfectly represent the "schizophrenic bind" R. D. Laing writes about. If the words are not genuinely taken seriously and only a pretense about them is kept up, this creates an impossible and corrupting cynicism very difficult for all except leaders to live with; if the commands are treated as genuine their insane and sadistic nature will unhinge all who try to act them out. This is perhaps what is truly meant by the phrase, revolutionary suicide—the killing in oneself of the uses of reality by submitting to "the program."

The film, *Ice*, and the novel, *Dance the Eagle to Sleep*, are both imaginary projections of revolutions and civil wars to come, and there is a coercive and mystical inevitability claimed, not directly but aesthetically, that links them with the program Huey Newton gives to his followers. And the concentration upon revolutionary "balling" in the novel goes back in my mind to the poor professor in his classroom, to the mysteriousness of the girl's answer to the professor's worries.

In *Ice* there is a deliberate lack of art, decoration, plot, characterization. All of these elements are missing and in their place is revolutionary dedication. Dedication to the revolution *is* the plot, *is* the characters. They have surrendered personality, differences, past and future history, and this mingling of people with their guns, their propaganda, their "actions," and their indistinguishable faces and voices is the substance and the interest of the work. Everything moves by the pulsing of "inevitability" and the pretense of belief in the coming revolution. The belief is not directed at the public but is simply a picture of the mind of the creator, Robert Kramer. *Ice* is filmed as if it were something on the TV evening news, something that has already happened.

In the film, the United States has become involved in a military intervention in Mexico, and proceeds with force against leftists or peasants, whoever is rising up there and threatening "imperialist" interests. In New York, and no doubt in other cities, the young radicals have opened up a second front of guerrilla warfare against their own government. The scene is upper Broadway, the courtyard of the Belnord, the New Yorker Bookstore at 88th Street, and a large apartment house in Greenwich Village. The actors look like Columbia or Hunter students, but not teen-agers by any means. They might well remind you of people about to get their licenses to teach in the New York City public school system since they have about them an oppressive and oppressed look, an air of dissatisfaction coupled with dedication, a feeling for work that is necessary, directed toward the welfare of the person and the community but which is, revolution and school alike, somewhat unappetizing.

Some scenes from *Ice*: The revolutionaries occupy an apartment house in Washington Square. They go up and down the halls with machine guns, blocking elevators and escapes, beating on the doors of the hard-pressed, random tenantry of New York City. They gather together some of the people—middle-aged men in undershirts, women in wrappers—and a revolutionary says to them: "You are closer to the Mexican students than to your own country." This is a reading lesson to a class watching the clock, and a complete falsification of the experience and nature of the tenants, who can't speak Spanish, and who aren't students. What is interesting about it is the lack of questioning on the part of the radicals, the survival in them of the grim sectarianism of the Communist International thirty or forty years ago.

The value of constantly predicting revolutions, civil war, violent accountings is to give a sense of power to the powerless. Sukhanov, thoroughly involved in revolutionary life, was sitting at his desk in February, 1917, sure that the revolution was decades away. And those to be overthrown were not in a state, either, of practical, counterrevolutionary readiness. Trotsky quotes Prince Lvov's account of a visit to the Tsar at a time when everyone could see the monarchy was collapsing: "I expected to see the sovereign stricken with grief, but instead of that there came out to meet me a jolly, sprightly fellow in a raspberry-colored shirt."

The activism in *Ice* and *Dance the Eagle to Sleep* is not a replacement of deadening alienation but simply an addition to it. Even though *Ice* was filmed in the basements and bookstores and streets of New York City, one often feels in it a memory of the suffocating boredom and darkly sexual crowdings of an old army post, the kind of waiting and frustration that made soldiers before Vietnam long for some action. So, after a few years of threats and promise of revolution, rebellion, change, militant encounter, *Ice* and *Dance the Eagle to Sleep* are tours of active duty at last.

Another scene: A young revolutionary is trapped in a basement by the enemy—powerful, short-haired policemen or rightists—and subjected to terrible genital torture. We hear the screams of pain and the horror of the scene makes it difficult to watch. Later another radical is in bed with his girl. He tells her that he is sometimes afraid. Our mind goes back to the torture. "You know what they do to you," he says softly. The girl, rather heavy, depressed, touches the boy's arm and mumbles, "You can't let it get to you."

Ice is as cold as its title, a glassy radical vision, austere, masochistic, longing for the "inevitable." To think of the revolution is to prepare to die. "They kill; we kill." You endure approaching death in a fantasy of activity: "regional offensive," arrival of "the Mexican footage," admitting "We had some bad losses." One of the most interesting things about it is that it is old-fashioned, humorless, like Maoists or the Progressive Labor youths, and we are thus spared endless fornications and commune banalities.

This is not true of *Dance the Eagle to Sleep* by Marge Piercy —a harsh and sentimental "youth" novel, vaguely set in the future but quite openly counting on the reader's acquiescence in the reality of its themes and obsessions. Actually many of the reviews thought the book was needlessly cast into the future and seemed to want to allow the fantasy the status of fact. The novel is about a pathetic group of "acid revolutionaries," all very young, most of them in high school. It is a destructive fantasy, full of suffering, dreary phallic obsessiveness, and it is meaningless in a political sense.

Still, the book's claim to immediacy is insistent and its scenes of brutal police activity, school occupations, drugs, communes are true enough. However, the real source of the action is a sado-masochistic death dream. The people in *Ice* seem to be Marxists, but in *Dance the Eagle to Sleep*, they are "tribes" brought together by the visions of a young Indian boy named Corey. "We belong to a new nation of the young and the free, and we're going to win!" The radicalization of some of the students starts at a police gassing and beating up in Tompkins Square, the others at the occupation of a high school in New York: both of these occasions not only solidify political activism but offer some pretty good "sexuality" as well. The young people set up a commune in New Jersey, and send out others to keep organizing "tribes" all over the country. The principal activity at the commune, or at least the ritualistic experience that shapes the movement, is a tedious and often repeated evening of drug-taking, nude dancing, and sexual excitement.

The language of the book has, in the dialogue, a coarse power, but the exposition, the thought, and the structure are very weak. Almost every idea or opinion in the book is a banality from one side of the gap or the other. Here is the dreaming mind of Corey, the Indian boy, leader of the tribe. "Just stride into school cool and easy some morning with the rifle on his back like a guerrilla fighter. Better a machine gun. Line up the faculty. Torture the principal to learn where they kept the anxiety gases and the chemicals they put in the soup to make the kids stupid and passive." When you get to "the anxiety gasses," and the chemicals that keep the kids "stupid and passive," you have passed, amateurishly, from the boy's dreams to mere opinions about our schools. It goes on, smothering teen-age life in the spelled-out opinions about that life. "Keep your hands to yourself. Don't look like you're enjoying yourself, ever. Don't laugh out loud over your peanut butter sandwich; don't get into excited conversation about anything you care for."

It is the intellectual assumptions of the book that interest me rather than its literary quality. A reviewer, leaning on the staff of comparison, mentioned *Lord of the Flies, Lord of the Rings* and . . . *Moby Dick*. The dreary sexual scenes go from, "Her cunt ached," to formal cadences in the late Hemingway manner: "She had prepared herself carefully, and he would wait for her. He would spend the night with her, he decided. She was plump the way he liked and he liked too that she had stopped to make herself ready." Symbolic moments are of a surprisingly handy sort. Corey has attacks of suffocation and panic. "It was an eagle [America?] that stooped on him as he slept and tore into him, that carried him bleeding high up so he could not breathe, and dashed him to the ground." The book ends—after Corey and Billy and others have been killed, Joanna has gone over to "them," and everything is destroyed—with one of those odd but oft-remembered finales of contrived hope, the birth of a baby. "The baby lived and she lived and it was day for Marcus and for him, it was day for all of them."

There is a brutal murder in the book. Joanna, Corey, and Shawn—the principals of the novel—participate in the torture and shooting of one of their members because he has been selling "bread"—the hallucinogenic drug the tribe manufactures—for his own profit. This scene has a moral numbness and indifference to physical pain quite characteristic of all the works I am concerned with. After the comrade has been shot and thrown into a grave, Joanna makes a smooth, "literary" switch to sex and takes that moment to tell her lover, Corey, that she once "made it" with Shawn, the other participant in the crime.

Remember the opening of Malraux's *Man's Fate*, the foot sticking out from under the mosquito netting, its throbbing life stinging the consciousness of the assassin. The foot. . . . What repels in the new works is the loss of pity for the poor body, of respect for its life, its suffering. Perhaps this is the underside, just as it was in Sade, of the worship of the body, of reverence for its sensations.

Notes on *Trash, The Groupies, Gimme Shelter*

Trash is a homosexual film produced by Andy Warhol and directed by Paul Morrissey. *The Groupies* has to do with deranged, obscene girls who follow rock stars around, hoping to sleep with them, if one may use such a drowsy, untimely phrase for these wandering, never-sleeping hunters. *The Groupies* is a documentary, although there is considerable staginess in it; *Trash* is a concoction that is also a real life thing part of the time.

The nature of sexuality is repetition. Phallic compulsiveness is an exaltation of repetition and yet a reduction to routine of the most drastic kind. Still, novelty and challenge never lose their hold on the imagination and in the phallic hell the center of interest will be reserved for the refusing, even for the impotent. The hero of *Trash* is an impotent junkie. He wanders through the long hours of the film. He is quiet, handsome, mysterious, stoned, but arouses almost insane desire in everyone he meets. In a world of compulsive sex, dramatic interest can only be achieved by complications, particularly since every frontier of practice has been crossed.

In *Trash*, the little drag queen, Holly Woodlawn, pursues, waits on, loves the impotent junkie, Joe Dallesandro, with an air of blind necessity, like that of an animal running on and on in the plains in search of food. Joe's drug addiction has released him from "performance," and although he keeps trying in a nodding fashion it is never because he himself feels the loss but rather that he is a nice, passive boy and the frenzy he arouses in others makes him attempt an accommodation. Joe has the charm of silence—he also talks very little—in a room of screaming deviates.

In *Ice* one of the revolutionaries has a "hang-up" and one of the girls sneers (in the sort of folk poetry that decorates all of these works), "If you're having trouble with your prick, don't take it out on me!" It is almost impossible to keep face, statement, and shadow of personality together in one's mind about *Ice*, but if memory serves, the troubled young man was far from being weak and inadequate and was instead particulary zealous, concentrated, and effective. In *Dance the Eagle to Sleep*, the girls are constantly available and practical—I'm afraid rather like a jar of peanut butter waiting for a thumb. Billy, the most intelligent and the most violently intransigent, is by comparison with the others noticeably reserved sexually, partly out of temperament, and partly because he gives thought to other matters. The revolution, at least in the beginning, is for puritans. . . . Later. . . .

In *Gimme Shelter*, Mick Jagger, Grace Slick, Tina Turner—
the rock stars—are a disturbing contrast to the dull, sullen,
angry hundreds of thousands who have come to hear them. For
one thing the performers are *working* and even if the pay is outrageous, and the acts somewhat tarnished by time, there is still
discipline, energy, travel, planning, and talent. Each one is a presence, unique, competitive, formed by uncommon experiences.
The crowd, however, is just a huge clot of dazed swayings,
fatuous smilings, empty nightmares, threatening hallucinations,
and just plain meanness.

There is death everywhere, and of every sort, in the dead,
drugged eyes and in the jostling, nervous kicks and shoves.
Everyone is a danger to himself and to others. One could be
stabbed by a "mystic" who thought he was God or Satan; or
choked by the lowering, alcoholic violence of the Hell's Angels
just for brushing against one of their sweating arms. Someone
is having a baby—another corny freak-out, you find yourself
thinking. The owner of the Altamont Speedway, where the
concert took place, wants the birth mentioned in the media as a
"first." "Easy, easy," Grace Slick pleads from the stage. "Why
are you people fighting?" Mick Jagger wants to know. After the
concert, two young boys were killed when a car left the highway and crashed into their campfire. Another young man,
drugged, fell into a canal and was drowned.

Thinking about the predatory girls who call themselves "the
groupies," remembering their obscene reveries and their moronic
self-exploitation, one wants to hold back from description. One
of the young men connected with the film said, in a press interview, that he was horrified by the girls and that they were
stoned out of their minds all of the time. The girls are hoarse
and coarse and not one arouses pity of the kind we feel for the
pimply, snaggle-toothed synthetic girl, Holly Woodlawn, in
Trash. All are despised by everyone, by the cameramen, the

producers, the rock stars, just as Holly is despised by Andy Warhol and Paul Morrissey.

The main life of *Trash* comes from the perverse, proletarian vitality of Holly Woodlawn, who comes across to us as rotting skin and bones, kept alive by the blood of mascara and the breath of discarded clothing from the city's trash barrels. Still, the people in charge of the film show their hatred by a long, boring, hideous scene in which Holly buggers herself to some sort of satisfactory exhaustion with a beer bottle.

The "groupies" take plaster casts of the parts of rock stars—or they claim the stars as the origin of their "collection." The idea came to one of them, she says into the waiting microphones, when an art teacher said one could make a plaster cast of "anything hard." "Wow," grunts the groupie. She later describes herself in the more delicate moments of the casting as being "very gingerly."

Certainly these girls are in extremity, pushing out beyond the horizon. Yet they are not much more freakish nor are they more obscene than the teen radicals in *Dance the Eagle to Sleep*. In the novel, Joanna, the girl most admired and desired by the boys, is serenaded with a little song that goes:

> Joanna has a hairy cunt.
> It's the kind of cunt I want.
> I get on my knees and grunt
> For a touch of Jo-Jo's hairy cunt!

The groupies contain in every swagger and delusion genetic reminders of their parents, longing for the kiss of celebrity; aging Stalinists seem to haunt the memories in *Ice*; Holly Woodlawn says in the film she was born on welfare and while that is probably a fiction there is no reason why she might not have been. Hell's Angels and the vaguely disoriented crowds are both caught up in the mindless anarchy. What can one make of these deaths, since death is the feeling most clearly projected by radical and freak, girl and boy: death by drugs, by the misery and dreariness of the commune; death *by* political enemies, death *to* political enemies, death in "regional actions," by helicopters raining destruction on teen tribes, death at the free rock festival, in the eyes of Miss Harlow, the little groupie with frizzy hair.

At his trial, perhaps feeling the sorrow of his complicity in the death of Che Guevara, Régis Debray said: "The tragedy is that we do not kill objects, numbers, abstract or interchangeable instruments, but, precisely, on both sides, irreplaceable individuals, essentially innocent, unique. . . ."

Something pitiless and pathological has seeped into youth's love of itself, its body, its politics. Self-love is an idolatry. Self-hatred is a tragedy. But the life around us is not a pageant of coldness and folly to which we have paid admission and from which we can withdraw as it becomes boring. You feel a transcendental joke links us all together; some sordid synthesis hangs out there in the heavy air. No explanation—the nuclear bomb, the Vietnam war, the paralyzing waste of problems and vices that our lives and even the virtues of our best efforts have led to—explains. Yet it would be dishonorable to try to separate our selves from our deforming history and from the depressing dreams being acted out in its name.

After the squalor of *Trash*, *The Groupies*, and *Dance the Eagle to Sleep*, one comes back to the girl in Professor Adorno's class. What did she think her bare breasts meant? What philosophy and message could this breathing nude embody? In one of his last essays Adorno wrote, "Sanctioned delusions allow a dispensation from comparison with reality. . . ." And he also said, "Of the world as it exists, one cannot be enough afraid." The students may have known all about the second idea, but perhaps they could not forgive him the first.

The Portable Canterbury

Billy Graham: A Parable of American Righteousness is the title of Marshall Frady's biography of the truly far-flung evangelist. "Whatever else," Frady writes about Graham, "he has transmuted into a peculiar sort of megacelebrity, megastar of his age: his rangy wheat-haired form has been personally beheld, the reverberant bay of his voice immediately heard, by more people over the face of the earth than any other single human being in the history of the race." Yes, yes. As Robert Frost once said, "Hell is a half-filled auditorium."

The swollen corporate evangelism of today, first perhaps understood by Billy Sunday whose organization in its time was found to be second in efficiency only to National Cash Register, is a graceless computation with rolling, gathering zeros of cost to be met by love offerings, books, pamphlets, bumper stickers, salvation kits; and always by bold invasions of the pocketbook, conducted with the insolent insistence that appeals when honored are the way to spiritual safety, second, if indeed that, only to prayer, still a free enterprise.

Billy Graham is an outsized statistic. Number gives him a definition somehow beyond his calling, or at least inseparable from it. Arithmetic precedes him with its flash; arithmetic follows him. Past numbers tend to create future numbers.

The long, hectic pilgrimages, or "crusades" as the preferred word has it, to India, the Soviet Union, South Africa, Australia, Korea (South), and even to the foreign territory of Madison Square Garden in New York: these are his biography. And Graham himself is a sort of double emanation: he is both the pilgrim and the shrine, the portable Canterbury to be visited and experienced. For God's Star it is an iron routine, with the shape and the form of the appearance settled and unchanging, except for various scriptural texts read out and briefly connected to a generality, and sometimes for conservative political asides suitable to the nation under the siege of the crusade. This is, as it must be, a long-running play, sustained by the inspiration that comes to Graham, as it does to gifted actors, from the presence of the audience.

Dislocation, variation, and change are to take place out there in the souls of the crowd. Still, the disagreeable reeves or drunken millers who may have "come forth for Christ" at this peculiar Canterbury will never be known to us as souls residing amid the shambles of their singular characters. Since the changes and revelations take place in bulk, so to speak, the pilgrims and the saved are reduced to number. "Responses" and "decisions" are carefully, laboriously recorded, offerings are counted, and all is filed away. The size of the crowd, the weight of the offering lead—after the unknowable workings of the inner light upon a single soul—where? Certainly to the next crowd and the next offering.

Like number itself, Billy Graham's life is repetition. A shock, a quivering of the seismograph—Richard Nixon, for instance—are calmed by prayer, prayer that is itself inevitably of repetitive, long-uttered diction, at least if one may judge from the public and published prayer-diction. "Guidance" appears upon request and its usefulness seems to be not so much to form opinion as to soothe anxiety.

Billy Graham's "ministry" and his life are circular. The circular life is concerned to defy distraction and temptation in order to return to where it started. Perhaps that is why Graham in his circlings often sounds like the orbiting astronauts, or it may be that they sound like him. Graham speaks of the visionary, the heavens and the depths, of dedications and revelations in a predictable swelling and falling of cadence, in a reiterative language that is scarcely language at all, or at least seldom the abrupt, broken searching of speech as it turns and twists to meet experience and thought.

From Marshall Frady's brilliant biography of Graham: ". . . equally generic to Graham's enthusiasms, and elemental to maintaining the vigor of his evangelism over the years, has been a certain cheerful imprecision in his apprehension of the actual —some lack of a final fine close-up focus register in his sense of things." And Frady on Graham and his group: "Their only sense of any mystery in life ranges no farther than incessant reports among themselves of wondrous and pleasant coincidences."

Among the "Praise the Lord, wasn't that a miracle?" happenings are such matters as a family without crusade tickets being suddenly offered nine spare ones. Sometimes coincidence reaches out to "a certain appreciation for the blank dead ends of the terrible." This was the case with Noel Houston's critical profile of Graham in *Holiday* magazine in 1958. "Graham's face briefly took on a grave and remote look—'Yes, and you know, very soon after those articles of his came out, he dropped dead of a heart attack.'"

In Graham's life and in his enterprise it is as if one were to make a large footprint with one's initials on it signifying a single choice under which all the rest of experience would somehow be subsumed. This in many ways makes Graham a resistant object for Frady's intense contemplation. First of all, if Graham is in a sense deprived by the habits of his mind, cut off from the vitality of struggling language, Frady is all language and flowing connection. Fluent sentences and paragraphs, a streaming abundance of imagery, a Faulknerian enchantment with the scenery in which these bare lives flourish. Frady's biography of George Wallace and the present large work on Graham are outstanding works of literature, not quite like any other in their intention and quality.

Imaginative saturation, a special kind of interest and intelligence, much that is quirky and novelistic, high creative ambitions are brought to bear on his charmless, driven Americans, Wallace and Graham. Wallace's nastiness and gift of tongues almost accumulate in Frady's fascination with speech, rhythm and anecdote into a kind of charm.

"He don't have no hobbies," declares an old crony from Wallace's hometown. "He don't do any honest work. He don't drink. He ain't got but one serious appetite, and that's votes."

In both books the surrounding characters are unique bits of American portraiture—in the Graham book, the cranky old evangelist, Will D. Campbell, for instance. A profound attention, a sort of respect, and finally a devastating looking: in this way these original works are created. Frady gives Billy Graham everything and yet concedes nothing. No secrets are uncovered, the person remains whole and is not found to be dishonest or insincere; instead he is *impervious*. Unthinkable that Graham, reading the book, would not fall to his knees a dozen times, asking for guidance through his feelings of unease.

Graham, accustomed to giving and receiving only in the glare of his definition of self, has of course his official biographer, John Pollock. A second Pollock volume on the "decisive years" from 1970 to the present is to be published this year [1979], perhaps to compete with Marshall Frady's. "Absolutely indispensable for the millions who follow Billy Graham's ministry and wonder about the man behind it."

Millions console, not to say *consolidate,* also. Yet, in weaving his way through things, Graham finds that lesser numbers are also valuable. When accused of being repetitious, he answers, "I am consoled by the fact, pointed out once by an eminent theologian, that Jesus repeated himself five hundred times." In his foolish book *Angels: God's Secret Agents* (over one million copies in print, says the jacket; in all of Graham's published work, the number of copies in print serves as a sort of subtitle), addition asserts that the Bible mentions angels three hundred times. There may be something here meant to wash clean the stain of the Middle Ages and the Papacy that discolors the subject. On the matter of appealing for funds, Graham says, "One fifth of all the teachings of Christ was given over to money and stewardship." One fifth.

It is not known whether the arithmetic comes from the old biblical concordances or from the computations done by the machinery of BGEA (Billy Graham Evangelistic Association) in Minneapolis. "Graham's ministry is administered from Minneapolis in a manner that has become a mix of IBM, McCann-Erickson, Sears Roebuck, Blue Cross, and the morning devotionals at Vacation Bible School."

Billy Graham's parents were pious, dogmatic North Carolina farm people. About his father, Graham observes, "I never once heard him even use a slang word, much less a profane one." Marshall Frady is, of course, a good deal more thoughtful on the elder Graham: "So he abided on through the years of his son's magnifying renown with a kind of peaceable and oblivious remoteness—a figure as lean and plain as a yard rake, with a long flattish face and narrow age-freckled forehead under a dim patina of zinc hair. . . . His chief occupation during his last years seemed to be passing his day ambling amiably among the tables at the S & W Cafeteria in the nearby Park Road Shopping Center."

Graham had in his youth several hapless excursions into love. As one of his relations put it, "If you ask me, Pauline was the greatest love to ever hit him. She really sent him into somersaults." In the midst of his attachment to Pauline, Graham was converted. ("I'm saved, Mother, I got saved!") This took place at a tent revival under the command of Reverend Mordecai Ham: "A tall, strapping, rigid figure, bald and fractious-tempered and florid of face. . . . He derived directly, in fact, out of the old furies of those brush evangelists of the frontier, having presided once at a bonfire of dubious literature in Mineral Wells, Texas. . . . Not incidentally, he also served in that long unspoken collaboration in America between gospel drummers and the baronies of commerce. In particular, he was one of his era's most gaudy and livid anti-Semites."

It is not suggested that Graham had any notion of Ham's secular obsessions or that he was aware of anything except "the majesty of God, I think, that hit me as I heard Ham preach about it." Graham's own conversion shares the peculiarity of his later evangelistic successes; the conversion of people already pious Christians. In the Crusades, it is not reckoned that Jew or Moslem or Hindu will depart from error and it is hard not to believe that most of the thousands entering the tabernacle, astrodome, or playing field are more than "almost persuaded" as they enter. The "coming forth" to sign with Christ as your "personal Savior" is what the event is all about. It takes up most of the time when the lines are long, as they usually are.

Pauline, the first love, could not go along with the way salvation took hold of Graham, and she eventually "married an army aviator . . . who soon joined Cal-Tex Oil. Her life with him then proceeded as an uninterrupted thirty-year gambol of champagne receptions in Singapore patio gardens, sundown parties on the jasmine-spilled terraces of Kuala Lumpur."

Graham's conversion meant preaching, Bob Jones College,

and later the Florida Bible Institute where Graham met Emily, a plausible religious girl, but alas another heartache. Emily gradually began to "evince certain signs of restiveness." When she broke with him, the expression on Graham's face "was that of a harpooned seal." Traumas gathered but never without the provision of the instruction that might be gained from them. At the Bible Institute two young Christians were discovered in a situation of "serious moral defection." Proper deportment in matters of language, smoking, drinking, and sex as the message of the Crucifixion no doubt did not begin with the shock at the Institute. In such matters, Graham always seems to be re-learning what he has always known.

Graham found his mate in Ruth Bell, found her at Wheaton College in Illinois, "a doctrinal evangelical conservatory set in the tawny plains south of Chicago." She was the daughter of Presbyterian missionaries in China, "born in the muddy provincial city of Tsingkianpu in the wind-raked reaches of north-eastern China." Ruth seems to have had every quality hoped for. "Reared in such a running hyperbolic moral dialectic between their own churchly decorums and the lurid brutishness [of China] around them, Ruth and her sister were instilled somewhat precociously with a rather livid sense of righteousness and perdition." One of Ruth's uses for Graham turned out to be the very circumstances of the geography of her birth. It provided, then and now, a nice ornamental root of Chinese place names and exotic missionary anecdote to the scrabby shrub of Graham's written and spoken discourse. "My wife, who was born and raised in China, recalls that in her childhood days tigers lived in the mountains." And so on.

Validation by the powerful and well-known is a natural wish of one absorbed in number, one for whom any remaining pocket of smallness or obscurity is a defeat. And this need for validation will multiply in those lives that are marked by the exploitation of personality. Graham is anything but an exception. His "vulnerability was that, while he contended that he looked on all his associations in government and commerce as mere openings for a fuller propagation of his ministry, at the same time he also was given to a compulsive entrancement with all those larger affairs and offices of the world."

Current evangelism is as far as one can go in the pursuit of faith without works. Graham has brought to perfection the notion of a global parish, that is, no parish at all. He is relieved of the need to make private visits, to gather boxes of old clothes in the church basement, to perform weddings, bury the dead, to encourage rummage sales and pie-suppers. Not only is he relieved, but the saved are also, if they like, outside the demands of works in community with others. With their salvation kits, they are like patients making a single visit to a clinic and who are thereby recorded in the cure statistics. The commitment does not require one to attend Mass or to go about ringing doorbells, selling *The Watchtower*, refusing blood transfusions and military service, making hasty recalculations of the procrastinating Day of Judgment.

In the matter of charities, the very rich Graham organization is again rather impersonal and drawn to the global and far-flung. Floods, earthquakes, and famines have brought forth checks from Minneapolis. The occasions are noted by John Pollock and others but since few figures are given perhaps the charities do not make a point in this world of digits. In many respects, evangelism itself is considered a charity. Under "social concerns" in the index to Pollock's official biography, one is led to several pages that describe evangelistic conferences, given over for the most part to evangelism's organizational and theoretical problems.

The early Civil Rights Movement, despite its religious groundings, did not seem to stir Graham—except perhaps to stir to alarm. Bleached optimism, complacency about the "greatness of America," and the almost divine dispensation of citizenship, an aggressive acquiescence in the least adventurous possibilities of propriety: all of this gives to Graham a special *whiteness* of style.

In speaking of demonstrations, he was inclined to promote his own large gatherings. "I have been holding demonstrations myself for fifteen years—but in a stadium where it was legal." At a meeting with Martin Luther King, he said, "So let me do my work in the stadium . . . and you do yours in the streets." Perhaps Graham feared some usurpation of his authority and of the national attention as the cameras directed themselves to the hymn-singing "fellowship" in Selma and other southern cities.

Marshall Frady, with his high sense of American scenery and his creative ordering of the meaning of character as it displays itself in history, writes about Graham and King that they were "like the antipodal prophets of that continuing duality in the American nature between the Plymouth asperities and the readiness for spiritual adventure, between the authoritarian and the visionary." Of King: "The genius of his otherwise baroque and ponderous metaphors was that they were the rhetoric of the human spirit gathering itself to terrific and massive struggle."

Nixon: for Graham's involvement here perhaps "ordeal" is too strong a word, but certainly he experienced personal bafflement and embarrassment. Graham was powerfully attracted to Nixon, who first of all was the President. They may have had little in common, but then neither of them has much in common with others. They shared successful impersonality. Graham's "polyethylene blandness" met Nixon's polyethylene deceitfulness and these impervious surfaces were very agreeable. Conservatism, self-righteousness, simplification, tirades against Satanism—sufficient bonds, perhaps.

To the numb and static vocabulary of Graham, the bad language of the Nixon tapes was a personal affront and a spiritual distress of the first order. Or perhaps it was the first and last order. The will to power cannot be admitted by Graham, who in his own driven will falls back upon the "stewardship mentioned so many times by Christ." And what did he decide when he could no longer fail to name *something* askew in Nixon? "I think it was sleeping pills. Sleeping pills and demons." As Frady expresses it, "Thus he has made his final peace with it: it had all been an exterior, artificial, demonic, chemical, intervention. The fault had lain, not in Nixon, but in the dark stars and dark winds of the underworld."

As the emblem to the Graham biography, Frady quotes from *Billy Budd*. And he returns to this theme in that matter of Nixon, telling of a visitor to Graham reading out Melville's passages on Claggart's evil. The visitor must have been Marshall Frady himself. *Who else?* In thinking of Graham, he writes: "There was also something about his equally abiding eager innocence throughout his relationship with Nixon that somehow strikingly evoked, more than anything else, Herman Melville's moral fable *Billy Budd*."

It must be said that Billy Budd's innocence is of a very different quality from the innocence that may perhaps be blinking behind the glare of Billy Graham. Billy Budd's radiance is inseparable from the symbolic nature of his condition. The Handsome Sailor and his miraculous glow are part of the mystery of being and he is unaccountable, without a past, without connections. He is an orphan; he is illiterate; he has a tragic but necessary flaw of nature, the stutter that overcomes him in moments of excitement. His innocence cannot protect itself against evil because he is literally struck dumb.

Billy Graham is always speaking; that is his profession, if one may use the word about his "calling." He is in a constant witnessing for God through himself. His "glow" is shrewdly protected from harm and even the house in which he lives is surrounded by high fences and patrolled by guards and by killer dogs. The anonymity of the Handsome Sailor, his strange sweetness and his lack of all the instincts and powers of self-protection seem almost the opposite of the driven, blameless, if you like, life of Graham as he lives it out in incorporated goodness.

A daily acquaintance with the Bible and its language: for the evangelist of our day some impediment, a sort of sheetrock of linguistic impermeability refuses assimilation. Words and rhythms, the parabolic intensities of the sacred book are set apart like old stained glass windows shining in a slab of concrete. The gorgeous utterances of the Scriptures live amidst the indolent preacher-diction in a barbarous union, illicit and shameless. Evangelism is a world of only one book and thus even the Bible becomes, in its solitary fluency, an object, a thing. It is property.

In Billy Graham's words, angels are God's "secret agents"; they are God's "heavy artillery" in the battle against Satan. The meeting of the beautiful word, angel, with heavy artillery and secret agent is the music of current evangelism. To leave aside words and encounter some of the "ideas" of Graham's thoughts: UFOs may be angels, although it is not certain; and do not forget the winged gull that made a dinner for the beleaguered Eddie Rickenbacker adrift in the South Pacific.

All of that is now. And what is the future, the final disposal of the old crusader? The philanthropy is to be "that immemorial last ambition of the powerful and notable," in this case the fourteen-million-dollar Billy Graham Center and Library. It is to be "a great auto-battery-shaped edifice of tannish brick with long thin arched windows like Popsicle sticks extending from ground to roof."

The television ministry: "the means of Graham's greatest single impact on his own country." It is "a massive closed system with its own vision and terms of evaluation and its own independent dynamic for self-preservation." Almost impossible to recall the lonely and stricken aspect of the old evangelical tent and street corner, the listeners with hangovers and prison records, the hand-organ performances on a desolate evening, the forbidding, charitable soup kitchen. Or the rural gravity of Dinah, the anxious refinement of the elder Gosses.

Coda: my own recent experience of the "intense inane" of television preaching. During a miscellaneous, mere two hours: the coarsest beggary and the most impudent misappropriation of the Scriptures.

I am watching on the coast of Maine. First a local, out of Bangor, Pastor Ronnie Libby with his resentfully modest question-and-answer program about "God's Plan." The first question addressed itself without discretionary pause to the everlasting content of TV evangelism. It arrived under the name of tithes, or "the first dime of every dollar." The old prophet Malachi was imported, dragged along by his ancient hair, and without mercy. "Bring ye all the tithes into the storehouse, that there may be meat in mine house, and prove me now herewith, saith the Lord of Hosts, if I will not open you the windows of heaven, and pour you out a blessing, that there shall not be room enough to receive it."

What is the storehouse? asks Ronnie Libby for us, in the way of evangelists. The storehouse is where you get your spiritual food. And where do you get your spiritual food? "Well, more and more get it from a television ministry like this. So that is where your tithes will go, if you would not 'rob God,' as Malachi expresses it." Box number in Charleston, Maine.

Pastor Libby goes on to a few inchoate questions, one about Ezekiel's interesting "wheel in the middle of the wheel." He gives a puny answer. Soon, "a break for funds." We are told that "God is using this Thursday night program. He wants us to continue." The credits roll by: Wardrobe by Henry Segal; transportation by Chrysler/Plymouth; flowers by Bucksport Nursery.

Sunday morning and the air is shaking with the videotapes of elaborate, competitive, well-known national ministries: Robert Schuller, Rex Humbard, James Robison, Oral Roberts, Jimmy Swaggart, Ernest Angley, Jerry Falwell. Personal style and regional colorations provide a sort of choice on the channels. A single evangelist will have short presentations on the smaller stations, programs that rant and beg a bit more openly than the same preacher's hour-long service before live audiences seen on the larger subsidiaries of CBS, ABC, and NBC.

Robert Schuller—in bluish-gray and black velvet academic robes he has the gray-haired assurance and look of comfortable health, in the face of administrative and building costs, that college presidents either have or acquire. His large California audience of well-dressed, pleasantly worshipping citizens looks out upon the minister amid real fountains, gladiolas, and tropical plantings. Schuller is a West Coast Norman Vincent Peale and his "Hour of Power," with its theme of "possibility thinking," is not far from copyright infringement. On one of his programs he was offering "God's Gift for Your Self-Esteem," and this morning a rather more murky title, "Trust the Crust"—the crust of bread that somehow through trust manages to augment.

"Nobody has a money problem, only an idea problem." Schuller is drawn to words like "management" and to other suggestive business-school locutions. His present establishment gradually came about by way of "10,000 of $500 each, and then a million dollar gift and then another million dollar gift." This year, 1979, he is on his way to the construction of a huge cathedral made entirely of small pieces of glass—and for this some millions are still to be gathered in. The architect is Philip Johnson.

Rex Humbard, out of Akron, Ohio, offers a family-style program, with children and grandchildren singing in lacy dresses. His importunate, very successful, work is called "Outreach Ministry." On one of his smaller programs, he spoke, in a mood of frantic solicitation, of his acute need. He wants over a million for his ministry—and soon. In a variation on the tithing system, he suggests for his "seven-day crusade to save America," that one consider "a dollar a day for seven days, or ten dollars a day, or a hundred dollars a day . . . depending, of course."

"Rex, here is my vote of confidence and my special gift." In an unexpected manic aside, he suddenly reduced, so to speak, his vision and called upon those who were *illiterate* or *blind* to send their offering and find a friend to read the message that would be sent forthwith. A toll-free number flashes on, holds. One number for Akron, and one for Toronto and the Canadian trade.

Ernest Angley, a dreadful and menacing faith healer. This dumpy little primitive in a wig specializes in screams and awful slaps to the head of sick Christians. Thump, "I command no more sugar in the blood." Soon, he is pulling someone's deaf ear and saying, "See, he can hear." Then a back pain victim is slapped on his head, thump. "I dare yuh to find yuh back pain. Bend over any way yuh want. It's gawn."

"Stand up with yuh walker, yuh cane, yuh wheel chair. Get out there and come walking." To one woefully thin man, a blow on the head: "I command no more cancer. I command yuh to gain weight."

Jimmy Swaggart, a hysterical, good-looking, youngish preacher from Baton Rouge, combines loud, gasping old-time gospeling with shrewd, good country-music new-time gospeling. For his Study Bible, the complete King James version, with two hundred pages "plus" of new annotations, many of them helpful messages from himself, you will need $40 here and $50 in Canada. (Credit cards acceptable, toll-free number.)

On the other hand, Swaggart rages over "money ministries" and "merchandising the Gospel." He says, "I don't care where I am on the ratings" if to rise higher he would have "to trim the sails of This Book," the Study Bible.

Swaggart is the cousin of singer Jerry Lee Lewis, who "in 1957 was edging Elvis on the charts," but who has gone down from drinking. Why do you drink so much, Jerry? Why the pills? Jerry answered, "I do it because I keep passing the casket. My mother, my little boy, my older son, Jerry Lee Lewis, Jr.— all dead."

James Robison, out of Fort Worth, is a handsome, distressing, successful preacher with many things to sell, many needs, and troubling matters on his mind. He offers a bumper sticker reading: Freedom of speech, Freedom to preach. The admonition desperately relates to his outrageous beggary, and also to his legal problems. Without giving a clear notion of the indictments against him, Robison squanders a good deal of his costly TV time announcing that he has hired the luxurious services of the famous criminal lawyer, Richard "Horse Race" Haynes, whose most notorious recent employment (not mentioned) was the successful defense of millionaire J. Cullen Davis on a murder charge.

"James, why would you need a famous criminal lawyer?" Robison asks himself, again speaking for us. There is a drifting hint that "Horse Race" has some spiritual inclination in the case, but also he is "well versed in constitutional as well as criminal law."

One of Robison's brazen inspirations is the notion of "selling out for God." Luke 14:31 assists him in the discussion of the terrible inflationary cost of "discipleship." The verse reads:

"What king, going to make war against another king, sitteth not down first, and consulteth whether he be able with ten thousand to meet him that cometh against him with twenty thousand?"

"Selling out for God" does not appear to be a loose and fortuitous metaphor in the haphazard vocalization of spiritual transactions. Instead, it seems to have literal intention, urging a quick gathering of assets and a more hasty transfer. Robison told of a man who sold his business, giving everything to his "commitment" to the Robison ministry. The man's son, David, was compelled to find another job, now that his father's business was committed. The first day on the job, David picked up "an innocent looking wire" and was electrocuted. "I called the father right away, of course, and asked if he thought his commitment had killed his son. And the father answered: 'Satan tried to pull that trick on me, but I didn't buy it. I know where my son is.'"

Robison wants fifteen million dollars to pay for his assaults on the Bastille of Prime Time* and for whatever assaults upon himself he has hired Richard "Horse Race" Haynes to counter in the courts.

A remembrance from a story about Ruth Carter Stapleton and her therapeutic ministry. To a woman not looking her best, Mrs. Stapleton advised: "Jesus wants you to have some conditioner put on your hair. He wants you to get some make-up. He wants you to look nice." Poor He, poor He.

---

* Prime Time is the celestial goal, the evening star, of the rich evangelists. "You Are Loved," a Humbard one-hour "special" of benign, more or less secular boosterism, indeed appeared recently up in Maine, coming on immediately after the CBS Evening News and the Abbé Cronkite, as someone, Malcolm Muggeridge, I think, once called him. It was a vastly expensive Humbard Family vanity show, with Liz Humbard singing in front of Mount Rushmore and Mrs. (Maude) Humbard doing "God Bless America" very near to the Statue of Liberty, and "our special guests" Roy Rogers, Dale Evans, and born-again singer B. J. Thomas. Someone has been tithing for Rex and for America—no advertisements, only the "offerings" of the "You Are Loved" pin from the toll-free number.

part two

❖❖❖❖❖❖❖❖❖❖❖❖❖❖❖❖❖❖❖❖❖❖❖❖❖❖❖❖❖❖❖❖❖❖

Lives and
Local Scenery

Ring Lardner

When Ring Lardner died in 1933, Scott Fitzgerald wrote an interesting and somewhat despairing tribute to him. "The point of these paragraphs is that, whatever Ring's achievement was, it fell short of the achievement he was capable of, and this because of a cynical attitude toward his work." Fitzgerald thought Lardner had developed the habit of silence about important things and that he fell back in his writing on the formulas he always had ready at hand. It is easy to imagine how this might have appeared true thirty years ago when the memory of the great short story writer working away at his daily comic strip text was still painfully near to those who cared about him. Lardner was a perplexing man, often careless about his own talents. How to account for the element of self-destroying indifference in the joshing preface to *How to Write Short Stories*, a volume that contained "My Roomy," "Champion," "Some Like Them Cold," and "The Golden Honeymoon." Edmund Wilson's review of this volume in *The Dial* spoke warmly about the stories and mentioned the disturbing unsuitability of the preface, which he found so far below Lardner's usual level that "one suspects him of a guilty conscience at attempting to disguise his talent for social observation and satire." If Lardner knew of this criticism, he was unmoved by it and introduced *The Love Nest* in a similar manner. (That volume contained, among others, "Haircut" and "Zone of Quiet.") The palpable incongruity of the jocular prefaces as an introduction to the superlatively bitter stories serves as a mirror to the strangeness of Lardner's personality and work.

Reading Lardner again now is almost a new experience. Somewhat unexpectedly one finds that he has a dismal cogency to a booming America: his subjects are dishonesty, social climbing, boastfulness, and waste. For that reason, Maxwell Geismar's new collection is valuable as a way of bringing Lardner once more to public notice. This new volume, because of larger print, is easier to read than the Viking *Portable Ring Lardner*, but it is not otherwise an improvement. Indeed the Viking *Portable* has the advantage of the complete text of "You Know Me, Al" and "The Big Town." Geismar's preface does not supply more than the usual demand; nevertheless his selection will not fail anyone who wants the unsettling experience of discovering Ring Lardner or of rediscovering him.

Out of a daily struggle to make a living by literary work of various kinds, Lardner produced many short stories and some longer works of great originality. These stories were also immensely popular and nothing touches us more than this rare happening. In a country like ours where there will necessarily be so much journalism, so much support of the popular, the successful, we are complacently grateful when we find the genuine among the acceptable. And with Lardner there is something more: he made literature out of baseball, the bridge game, and the wisecrack. Of course he was terribly funny, but even in his funniest stories there is a special desolation, a sense of national spaces filled by stupidity and vanity.

Now, in the 1960s, the distance from the twenties reduces

some of the journalistic aspects of Lardner's writing. We are struck most of all by his difference from popular writing today. His is a miserable world made tolerable only by a maniacal flow of wisecracks. "That's Marie Antoinette's bed," the four-flusher says as he shows a couple around his Riverside Drive apartment. The wisecracker asks, "What time does she usually get in it?" When the wife says, "Guess who called me today?" the husband answers, "Josephus Daniels or Henry Ford. Or maybe it was the guy with the scar on his lip that you thought was smiling at you the other day." Out of the plain, unabashed gag, and the cruel dialogue of domestic life, Lardner created his odd stories, with their curious speed, rush of situation, explosion of insult and embarrassment.

Lardner's characters have every mean fault, but they lack the patience to do much with their meanness. The busher is boastful and stingy, and yet quite unable, for all his surface shrewdness, to discover his real place in the scheme of things. He is always being dropped by the women he had boasted about and all his stinginess cannot help to manage his affairs. Lardner's stories are filled with greedy, grasping people who nevertheless go bankrupt. You cannot say they are cheated, since they are themselves such awful cheats. The Gullibles have the fantastic idea of going to Palm Beach to get into "society." Mrs. Gullible does at last meet Mrs. Potter Palmer in the corridor of the hotel and Mrs. Palmer asks her to put more towels in her suite. The squandering of an inheritance by the characters in "The Big Town" shows a riotous lack of elementary common sense. The husbands usually have some idea of the cost of things and of the absurdity of their wives' ambitions. But they cannot act upon their knowledge. It comes out only in the constant static of their wisecracks. Wildly joking, they go along with their wives into debt and humiliation. It is hard to feel much sympathy and yet occasionally one does so: the sympathy comes, when it does, from the fact that the jokes played upon these dreadful people are after all thoroughly real and mean. Even the language they speak with such immense, dismaying humor is a kind of joke on real language, funnier and more cutting than we can bear.

Vanity, greed, and cruel humor are the themes of Lardner's stories. The lack of self-knowledge is made up for by a dizzy readiness with cheap alibis. No group or class seems better than another; there is a democracy of cheapness and shallowness. Lies are at the core of nearly every character he produces for us. The only fear is being caught out, exposed to the truth. Love cannot exist because the moment it runs into trouble the people lie about their former feelings. Because of the habit of lying, it is a world without common sense. The tortured characters are not always victims. They may be ruined and made fun of, but they have the last word. They bite the leg that kicks them.

"Haircut" is one of the cruelest pieces of American fiction. Even Lardner seems to have felt some need for relief from the relentless evil of the smalltown joker and so he has him killed in the end. This cruel story is just about the only one that has the contrast of decent people preyed upon by a maniac. "Champion" is brutal and "The Golden Honeymoon" is a masterpiece of grim realism. Alfred Kazin speaks of the "harsh, glazed coldness" of Lardner's work. He wrapped his dreadful events in a comic language, as you would put an insecticide in a bright can.

Lardner's personality is very difficult to take hold of. In spite of poor health that came, so far as I can discover, from his devastating drinking, he had the continuing productivity of the professional journalist. He went to work every morning. Why he drank, why his views were so bitter are a mystery. He came from a charming, talented family and married a woman he loved. He was kind, reserved, hard-working; his fictional world is loud, cruel, filled with desperate marriages, hideous old age, suburban wretchedness, fraud, drunkenness. Even the sports world is degraded and athletes are likely to be sadists, crooks, or dumbbells. The vision is thoroughly desperate. All the literature of the thirties and forties does not contain such pure subversion, snatched on the run from the common man and his old jokes.

Robert Frost in His Letters

Simplicity and vanity, independence and jealousy combined in Robert Frost's character in such unexpected ways that one despairs of sorting them out. He is two picture puzzles perversely dumped into one box and, no matter how much you try, the leg will never go rightly with the arm, nor this brown eye with that green one. Perhaps the worst you could say about Frost was that he could not really like his peers. The second circumstance the observer of "the man" must deal with is that, as an engaging but insistent monologist, he was not especially mindful of the qualities of his auditors and therefore spent a good deal of time in the company of mediocrities. And, further, you could say about Frost, as Dr. Johnson said of Pope, that he had the felicity to take himself at his true value.

If these faults are unfortunate, at least one must say that retribution has not been lenient or slow to come. During Frost's lifetime he was the subject of many astonishingly uneventful books and hopeful was the soul who imagined his death would bring an end to this. His friends were and are dismayingly disposed to sentimental reminiscences. People could not only listen to Frost and read his verse, they could also write about him as if they somehow felt he was not much better than they themselves were. No hesitation intervened and few complications of feeling arose. Frost was his own stereotype. He was already written, so to speak, and one had only to put it all down. He was the *spécialité* of many a comfortable *maison*—a college president here, a governor or two there, and at last even the great Chiefs themselves. Nice, successful people tended to see him as, simply, Robert Frost, a completed image. And as for his work, well, that too was clear. New England human nature he loved and next to nature, art—although as the most tenacious of old, old men he was never, not even at eighty-eight, "ready to depart."

Here are Frost's letters to Louis Untermeyer. They begin in 1915 and they end in 1961. That is a long time and it would take a heart very hard indeed not to agree that Louis Untermeyer, having set upon these eggs for forty-five years, was naturally impatient. His idea had always been to bring the letters to print at the earliest possible moment. Actually, relief had been promised in 1961 and Untermeyer, at that time, prepared the volume for publication. But Frost stalled and stalled. ("When the manuscript was ready for the printer, he made excuses for delaying the publication.") No matter, here they are. They are printed without an index and are very difficult to use for that reason. Still they are certainly quite "interesting." And one must confess, full of vanity, ambition and ungenerosity.

Frost was a good letter writer, but not a superlatively good one. Indeed, except of course in his poetry, he is untranslatable from the spoken to the written word and that is why those thousands, under the enchantment of what he *said*, will always be perplexed about how cold he appears in his letters and how dull in his biographies. He was malicious and capricious, but there was, hanging about it all, the famous blue-eyed twinkle, the liquid chuckle, the great head, handsome and important at all ages. And when he had said everything his hurt heart had stored up inside him, then he twinkled once more and took it all back, calling it "my fooling."

In 1915, when the letters begin, *North of Boston* had just been enthusiastically received in America (by Louis Untermeyer, among others, and therefore the correspondence) after the very important reception it had received the previous year in England. From that time on, Frost was recognized as a major American poet, even though, of course, he had the usual dismal scratch to make a living and there were many ways in which he endured the intermittent neglect of fashion and the narrow interpretations of some of his more complacent admirers. In 1915, when fame and assurance came, Frost was forty-one years old. That fact is often made to bear the burden for whatever limitations of spirit he may sometimes have shown as a man.

Until the publication of *North of Boston* in England, Frost lived a lonely and more or less isolated life with his wife and children. He had various jobs—always he worked as little as possible because he never had any doubt from the first that his fate would be to devote his whole life to writing poetry. He had started writing in high school and even after he was married he went back to Harvard to study the classics, to prepare himself for his clear destiny. He was never more than an indifferent farmer. He wrote slowly and did not flood the offices of magazines with his verse, only to suffer rejection. He was not immediately recognized and no doubt the tardiness was cruel; yet when fame came it was not dramatically late and it was certainly dramatically brilliant. One cannot altogether credit the indifference he showed to the claims of his fellow poets to an unbearably long wait for public approval. After the success of *North of Boston*, he began the rounds of readings, intervals at various colleges, appearances and so on from which he made a living—this, with his writing, filled up the rest of his life. He was to be the most gregarious of lonely men, the most loquacious of taciturn Vermonters, the most ambitious of honest Yankees.

Frost had a very active and expansive idea of the kind of figure he meant to cut, the kind of role a poet should play in society. His sense of public demand was always acute even though much of his best work, nearly all of it, grew out of his early days of isolation, his experiences with the farm people of New England. That was the treasure upon which he drew. The privacy of his earlier years was as much a reflection of his wife's character as his own. About his wife, Frost writes to Untermeyer: "Elinor has never been of any earthly use to me. She hasn't cared whether I went to school or worked or earned anything. She has resisted every inch of the way my efforts to get money. She is not too sure that she cares about my reputation. She wouldn't lift a hand to have me lift a hand to increase my reputation or even to save it . . . She always knew I was a good poet, but that was between her and me, and there I think she would have liked it if it had remained at least until we were dead. . . ."

Frost, even in great poverty and defiance, was as far as anyone could be from the *poète maudit* or the Bohemian. In his personality and in his conception of the dramatic possibilities of the literary life, he appears to have united two strains. On the one hand he shows a clear connection with the old New England sages in their role of public instructors. Emerson was a hero of Frost's and Emerson's great career as a lecturer was of course not lost upon his young admirer. The two men were indeed different, but Frost with his poems and his sagacious anecdotes meant, as much as Emerson in his lectures, to save the nation. The writer counted, he was an important public figure and his ideas were urgent. Secondly, Frost seems to have been stirred by the vast audiences, both literary and public, of men like Edgar Lee Masters and Vachel Lindsay. The sales of *Spoon River* were extremely annoying to him. The fantastic popularity of the manic performances of Vachel Lindsay made their point. (So greatly stressful has the life of a writer ever been in America that Lindsay, when his hold upon things began to weaken, drank Lysol, saying as he sank into death, "They tried to get me, I got them first.") E. A. Robinson and Frost gradually took the attention away from Lindsay and Masters. (Masters, in his quite unusually interesting biography of Lindsay, published in 1935, says that the Jews were to blame for the vogue of the New Englanders. To the Jews, "pioneers are objects of aversion. . . ." By "pioneer" he did not signify anything technical or revolutionary, but rather that he and Lindsay were Middle Westerners.) In any case, forensic powers were part of the writer's baggage as Frost saw it.

The relation of Frost to other poets was frankly one of rivalry —indeed one of frank rivalry. He had a certain good-natured, off-hand way of expressing this that saved him from any hint of fanaticism, but it must be said that he was quite anxious about E. A. Robinson's reputation. He made fun of Wallace Stevens' "Peter Quince at the Clavier." He was ungracious about Walter de la Mare ("I have been in no mood to meet Walter de la Mare. He is one of the open questions with me, like what to do with Mexico"), and even had the odd notion that De la Mare was an imitator of Edward Thomas, who in turn was Frost's most important disciple. In late life when Frost, visiting out in Ohio, was taken to see the old reclusive poet, Ralph Hodgson, he reported, "I couldn't see that it gave Ralph Hodgson much pleasure to see me. . . ." Frost was a man of great culture, of naturally good taste, and had the deepest seriousness about poetry —it was vanity and not simplicity of mind that led him to fear his great contemporaries. His praise went to Untermeyer, Raymond Holden, and Dr. Merrill Moore. That the Nobel Prize should have gone to T. S. Eliot and Camus he considered, as Unter-meyer tells us, "a personal affront."

Frost's private life was marked by the regular appearance of disaster. Except for his devotion to his wife and—what to call it?—the clamorous serenity of his old age, he was spared little. His sister went insane during the First World War. His letter about her condition is not sacrificial. "As I get older I find it easier to lie awake nights over other people's troubles. But that's as far as I go to date. In good time I will join them in death to show our common humanity." His most talented daughter, Marjorie, died late in her twenties and his wife never fully recovered from her grief. She herself died suddenly, leaving Frost utterly bereft and disorganized. Untermeyer describes this period: "It was hard for Robert to maintain his balance after Elinor's death. He sold the Amherst house where he and Elinor had lived; he resigned from the college; he talked recklessly, and for the first time in his life the man whose favorite tipple was ginger ale accepted any drink that was offered."

After a sad life spent in a futile attempt to become a writer, Frost's son, Carol, committed suicide. Another daughter broke down and had to be put in an institution. There is no doubt that Frost grieved deeply over these tragedies—horrors the audi-ences coming to see him and to read him knew nothing of. Still he endured and he gradually settled down to his spectacular old age and to those multifarious activities that made his final image.

His reputation as a poet was, one might say, put into order by the brilliant essays of Randall Jarrell. Those essays—so far as I can be sure without an index—are not mentioned in the letters to Untermeyer. They had a stunning effect upon Frost's reputation with the most serious young writers and readers. At the end, Frost was *in* with everyone, with Sherman Adams and W. H. Auden alike. This is a circumstance of great rarity in our literature. Of course, it was the nature of Frost's poetic talent, as well as the prodigality of it, that allowed this ubiquitous prospering of his work. As Yvor Winters puts it: "A popular poet is always a spectacle of some interest, for poetry in general is not popular; and when the popular poet is also within limits a distinguished poet, the spectacle is even more curious. . . . When we encounter such a spectacle, we may be reasonably sure of finding certain social and historical reasons for the popularity." Winters goes on to say that Frost writes of rural subjects and "the American reader of our time has an affection for rural subjects . . ." and so on. In spite of the misinterpretations of some of Frost's readers, he was at least to everyone *readable*. How difficult it is to imagine even so well-liked a poet as T. S. Eliot at the Eisenhower board. Perhaps Eisenhower did not even read Frost, but if he had he could certainly have understood at least some of his work; one cannot be sure of a patience for "Prufrock" or "Journey of the Magi."

One of the most arresting aspects of Frost's character was his genuine interest in power. And for him power did not lie, as it does with most artists, in the comradeship or the approval of the *avant-garde*. Also, he cared nothing for "smart" people, for chicness, for the usual intellectual celebrity world. What he liked was the institutionalized thing. He was perfectly serious in his relationship to power. When he was Consultant in Poetry at the Library of Congress he expected to be "consulted," and not about what went on the poetry shelf, but after important matters of state. So great was his idea of public possibility that he went beyond factionalism, serving Republican and Democrat in turn, in a spirit of poet-laureatism and also in some strangely conceived Public Spokesman mask. His political ideas were usually capricious. A certain coldness entered into his notions. If he had a consistent political theme it was self-reliance. The New Deal with its atmosphere of optimistic enthusiasm was antipathetic to him. But Frost was not in any way a fanatic. He never went very far; somehow inside him there was always the desire to please. Take Untermeyer for instance: layered over his person, like a house with its coat after coat of paint, is nearly every folly and every enthusiasm of liberal belief of the last forty years. Frost teased him; he never became angry with him or broke with him. The independent old Vermonter side of Frost has been exaggerated. He was indeed independent, but he wanted to count, to have importance: this gave him a steady flow of prudence. Frost did not even want disciples. That would be a two-way street and except for those in his family he didn't want to share himself. (Edward Thomas died in the First World War.)

The strain of some unnamed trouble that we feel in Frost is inexplicable. He was brilliant, adored, available, and even his resentments were not the sort that stripped a man of his charm. They did form his ideas to some degree. Somehow he had suffered and come through: there are no Welfare State lessons to be learned from that. There is, instead, only the example of individual initiative. Even his relation to those people who, like Ezra Pound, had the highest regard for his powers was touched by ambivalence. Amy Lowell wrote an early and very impressive essay about him, but he was, if pleased, not *entirely* satisfied. (Didn't like what she said about his wife and was not happy to share the stage with Robinson.) The only mention I can find—in Elizabeth Shepley Sergeant's book—that Frost actually made of Randall Jarrell is not about Jarrell's writing and is a bit querulous: "Randall Jarrell thinks poets aren't helped enough. But I say poetry has always lived on a good deal of neglect." We shall have to wait for other Frost letters to get his full opinion of Untermeyer.

But Frost was not a conservative, either. He was only a writer. He did not care for money, but for position, whatever

Sex and the Single Man

Poor Corydon is now in California, driving the freeways with a daydreaming ardor, attacking the ants with a Flit gun, and mourning among the hibiscus bushes. His name is George and perhaps he must be called the "hero" of Christopher Isherwood's new novel, *A Single Man*. George is chagrined, restless, grieving over the death of his lover and housemate, Jim, as a widower would grieve for his wife. George is an Englishman. He is ironical, middle-aged, and yet boyishly passionate. His is a fairly modest anal disposition, respectable enough, with a finicky, faggoty interest in the looks of things—far from the corruption and splendor of his type in French fiction. And yet perhaps he is a little corrupt and a little splendid, too. George lives in a hide-away cottage on Camphor Tree Lane. He knows all about the human and decorative insults of suburban California; his tastes are low but his Taste, of course, is reasonably high. He is a perverse mixture of arrogance and shyness, suspicion and indifference. Devastating revolts threaten in daydreams, but in truth he is controlled enough to get by. His neighbors, the Strunk and Garfein couples and their rackety children, are the object of George's fears and his satiric vexation.

George teaches at San Tomas State College in Los Angeles.

If he were not so "English," so plausibly bred, he might, as he faces his classroom of boys and girls lined up before him like bulldogs, be some S. Levin out of Malamud. His entrance into the classroom "is a subtly contrived, outrageously theatrical effect." When he gives his brittle, hysterical lecture on Huxley's *After Many a Summer*, we see that George is not a real teacher, but one of those American artists or writers, hanging by his fingernails to his academic and sexual freedom, making a diversive display to hide a natural leaning toward indiscretions.

George is abjectly presented. Indeed his first scene takes place on the john. ("George feels a bowel movement coming on with agreeable urgency and climbs the stairs briskly to the bathroom, book in hand.") The book is by Ruskin and from his throne George looks down upon Mrs. Strunk "emptying the dustbag of her vacuum cleaner into the trash can." It is not Isherwood's purpose to write a novel "about" homosexuality; rather, he appears to want to present, without "scholarship," or explanation, a homosexual who is, so to speak, just like everyone else, who claims his rights to be allowed to go about his homosexual life— a life curiously, in its little cottage, its domesticity, its social compromises, remote from angularity and singularity. There is a lot of Mr. and Mrs. Strunk—or is it Mr. and Mrs. Garfein?— in George and Jim. They too are emptying, day in and day out, the dustbags into the trash can.

So George is a natural man, compromised, self-conscious, irritable, but nevertheless keeping up his exercises (and his all too easily aroused hopes) at the gym, telling his little jokes and still heroically on the make. He is slight: that is to say we see him for only one twenty-four hour period as he struggles through his slices of life, all bare of poetic ornamentation and free of strenuous intention. The events of the day are mostly routine in the accepted sense; when they are unusual they are still routine to George's erectile existence. In a melancholy scene, George dines on "Borneo stew" with another English survivor of cocktail parties and dead love affairs: a lady named Charlotte—called "Charley"—who wears embroidered peasant clothes. They get very drunk and Charley, as prone to squalid, sexual hopes at the wrong time as George himself, begins to think—well, why not? Maybe? Who knows now that Jim has gone? "As they embrace, she kisses him full on the mouth. And suddenly sticks her tongue right in!" In the end, Charley defers to reality and changes the subject.

Late at night, staggering, George goes through his eternal return: a mystifying, exhilarating encounter with a normal man. At a bar he meets one of his students, Kenny, who has come to look for him. George's heart leaps up with excitement, wonder, joy. Is Kenny flirting with him? Are these teasing remarks full of invitation and promise? But Kenny disappears after a devastating (for George) swim in the nude and the questions are still unanswered. George is left with his onanistic explosion, a grateful moment in which he can, in imagination, order all the players about. "George hastily turns Kenny into the big blond boy from the tennis court. Oh, much better! Perfect! Now they can embrace. Now the fierce hot animal play can begin."

Mr. Norris with his perfume, his giggles, his wig, his moans of joy in the sadistic brothels of Berlin of 1931; Peter Wilkinson, the weak, spoiled English boy enslaved to Otto Nowak; the hinting end of *Prater Violet* ("Love had been J. for the last month. . . . After J., there would be K. and L. and M., right down the alphabet"). Isherwood's books have all been homosexual in spirit; even campy. Perhaps the surprising thing is that he has so often been able to be a serious artist at the same time. For instance, about Germany in the 1930s few works of fiction have told us more than these peculiar stories. Even in style, in form, his work was strikingly appropriate. He had found the way around falsity and exaggeration by simplicity and directness. One had the feeling, often, that this was not fiction at all. The stories seemed entirely natural and easy: they were simply strokes of good luck, seized upon by a clever author. The luck to have been in Berlin, the luck to meet Sally Bowles. Imagine knowing an outrageous man like Arthur Norris or doing a film with the director, Dr. Bergmann. And there, standing aside from the whippings and the abortions and masochistic brawls, was the austere, beautiful Landauer family, to whose strict and touching daughter, Natalia ("'You are lazy? . . . So? Then I am sorry. I can't help you.'"), Chris had the good fortune to give English lessons. In "The Landauers" Isherwood wrote one of the most poignant stories about the suffering of the Berlin Jews.

The easy manner—the use of his own name—gave the tone of journalism, of reportage, of a superlative ease. There was not much invention, but there was perfection, rightness. All the events in the early books, up through *Prater Violet*, seemed to be just life itself, without manipulation, without the temptation of the hope of aggrandizement by formal means. "I am a camera," he insisted. And one of the sections of a more recent book, *Down There on a Visit*, begins: "Five years have gone by—this is May 1933—and here I am, starting out on another journey. I am on a train going south from Berlin toward the Czechoslovakian frontier. Opposite me sits Waldemar." Involvement, spontaneity, actuality are all meant to be suggested by his manner, but it is a very special Isherwood autobiography, the autobiography of "experiences" rather than Experience. It is Waldemar, not ancestors, that seems at the center of everything. Perhaps it is natural that his straight reporting would appear less true than his fiction. In a travel book about Peru and Ecuador, *The Condor and the Cows*, a great deal seems made up, re-written, arranged, and so there is a loss of vivacity. The expected travel scene does not raise Isherwood's talent to a heat. "Last night, Mr. Smith and his wife asked us to a party at their house where we met Mr. Mott, the manager of the Shell Oil Company of Ecuador."

After *Prater Violet*, Isherwood began to choose more ordinary ground for his social comedy, particularly in his "straight" novel, *The World in the Evening*, and in the setting of the new one, *A Single Man*. (*Down There on a Visit* is something else. It is saturated with all the knowledge of vice Isherwood had somehow made into art previously, but here the scene is claustrophobic, decadent.) In the end we see that Mr. Norris is more real to Isherwood than the Coke drinkers before their television sets. Satire of the ordinary and the usual had for him as for other novelists the risk of trivializing genuine emotions. In *The Condor and the Cows*, he mentions a young American couple on their second honeymoon. "After years of accepted routine—office work, raising children, shopping, cooking—you take your marriage out of its little suburban frame and set it against a tremendous classic background of ocean, mountains and stars. How does it stand up? Is it self-sufficient, deep, brilliant and compact as a Vermeer? Or a messy amateur sketch which doesn't compose?" That cuts the young couple down like lightning. Better any old fat lady on the dance floor than that. In *A Single Man* he writes, as others before him have about America, "('old,' in our country of the bland, has become nearly as dirty a word as 'kike' or 'nigger')." When you are dealing with fundamental ideas, jauntiness of style may offend against the truth. It is the satirist and not his object who appears trivial.

In the earlier works, in *Goodbye to Berlin*, *The Last of Mr. Norris* and *Prater Violet*, everything pure in Isherwood's talent came together. His masochistic fascination with vice did not spoil his nature; he was a perverse and yet a liberal, free spirit. As time went on, the spirit seemed to tire a little. Compulsion, isolation defined his mood. The body had become a terrible enemy. *A Single Man* begins and ends with brute biology.

George's demeaning day opens as "fear tweaks the vagus nerve. . . . But meanwhile the cortex, that great disciplinarian, has taken its place at the central controls and has been testing them, one after another. . . ." In the evening, the unhappy vespers sound: "Within this body on the bed, the great pump works on. . . ." So, poor Aurelia's growing old. George will soon have a heart attack and his cruising, his longing, will be over.

Looking back over the novels, you see an Isherwood who is pleasure-loving and yet guilty. *Down There on a Visit* shows us that the life is Hell. The boys are really awful, pretentious, shallow, dishonest; the women are disgusting; and Hollywood, where one works, does not ennoble. The detachment—malicious but not forbidding—has changed to fatigue. What had been amusing is now seen by Isherwood as the trap, the humiliation. If *A Single Man* seems tired, it is also true in feeling. It is a sad book, with a biological melancholy running through it, a sense of relentless reduction, daily diminishment. From the morning toilet to the evening masturbation—that is its sadly swinging arc. . . . The Bhagavad-Gita, the California monastery, Gerald Heard—those flights of Isherwood's about which we have heard, the hope for peace, the escape, are not without point.

Domestic Manners

How are we living today? Of course, there is no "we" except for those who address us, advise us, praise us in the round, as "the American people." The phrase is a signal for the wary, doing as it so often does more honor to the exhorter and his plans than to those millions gathered in under the grand title.

Only the forgetful can easily ignore the duplicity practiced upon the defining imagination by the sudden obsolescence of attitudes and styles just past, styles that collapsed or scattered into fragments just as one had felt free to identify them as facts, changes, alterations of consciousness, shiftings of power or threats to power. These elements, at least at the moment of identification, had the shape of reality, of historical presence, of genuine displacements; and even though they could not be asserted as eternal they still could not be experienced as mere historical moments soon, very soon, to be reversed or simply erased. It is with some perturbation that one has to learn again and again that the power of external forces is greater than style, stronger than fleeting attitude.

"Confidence in the future" is a peculiar phrase, although in frequent use. It is not meant to signify the mere expectation of continuing existence, but rather to signify hope—perhaps for the stock market, for relations with recalcitrant and truculent foreign countries, for our own life as a whole, or for small groups, rich or poor, protected or beleaguered, who are in need of reassurance. It seems to mean that it is reasonable to assume the future will not diminish rewards in some cases or that the future will augment rewards in others. Most seriously it imagines that the future will, with all its attendant inequities and surprises, remain open to the understanding and to the effort of those leaders and advisers we have grown accustomed to and from whom, given the nature of things, we have generously not asked very much. These assumptions about the future are in grave disorder and "confidence" is merely a sentiment.

There is always the question of the will to understand first and then the greater will of society to undertake even the most reasonable alleviations, since alleviations on the one hand are the cue for disgruntlements elsewhere. Lacking the will, society waits for events to which it must respond, often in a final condition of fear and crisis and anger; or, in long, drawn-out, hopelessly tangled injustices and dangerous defaults it simply waits not to respond at all. Things reveal themselves in an atmosphere of grotesque folly. The persons exploiting oil in Arab countries are the same persons theatrically throwing pound notes on the ground in London rather than on the parched land of the poor of their own regions. The waste of Western capitalism is not always different, but America at least is used to the waste and looks upon the reduction of it with alarm.

To speak of persons as the "product" of their decade, or half-decade in some cases, is a severe telescoping of history, and yet it has an obvious descriptive usefulness, a conversational meaning that is measured by the clear recognition others give to the terms, a recognition coming out of the very grossness of the designations.

Certain persons and certain aspects of our society appear to be a product of the 1960s. The legacy of the period is intractable morally and socially in the manner of all history and it bears the peculiar opacity of its closeness to the present—that is, the period is *experience*, and its transformation into history is somewhat a work of the subjective imagination, a work close to autobiography in the way it reenters the memory.

There is sadness and regret in the memory of the sixties. For those who reached the age of eighteen in the last years of the decade the temptations to self-destructions were everywhere, bursting forth from what was called the "counter-culture." The hallucinations of LSD, deformations by drugs that lingered on in apathy, addiction, aborted education, restlessness; the deprivations and fantasies of numerous torpid "communes," the beginnings of hysterical youth cults—this still lies there behind us, for it seems that historical rubble is no more easily disposed of than the stone and steel and concrete of misbegotten highways, shopping centers, overweening towers for habitation. For those who in the sixties were "revolutionaries," it meant hiding, police records, death, exile, the delusions of youthful power that took little account of the brutal rebukes the genuine power of society can command. It meant disillusionment with "infantile leftism," with postures that time and the sluggishness of history outmoded.

For the youth of the sixties who remained outside the general reaches of a vibrating, rebellious youth culture, the decade meant death in Vietnam, mutilation, bad dreams, drug addiction, the bad faith of corrupted authority, and, at the least, a weird and agitating confusion of values. President Carter's campaign made an effort to give voice to the youth who accommodated the sixties, those who agreed with the old values in peace and war, those who suffered; but it was disheartening to realize how little he could find to say, how vague and unreal were the consolations, the approbations. If sacrifice is not to be praised as a value based upon its objectives, the gratitude of authority is therefore bound to be mixed with shame and to come forth merely as rhetoric.

Casualties of every spiritual and personal nature lay about as the legacy of the sixties. Authorities experienced much of the decade as a form of insult and fell into a state of paranoia. It was only by accident that the paranoids were removed from the domination of the state and from the determination to corrupt many of its institutions.

On the other side, the agitated scrutiny directed in the sixties to the arrangements of society discovered many pieties and hypocrisies which had claimed the aspect of eternity but which were, in fact, mere prejudices and matters of unexamined convenience. Many benign and practical refusals and reversals marked the period—the questioning of unnecessary, self-serving authority in the home and in institutions, the pure hopes of the Civil Rights Movement. Informalities of all sorts, trivial and important, could, it turned out, be more or less painlessly accepted and removed from the domain of social oppression. Tolerance of deviation, acceptance of a pluralism long ago established by ocular evidence, concern for the integrity and endurance of nature, ridicule of the endless consumption of redundant goods, personal relations, masculine presumption, the old and the young—the mere listing of customs and tyrannies challenged in the sixties is, as Chaucer said, like "trying to catch the wind in a net."

The children of the sixties had been brought up in the fifties and no doubt this earlier, seemingly plausible and hopeful, period floated about parent and child like an ectoplasmic memory. The fifties—they seem to have taken place on a sunny afternoon that asked nothing of you except a drifting belief in the moment and its power to satisfy: a handsome young couple, with two or three children, a station wagon, a large dog, a house and a summer house, a great deal of picnicking and camping together.

For the middle class the fifties passed in a dream, a dream in which benevolent wishes for oneself were not thought of as always hostile to the enlarging possibilities of others. The treasured child would do well in school and the psychiatrist could be summoned for the troubled. The suburbs offered the space and grass that would bless family existence. The cars and the second cars were symbols of power over one's life, as anyone can see who looks at the gleaming chariots that decorate the filthy, blasted streets of the ghettos.

The sixties seemed to grow, nationally and personally, upon the beguiling confidence of the decade just past. Wars to establish credibility are for the prosperous. Time was not slow, however, but speeded up, unreal, very much like time in the air; by the late sixties the happy child was scarcely to be distinguished as he went into his teens from the quarrelsome one. Complacent parents had, after all, expected more than they realized, more of their children and more of each other. And so a decade was only ten years. And a new year could be more like a tornado uprooting the grass than another period of growth.

But how *real* the sixties were, how dreadfully memorable the horrors, how haunting the alterations, everywhere, in feeling, in belief. Already the receding years have character, violently ambivalent, and beyond repeal. And how American, one is tempted to insist. In what way? Perhaps in the way destruction was created out of the pleasures of plentitude, assassinations out of the riveting excitements of leadership, diminishment out of a manic sense of expansiveness. What went down were people here, whole countries far away, and a few of the unnecessary follies that had been sitting in our lives like memorial plaques on the mantelpiece.

A strange decade indeed. How is one to set a value upon the

sensible pleasures of "informality" and the limited liberation of maligned groups against the slaughter of people? And what is the historical connection, finally? The connection between the rights of personal style in dress and living arrangements, the right to homosexuality, to marihuana, and the present nightmare in Cambodia? It was a terrifying decade, anarchic, brutal —and fortunately for all of us, the saving energy of a profound protest, sustained by youth and a few older allies, a protest against dehumanization, military control, political lying, and power madness.

The 1970s have passed their zenith. Did they take place— this handful of years—somewhere else, in another land, inside the house, the head? Fatigue and recession, cold winters and expensive heat, resignations and disgrace. Quietism, inner peace, having their turn, as if history were a concert program, some long and some short selections, a few modern and the steady traditional. For young people, it is common to say that things have settled down. *Down* is the key: accommodation, docility, depression of spirit.

Many people are going to law school, searching, one supposes, for the little opening, the ray of sun at the mouth of the cave. It does not seem possible that what our world needs is a generation of new young lawyers. In certain respects what is being honored, at least by the approving adults, is not always the actual profession so much as the sign of a willingness to begin and to persevere to the end for a practical purpose, to memorize, to master a process without the demands for the gratifications of supreme interest at each moment along the way. Yet, out there at the end are the litigious anxieties of the corporate world to which whole young lives are to be prosperously dedicated and consumed.

Advanced studies in the humanities are another matter. They are felt to be impractical—and that means that society does not find them necessary. There are not only enough of you scholars, it says, there are too many. To go on in the study of literature, philosophy, or history can be a personal passion, but as a profession it depends upon someone out there to teach and a supply of teachers in a reasonable relation to the waiting learners. At the present time, the Ph.D.s remind one of the feverish, superfluous clerks in Russian literature, anxious persons floating in a menacing void, waving their supererogatory diplomas. It is not quite clear that to come to the end of one's college years is to have arrived anywhere.

The seventies have not been free of definition; even drift has its direction. Intimacy, the validation of the self in a narrow, intense relation with a few others, or one other, is seen by many thinkers as a definition of our period. Very few of those who do the naming are pleased with the turn of the wheel. It is not the activism of the sixties that is mourned by conventional commentators but rather a wish for a more aggressive, outward-looking intrusion of the individual ego into the realities of power, into concern for a material grasp of self-interest rather than the vaporous transcendence of self-absorption.

The past reclaimed as an image, the opacity of life lightened by dichotomies, the fall and the rise. Our own time: "It is the localizing of human experience, so that what is close to the immediate circumstances of life is paramount." The quotation is from Richard Sennett's ambitious book called *The Fall of Public Man*, a fall which led naturally to the elevation of private man, ourselves, and "The Tyrannies of Intimacy."

The public life, as Sennett somewhat vaguely reconstructs its lost shape, was lived out of a rich variety of experiences and acceptances largely impersonal. The life of the city was possible then; intimacy, however, lives out of a fear of the unknown and the different and allows the self to retreat, nervously, into absorption in the private. Finally, one cannot in present history know others unless one knows them in a fearful closeness, accepts them as part of the returning reassurance of looking into a mirror. It is the nature of intimacy to be unattainable, a mood trembling with anxieties and insecurities because the self is insatiable. The city, along with many other things, dies, frozen by the retreat from the public domain.

Sennett's book is an abstruse effort in cultural history, designed to reach its destination—contemporary "narcissism." Narcissism, awareness, intimacy, new consciousness—these terms appear again and again in theoretical and autobiographical descriptions of the seventies. The words are strikingly varied in quality and seriousness—the least "serious" usually being revelations and transcendencies achieved in a few balmy autobiographies, the very process of "success" providing the despairing material of the more distant and critical theoreticians.

The self's unanchored demand for security and relief from psychological unease dominates the inhabitants of Christopher Lasch's brilliant essays on the "narcissist society." (It is part of the puzzle of current writing on the elusive present that Sennett's *reign* of private man is in many respects another way of describing Lasch's "The *Waning* of Private Life." "Private life" in Lasch's work appears to represent roughly what has been called "family life.") About the ubiquitous drift to narcissism, Lasch writes, "Having no hope of improving their lives in any of the ways that matter, people have convinced themselves that what matters is psychic self-improvement: getting in touch with their feelings, eating health food, taking lessons in ballet or belly dancing, immersing themselves in the wisdom of the East, jogging, learning how to 'relate,' overcoming the 'fear of pleasure.'"

The cultural analyst, Philip Rieff, has assumed the present under the notion of the "triumph of the therapeutic"—the hunger for personal satisfaction that imposes upon the will the privilege or the burden of escaping painful feelings. The "therapeutic" (strangely, at times Rieff speaks of it, or to it, as "him"), in the writing of the often-hectoring Rieff, means many things, among them that ideas, emotions, experiences take their moral and social value from how they make you feel. The contemporary soul escapes from anxiety, duty, orderly thought by means of therapy and by therapeutic assaults upon intellectual and social authority. All of these writers, naming the not-quite-measurable sense of the present, are different in tone and in the atmosphere of recommendation, warning, regret that is the surrounding mist of the intellectual, political, and temperamental inclination of the individual writer at his desk. There is not doubt that they all prefigure (in Rieff's case) and describe one phenomenon of the seventies—the demonic acceleration of investments in gurus, encounters, magical healings, diets, transcendencies and transformations that compete, like varieties of aspirin, for the remission of aches of the mind and psyche.

Life at home, domestic drama, sexual warfare are part of history, and the matter of fiction. Divorce statistics are little figures of decline that reveal more than mere legal possibility and fact. The numbers are rich in attitudes, assumptions, hopes and lost hopes. It is not necessary to seek a divorce in order to live out personally the deepest skepticisms about the future of marriage. Irony about romantic love is the inescapable soil of existence upon which both marriage and divorce grow simultaneously, shooting up in the same season like plants in the garden.

Irony represents the recognition of the shortened life of the feelings. It says that the attachment to a particular person, even the legal attachment, defines the moment or the years but is far from being the key to the future. Disruption may represent failure, but it also represents the sweet boundaries of new hopes. If we can trust fiction and film, our period is, like that of Restoration drama, *comic*.

An abundance of cynical wit and coarseness are the necessary conditions for verisimilitude about prevailing manners. In speaking of the cynical and coarse one is not investing the words with moral outrage; they are instead descriptive. With the appearance of a large number of licentious works by women, even the cuckold has returned as a familiar figure in literature. Certain types return and certain are lost forever, figures such as the awkward, trusting ingénue or country girl of the Restoration period. Don Giovanni's *mille e tre*, the once singular arithmetic of the frenzied aristocrat, appears as a natural accumulation of the normal sexual exuberance of men and women freed, instructed, and determined.

The comic destinations of romantic love are shown in Saul Bellow's last novel. In *Humboldt's Gift*, the most engaging of the novel's female characters, Renata, leaves the intellectual, Citrine, to marry a mortician. In Joseph Heller's *Something Happened*, the hero sighs and says it sometimes occurs to him that he got married so that he could then be divorced.

Ennui is an attendant of irony. Andy Warhol, the painter, said about his decision to abandon his emotional and sexual life: "I was happy to see it go." Love with its ancient distresses cannot be removed from the landscape by fashion. It cannot be separated from power, for one thing. Nevertheless, the pains of rejection and loss, representing as they do interferences encountered by the individual will, are not sympathetically understood as sufferings to be endured. And in no way does such suffering take on any of the sweetness of fidelity injured, loyalty degraded.

Improvisation, moving on, substitution, defiance, inner healing—characteristics of the strategies by which a sexually relaxed society copes with regret and denial—have a moral dominance in matters of painful love. A broken heart, caressed too long, is a dishonor often seen as a weapon of revenge, manipulation. "Anger" is the word psychiatrists give to assertions of the anguish of love.

Sex, sex—what good does it do anyone to "study" more and better orgasms, to open forbidden orifices, to experiment, to put himself into the satisfaction laboratory, the intensive care ward of "fulfillment." The body is a poor vessel for transcendence. Satiety, in life, is quick and inevitable. The return of anxiety, debts, bad luck, age, work, thought, interest in the passing scene, ambition, anger cannot be deferred by lovemaking. The consolations of sex are fixed and just what they have always been.

In the seventies sex has become information, about yourself, about others, about yourself in relation to others. The practices of "polling"—one manner of invading or pretending to invade the public mind—works here in the interest of sexual technique and attitude, giving a quasi-consensus, often to nothing more than the mere practice of polling itself. Questionnaires, reports, new studies, "probing surveys" (*sic*), the "real" truth about women, homosexuality, premarital and postmarital intercourse, about changing views and changing positions. These dubious statistics are an industry, and like the manufacture of other products there is little worry about repetition, need, accuracy, or significance. The title of each new book is very much like a new brand name for an old offering.

The most depressing part of the sexual information business is that, in the way of commerce, it is offered for our health and reassurance. Pessimism, naturally, does not sell, nor does skepticism—that, one assumes, the poor consumer can provide for himself, from his own experience. In the books and articles conclusions never fail to liberate, and if there is nothing new, whatever exists takes value from its mere occurrence, that is, if one believes the surveys give any true picture of contemporary sexual life. Piety, exploitation, complacency, triviality, and spurious objectivity deface these scrofulous enterprises.

Sexual Behavior in the 1970's is a study exposed to the public by Morton Hunt on behalf of the Playboy Foundation. The pastoral note on which the study ends is typical of this kind of work. "The changes that are taking place are none the less important and profound for taking place within the culture rather than breaking away from it; indeed, they may be more valuable than total sexual radicalism would be. For while they are bringing so much that is pleasurable, healthful and enriching into American life, they are doing so without destroying emotional values we have rightly prized, and without demolishing institutions necessary to the stability of society itself." More valuable, pleasurable, healthful, emotional values, stability of society. The sadness, the corruption, the meaninglessness of all this is one aspect of the 1970s.

To think of the family today is bewildering because the classes are so far apart in the scenery in which daily life takes place. For those in the light the uncertainties have to do with hanging on, imagining the future, imagining if possible the meaning of the generations, of youth and old age, money, and the menace of reduction. In the darkness below, within the family there are joblessness, crime, madness, cruelty, and despair. It is not easy to remember that these scenes are part of the same play.

When the politicians, the candidates, speak of the "poor" and the unemployed, of those on welfare, they are being no more empty than the rest of us in being unable to convey any sense of the experience of the condition, the misery and horror. There is still an inclination to see the poor in previous images, perhaps the more consoling ones of the 1930s: a wrinkled face, battered but benign; a worn body in which Christian doctrine still circulates in the veins; young families in decaying bungalows with an unpaid-for car in the drive. The sharecropper, the Okie, the miner, the laid-off factory force, memories from one's own family. Television, magical as it is for certain events in real life, cannot fully picture on its small frame the slums of the city, the menacing breakdown, the insanity, the brutality, the isolation. What has become unimaginable exists in images of fear, hatred, and withdrawal. Fear is sanctioned just now because there is much to be afraid of.

One thing that distorts our comprehension of the life of the poor is that on the street, in the supermarket, the marvelous disguise of the mass-produced American clothes gives a plausible surface, almost a shine, to what is really implausible and dark. On the evening news, the young thief or killer in his sneakers, his jacket, his jeans; his family in turtlenecks, jerseys. Together they appear in a state of health, often beautiful, well provided for, their clear and startling contemporaneity like a miraculous mask.

In the city slums it is the houses, the rooms, the halls, the very walls that define the actual life. It is here that everything necessary and hospitable to a decent life is lacking. This is home and family and relationship. It is here, inside, that deformations are so pervasive and inescapable, here that the devastations of character and purpose grow. Society is never asked to experience directly the misery and its attendant, hidden rages and abusive idleness.

In New York City the old, the very old have become victims of the very young. Poor, crippled people, eighty-two years old or even in one case one hundred and three years old, are beaten, killed for two dollars, ninety-five cents, for nothing. The age of the victims, the paltriness of the "take," the youth of the criminals, the bizarre equality of poverty between the robbed and the robber, outrages every sense of reason, even criminal reason, and makes one look beyond the act. Part of the choice of victim is that his weakness is immediately evident and is itself a sort of affront. An old and enfeebled, poverty-worn person is, apparently, to the battered children of the slums an object that is contemptible and finally not quite real, for to imagine old age one has to imagine life as a long flow, something protected by nature and therefore meaningful in its orderly progress from one stage to another.

Part of the preying upon each other comes from the familiarity of neighborhood, the known turf, known for its vulnerability, its exposure to every injury and insult. Middle-class neighborhoods in the city are places of warm beauty, utterly beguiling behind the curtained, plant-filled windows. The nice streets are a shimmer of light and power, taxis and doormen, smiles and golden belief—an obstacle in their foreignness, their dreamy protection and unassailability. Great sophistication, vigilance, imagination are needed to storm these heights, and the very young, poor criminals do not possess that felonious experience. The clever criminals of the old school are like figures in a film comedy. They drive up to expensive hotels in limousines, dressed in dinner jackets, in order to plunder the safes filled with diamonds; their actions are swift and efficient, and above all, mannerly, out of consideration for the quality of the loot.

Here in the city the worst thing that can happen to a nation has happened: we are a people afraid of its youth. One's own memory—the memory of a girl—was of turning about on a dark street at night, fearful of footsteps coming closer, turning and saying, Oh, it is only a boy. Relief. Now for a young man to be in his twenties or thirties, out of jail, is in some way a guarantee of accommodation to society—at least in the mass, if not of course in particular cases.

For the sick and dangerous young, the idea of "treatment" is a cliché, the joke of a psychiatry which does not know how to treat such devastating deviations, such appalling dislocations, such violence that baffles by its fecklessness. There is no will to undertake reconstruction of society. Not only is the imagination lacking just now, but the very terms of the reconstruction, the extent of it, freeze speculative thought and reasonable recommendation.

Revolutionary societies destroy or brutally "reeducate." Some countries like India have long ago learned to look upward and inward as they step around filth and hunger. The torpor of the Indian millions is a blessing for the prosperous. In America among the poor, there is a political accommodation, or at least no symptom of organized revolt. Instead there is random crime. Random—a felicitous phrase that gives no substance to the devastation.

The wild growth of dangerous criminal insanity in the cities is a comment on the meek young with their ashrams in old brownstones, on Moonies in costly hotels and country estates, on clean-cut groups quietly meditating. Poverty and its abuses to children have their transforming power. Young persons stab and kill, throw each other off the roof, beat each other to death on the playing ground, rape, mutilate, set buildings on fire. To allow the facts to enter the mind is a guilty act, as if one were recording the scene of a porn film with a suspicious degree of imagination. And from the public pathetic screams for protection, when there is no protection. In the cities there has been a profound derangement of whole generations of the urban poor.

We cannot take it in. All we had planned on was Appalachia and the sweet, toothless smiles, the pale, white faces, ragged dresses, bare feet, hungry glances. No matter—a vibrant, ferocious, active, heartbreaking insanity is as much a part of the seventies as intimacy, retreat to the private.

It is always a relief to return to the middle classes, to ponder the way culture, economics, fashions work upon these citizens who are a mirror, returning what society puts before them.

To think of our domestic life is to ask what sort of person is actually needed by society. What parents, what children, young adults, workers. What makes sense—the tough and practical, the unsure and idealistic? The inner-directed and the outer-directed, to use David Riesman's terms, seem merely private, accidentally characterological, as one may be stingy or generous. The work ethic describes one who lives in a society that invests work with great spiritual and historical necessity, seeing in toil, advancement, tenacity, a virtue beyond material reward—the definition of self. All must work, but how hard and at what and with what motivation beyond dollars? In the late sixties many young people answered the question of dollars by casual work quite unrelated to their advancement, their interests, and their future: driving cabs, working as waiters, making jewelry, teaching transcendental meditation, walking dogs, playing the guitar. Marginal occupations are suitable to prosperous times and have little reality in inflationary, unstable periods.

"I love long life better than figs," Charmian, Cleopatra's attendant, says in Shakespeare's play. If things go on as we reasonably expect, young people will experience long life as an unruly challenge to morals, possibilities, fantasies. They will, in huge numbers, live way up into their seventies and that means they will have three lives, with each one perhaps wiping out the one before as though it had never been. Who can easily imagine a young son or daughter marrying and living with the same person for close to fifty years? Or with two for twenty-five years each? This is not the way of hearts in love with the shifting demands of the ego, with painful pressures for new experience, second and third chances, lost hopes that are an accusation to self-esteem.

In a long life in which little can be taken for granted, it is not reasonable to project a fearful clinging to the known on the part of the contemporary sensibility—so far removed from the peasant-like stasis of times past. Instead, a nomadic search for the new waters and pastures of each period of life leads one on, running from the dryness of the past. Hell is no exit—and without social, moral insistence many would not wish to honor the contract of youth.

It is no wonder that with parents authority seems to have become a burden. Part of it is the peculiar melding of parents and young adults in the way they look and dress, in their common reverence for sexual experience, which they have been told need never end for the good and the healthy. Custom is shattered by the parents' fear of age and the children's disaffection about age's wisdom, difference, and virtue, by the vacation spirit of a people who are not sure that society needs its work, by the blurred future of the species—on and on. Coolness rather than domination is the complaint of children against parents, neglectful confusion rather than insistent assertion. Those who imagine that this can be reversed by the will, by mere opinion, are not credible because the will to rule has itself collapsed along with the painful recognition of limits everywhere of every kind.

The women's movement has crystallized in domestic life changes that have been going on for decades. Historically, the political and social expression of the themes of women's liberation coincides with the needs of a world in which there are almost as many divorces as marriages, with smaller families, longer lives, the economic expansion desired by the average household for which two incomes are required, education of women, diminishment of the need for heavy muscular work, which meant that the lives of men and women—talking on the phone, sitting at the desk, managing—became more and more alike.

The inner changes within women can scarcely be exaggerated. Ambition is natural to new groups freed, or demanding to be free and equal. No group demands equality for nothing, as a simple adornment of status. The arrival of women's ambition, transforming as it does private life, inner feeling, and public life is not at all simple but instead resembles the subtle shiftings of human thought and life brought about by enormously challenging ideas such as evolution and Freudianism. Many hang back; just as many would stand on the literal truth of Genesis; but no matter what the ideological reluctance may be, every life is an inchoate but genuine reflection of the change. We begin to act upon new assumptions without even being aware of the changes.

Society does not want women to lead a long life in the home. It is not prepared to support them and cannot give the old style true sanction. Children do not want their parents' lives to be given to them forever. Husbands cannot take the responsibilities for wives as an immutable duty, ordained by nature. Women's liberation suits society much more than society itself is prepared to admit. The wife economy is as obsolete as the slave economy.

But more than dollars are at stake. Power, the most insidious of the passions, is also the most cunning. The women's movement is in some respects a group like many others, organized against discrimination, economic and social inequities, legal impediments: against the structural defects of accumulated history. Perhaps it is that part of the movement the times will more or less accommodate in the interest of reality. The other challenges are more devastating to custom, uprooting as they do the large and the small, the evident and the hidden. The women's movement is above all a critique. And almost nothing, it turns out, will remain outside its relevance. It is the disorienting extension of the intrinsic meaning of women's liberation, much of it unexpected, that sets the movement apart. It is a psychic and social migration, leaving behind an altered landscape.

In the 1970s the insecurity of life, the rapid using up of resources, the alienating complexity of every problem from nuclear proliferation to falling reading scores, can scarcely fail to bewilder and lacerate relations between people in the family, in the streets, among the classes. When one tries to think of "domestic manners"—all of the rules and customs and habits which people have assumed as a group—one cannot imagine just who is sure enough of his ground to pass on the beliefs that grow out of reasonable certainty. And to whom are they offered, these beliefs and customs? The life of the young is far more complicated and murky than the life of those older. One thing looms out of the shadows: the reluctance of so many *promising* young people to have children.

A Bunch of Reds

Are you an *American* American? Lenin asked John Reed. The revolution would not be unmindful of the "human interest" attaching to the spirited and sunny Bolshevik from the United States. Clearly Reed was something apart from Lenin's Russian and European experience bitterly acquired in prison and exile and recorded in his florid, vitriolic disputes in the old *Iskra* and elsewhere. John Reed was not a Pole, not an Italian anarchist, not a Jew, not a Menshevik, not a socialist revolutionary. In truth he was what he appeared to be, a charming enthusiast of the revolution, a genuine American with no jarring memories of Zimmerwald debates, of Kautsky polemics, of Rosa Luxemburg.

Could he even be called a Marxist since he was not attracted to exegesis or to study in some American equivalent of the British Museum, or the libraries of Zurich? Nevertheless he was a revolutionary, not just a leftist, and certainly not an "infantile leftist" with their accusing utopianism. And, of course, like so many others, he was a world revolutionary, believing in the overthrow of capitalism, first here and then there, by way of strikes and insurrections. The gradualism of the Socialist Party was not agreeable to Reed's temperament and he was, after the victory in Russia, determined upon its replacement in America by some form of the Communist Party, recognized and unified, as it were, by the Comintern.

Reed is a curiosity and his political biography is held together by theatricalism and by his seizing upon, as a journalist, the dramatic moments of the class struggle; that is the moment when the stage is lit by a strike, by Pancho Villa and his horsemen in northern Mexico, and by the Bolshevik seizure of the government in November, 1917. Certainly these are natural landscapes for the reporter-participant, the brilliant, early master of radical "new journalism."

And circumstances made Reed what is called a legend. Even so striking a book as *Ten Days That Shook the World* could only make the author famous, celebrated, widely known, still one among others. It was early death that made him legendary, always bright and free of the ruins of time. At thirty-three he died in Soviet Russia of typhus and was buried in the Kremlin. So here is a radical American idealist, an activist with youthful, beguiling impetuosity; and all somehow illuminated, charmingly colored by his having been a treasured child of the American bourgeoisie, a westerner from Oregon, a graduate of Harvard, tall and good-looking in the old Greenwich Village gifted days.

Reed died in 1920, his book and his *persona* lived on, but there would inevitably be sixty years later some sketchiness in public memory. And now, in 1981, he has been revivified in Warren Beatty's film, *Reds*, an expensive, ambitious, romantic celebration of American radicalism, a celebration of love, vitality, and bohemianism. "Who were they? Were they socialists?" Adela Rogers St. John asks about Reed and his wife, Louise Bryant. She does not remember them and yet she is, we must say, on the right track. Had the film been made in her earlier days Mrs. St. John, a Hearst reporter very knowledgeable about Hollywood, would indeed have remembered. Pictorial, synoptic, imagistic history, united with the extraordinary grip of the visage of screen actors on the memory, lasts a generation at least, and often longer.

Reds—the candid title, connected in the mind with "a bunch of"—sets the good-natured tone of this representation of a bloody, suffering, unbearably complex historical period, the period that ended for Reed with the Russian Revolution. For radical Americans in love like John Reed and Louise Bryant the catastrophic time of war and devastation of the past of Europe was washed in a silvery light, the light of "when we were young and believed in something."

Warren Beatty, in so far as the mind can concentrate a film personage, does not appear to be in reality a violation of the historical John Reed. Indeed they are both "making history" in accordance with the useful and possible media at hand, and the sixty years intervening are interestingly foreshortened by the persistence of type. It is no wonder Beatty took upon himself so many of the professional duties of the enterprise; it is as if he feared the intrusiveness of alien spirits born, as it were, under the wrong sign. A like sense of osmotic recognition perhaps directed his most successful invention, the inclusion of persons, some of whom had known Reed and some not, who were alive at the time of World War I and who in their stray, broken, lifelike remarks attest to the past in the present, to the fading but not yet extinct silvery world—the way we were.

The witnesses do not reveal so much about Reed as about the endurance of the mask and its meeting with opinion which are finally personality—the quintessential union achieved by John Reed in his youth. Henry "Fucking" Miller, working-man Heaton Vorse, the old swaggart Hamilton Fish, the refined, liberal Roger Baldwin, and above all the restless individuality of two distinguished Englishwomen, Dora Russell and Rebecca West: these persons act in the place of the conventional news-reel, banner, and headline to establish the mood of history and the claim of a certain root of factuality.

Trotsky at the end of *The History of the Russian Revolution* writes: "Parliamentarianism illumined only the surface of society, and even that with a rather artificial light. In comparison with monarchy and other heirlooms from the cannibals and cave-dwellers, democracy is of course a great conquest, but it leaves the blind play of forces in the social relations of men untouched. It was against this deeper sphere of the unconscious that the October Revolution was the first to lay its hand."

The "deeper sphere of the unconscious" laid its hand upon revolutionaries, on individuals, rather than upon the state, the embodiment, which had no relief from a conscious, wary, cunning, and unending struggle for power. As the Russian poet Alexander Blok wrote, in a revolution "everything is confused as in a tavern, a fog." But the enthusiast, whether of the right or of the left, is frightened of the fog and naturally sees it as an impediment to forward, march.

Reed, the enthusiast, seems to have discovered his political self when he met Big Bill Haywood in 1913. Haywood, the leader of the IWW, was at the time of the meeting leading a strike of 25,000 textile workers in Paterson, New Jersey. Haywood himself had outstanding courage and revolutionary political ideas; he also had a useful working-class charisma that riveted the attention—a "massive, rugged face, seamed and scarred like a mountain." In Paterson, where police and company brutality was extreme, Reed went to report on the plight of the mostly foreign-born workers who had been organized under the banner of the IWW. "Immediately Reed fell in love with these Italians,

Lithuanians, Poles and Jews, small, dark, tough, boisterous men who cheered the IWW, incessantly sang union songs and fearlessly denounced their jailors."*

He was arrested for some minor interference and jailed for four days in the same cell with the noted Italian radical, Carlo Tresca. (Tresca was assassinated—some said by the Comintern, some by the "mob," acting for fascists—in front of his office on lower Fifth Avenue in the 1940s, and one of my own New York memories is of the twilight gathering of a small group, always including Norman Thomas and Dorothy Kenyon, on the spot of his death for an anniversary memorial service.) From the IWW and the experience at Paterson Reed received what appears to be his only cluster of political principles: syndicalism. This lasted throughout his life, even after he and a good many of the Wobblies were consumed by the Communist Party after 1917.

The principles were One Big Union and open war against the excluding craft unions of the conservative AF of L under Samuel Gompers; direct action by way of strikes and boycotts for the overthrow of capitalism; opposition to mediation, parliamentarianism, running for office as a minority political party; antimilitarism and opposition to America's entrance in World War I, the war of "profits." These principles dominated Reed's distaste for the Socialist Party, even though as early as 1912 Debs had received 900,000 votes as a candidate for President and was to receive 914,000 when he ran from his jail cell in 1920. And most importantly the principles and his experience of

---

* Much of the information about John Reed in this article comes from *Romantic Revolutionary*, by Robert A. Rosenstone (New York: Alfred A. Knopf, 1975; Vintage, 1981). Rosenstone's research in articles, manuscripts, foreign sources, and Reed bibliography is exhaustive. His biography is an exemplary source of interest and fact for anyone who wishes to reflect upon Reed's career.

them in America informed what seems to have been Reed's only serious dispute with the direction taken by the Bolsheviks after the victory of 1917: that is the decision that the radical American workers, whom Reed emotionally and ideologically saw himself to represent, should "bore from within" the more powerful AF of L, which Reed detested. By these alliances they were to achieve a mass following.

Also at Paterson what might be called the popularity of Reed's personality, the *noblesse* of it, was immediately manifest. He was *noticeable*, vivid, under a sort of enchantment with his princely dash and large sympathies. Perhaps because he held whatever political ideas he had in a haphazard and personalized manner, Reed was not attracted to the urge for organizational power, an almost inevitable handmaiden to the theorist in action. In political activity what are abstractions good for except to be imposed upon groups, opponents, the flow of events? Or to provide substance to the *critique*, a mental activity, souring enthusiasm, and uncongenial to the expressive sans-culottism of Reed's nature.

His moment as a radical journalist is the *showdown*, the possibility of a reversal of power and the appearance out of the darkness of the forest of powerful men, with the object always of redeeming, reversing the sufferings of the powerless. Reed enters the showdown with a happy receptivity, always, even at Paterson, under the star of his own *engagé* foreignness. He is a striker at Paterson, one of *los hombres* with Pancho Villa in Chihuahua, and an instant Bolshevik in Russia. He is trusted because he is not disputatious and indeed he has brought with him to the scene only the wish that the revolt, the insurrection might succeed. He is the troubadour of the main event and it would be withholding to stifle the spirit with too great a pause for "details" that trouble. The *torrent révolutionnaire*, the mob, *les malheureux* in the streets, at the barricades, ragged armies, strong leaders—for these his gift is ready. Reed does not seem to know much about past history and the only historical reference in *Ten Days* is to Carlyle, very briefly.

When he meets Pancho Villa he is impressed with "the most natural human being I ever saw—natural in the sense of being a wild animal." In turn Villa is impressed and soon Reed is riding with *la tropa,* sleeping with the *compañeros,* and writing: "I made good with these wild fighting men and with myself." There is banditry, expropriation, revolutionary justice by execution; and there is Justice, the turnover, the awakened peasantry, the blaze of a new dawn. Reed's account of the Mexican Revolution is brilliantly alive and moving. Walter Lippmann wrote about it: "The variety of his impressions, the resources and color of his language seemed inexhaustible . . . throngs of moving people in a gorgeous panaroma of earth and sky."

Because Reed wrote in a powerful, rhythmical, descriptive style he is again and again spoken of as a poet, "the poet of the revolution," and so on. When he goes about the country agitating against conscription and about the Russian Revolution, he is reminded by his friends that he is, essentially, "a poet" and he thinks of himself as such—at times. The truth is that his uniqueness was precisely fulfilled in his prose and he is in no sense genuine otherwise. His love poems are conventional and quite expendable, along with, except for information, such of his letters as appear in books devoted to his life. His efforts to command the inclusive Whitman style are boasting and predictable in language.

I have shot craps with gangsters in the Gas-House district. . . .
I can tell you where to hire a gunman to croak a squealer,
And where young girls are bought
    and sold, and how to get coke
        on 125th Street. . . .

The generalized experience offers little to this writer who needs the landscape of heroic action in what he sees as a just cause. To describe, feel, and experience is his gift; to heighten observation by a free and lovely fluency of language at a moment when all is given, accepted, beyond reflection. World War I, which he covered in a desultory manner, was not a source for his literary inspiration. The long, slogging, murderous destruction of men and history was lamentable, but, for his talent, it was not dramatic, being too dense and blurred.

The narrative power of *Ten Days* is astonishing when one considers the amount of information needed for Reed's audience —not to mention the need of the author himself when he gets down to the page—and the effort to organize the documentation, the decrees, shifting alliances, committee meetings, newspaper accounts, without which the book would be only a dazzle. The *esprit* is unflagging; the rush through history and chaos is the rush to victory. The pace of the book is the pace of the victorious tide. It is all youthful, high-spirited, with none of the disfiguring vehemence of the polemicist because Reed is a mind too newly born for moral carping. And he is a comrade without memories. In truth Reed doesn't really know a soul there in the "vastness"; he hasn't a single Russian friend and is not humanly acquainted with a foot of the earth.

For the others it was not so fresh and always blooming. When Angelica Balabanoff, the daughter of a wealthy land-owning Russian family and a revolutionary since her youth, is sent by the Party to work in Odessa, "the mention of Odessa made me shudder." Her relatives, from whom she was long estranged for political differences, had gone to Odessa in order to be able if necessary to escape to Turkey. (Her mother escaped to Turkey and died of starvation there.) Madame Balabanoff dutifully goes to Odessa and while outside her office she can hear the shouts of Long Live Comrade Balabanoff, her anti-Bolshevik sister is ushered in, a sister dressed like a beggar and so miserably altered she is hardly recognizable.

It is no diminishment of his stunning reportage to say that for Reed the October Revolution is pageantry from a moonscape. "In Smolny Institute the Military Revolutionary Committee flashed baleful fire, pounding like an overloaded dynamo." And, "Vast Russia was in a state of dissolution. . . . Old Russia was no more; human society flowed molten in primal heat, and from the tossing sea of flames was emerging the class struggle, stark and pitiless—and the fragile, slowly cooling crust of new planets." Power, vastness, newness, throbbing, rushing, rising, unrolling are the signifiers of the grand purpose, the necessity, the destiny of history. Petrograd falls, and then the bombardment of the "holy" Kremlin itself, and then the pause for the funeral of the Martyrs of the Beginning of World Revolution, and then: "I suddenly realized that the devout Russian people no longer needed priests to pray them into heaven. On earth they were building a kingdom more bright than any heaven had to offer and for which it was a glory to die. . . ."

There is revolution and then there is also love. With the leaders in Russia, love stories are not often in the advance guard of experience. Lenin's mistress, Issa Armand, is not even mentioned in Trotsky's biography of Lenin or in his history of the Russian Revolution. Trotsky must have known of her death from cholera in 1920 and of Lenin's stony grief, mentioned by other memorists, when she is taken to be buried in the Kremlin, near to the grave of John Reed. As for Lenin's wife and comrade, Krupskaia, she lived on, a survivor sometimes troublesome enough to lead Stalin to say that if she didn't watch out, he would find someone else to be Lenin's widow.

Rosa Luxemburg's biographer spoke of her love for her husband, Leo Jogiches, as one of the "great and tragic love stories of socialism." And certainly Emma Goldman was a lover. Her account of her life soon after she arrived in America as a young woman is detailed by short headlines at the top of the page. They read in breathless succession: Sasha Makes Love to Me; I Respond to Fedya; and Most [Johann] Confesses Love for Me. Most was an anarchist-terrorist—"propaganda of the deed"—whose criticism of Sasha (Alexander Berkman) after he had shot Henry Clay Frick led to the next Emma Goldman autobiographical headline: I Horsewhip Most. As she did on the stage of one of Most's lectures, ending the scene in a majorful manner by breaking the whip in two.

In *Reds*, the love of John Reed and Louise Bryant is not one of the great stories of socialism. Its landscape for the most part is the America of Oregon, Greenwich Village, Croton-on-Hudson outside New York. Much of it is out of classic film romantic comedy—fighting and making up, husband sent to the sofa, husband in the blazing kitchen, and in this case the historically permissible "free love" infidelities of Louise Bryant.

Louise Bryant met Reed when he was on a visit to his family in Portland. The meeting was brief and thoroughly *fateful*. She left her husband, went to New York, and married Reed not long after. Louise Bryant is interesting as an American woman who was not so much complicated as murky and given to the improvisations of survival.*

She came from the working class and while this might be a picturesque idea to some of the Greenwich Village intelligentsia, Louise Bryant knew it to be a soot-flecked reality. Her father was born in the mining region of Pennsylvania, worked in the mines, and by self-education became a school teacher and a reporter, finally working on newspapers in San Francisco where the daughter was born, before he vanished completely from the

---

* *So Short a Time*, by Barbara Gelb (New York: W. W. Norton, 1973; Berkley 1981), is the only biography of Louise Bryant and it is a necessary source for her life.

family scene. The destruction of records in the San Francisco fire was a release to the imagination and in Granville Hicks's biography of Reed, Louise gave out the information that she had been "brought up by her grandfather, the younger son of an Anglo-Irish lord." Instead she was brought up by her mother and stepfather, a railroad conductor, in Wadsworth, Nevada, and made her way *out*, to the University of Nevada and the University of Oregon. When she married her first husband in Oregon she was twenty-two, but preferred to be thought nineteen. In New York with Reed she was twenty-nine, but chose to be twenty-five.

Louise Bryant's life is like a traditional realistic novel of which she is the heroine under the domination of an ordained curve of fortune. Unpromising beginnings, sloughed off gradually by charm and by a fierce feminist determination for a worthy self-identification; romantic dishonesties, either profitless or gratuitous, but meant to ensure against something; the upward swing of many successes and no more relative than usual in "success"; and a truly terrible ending, without necessity, without preparation as it seems, except in a Hardy-like fate.

The triangle, supremely interesting in real life and so often the very blood of literature, was a natural mode for this driven coquette from the provinces and at almost every important point in her life with Reed the inclination, with its more or less forgivable deceptions, goes along like a handbag. Her affair with Eugene O'Neill began when the three of them were in Provincetown, continued "heavily" when she invited O'Neill to the house in Croton while Reed was in a hospital in Baltimore for the removal of a diseased kidney. When she returned, two months ahead of Reed, from the first trip to Russia, her immediate action was to get in touch with O'Neill. The way of the world had intervened; O'Neill had taken up with someone else and the affair was not resumed. In *Reds*, Louise Bryant's character is given a greater degree of common sense than one can document. Also in certain fluent declamations and in the hintings of moments of "concerned" silence, she is made to appear the possessor of political wisdom, a sort of intuitive feminine guardian against the follies of radical enthusiasm.

In the group of artists and writers in the Village, more was necessary for a woman than attractiveness and compatibility of views, views about love, women's suffrage, and so on, which Louise had come to before she met Reed. Still it was necessary to be something, if only rich like Mabel Dodge. So, without spectacular talent but with a steady energy she became a political journalist. In Petrograd with Reed she found her subject and *Six Red Months in Russia*, her book of dispatches based on her *four* months in Russia, came out in 1918, a year before *Ten Days*, published in 1919.

The stories, as she calls them in an introduction, "gathered together on the edge of Asia, in that mystic land of white nights in summer and long black days in winter . . . ," are naive and written in the style of light feature-journalism, with many exclamation points that serve sometimes as irony or as a clue to excited emotion. "Kerensky again in the limelight! Kerensky visiting the world's capitals and hobnobbing with the world's potentates!" An effort is made to sort out the unnerving complexity of the political parties, to explain the Democratic Congress and to "explain away" the dissolution of the Constituent Assembly, but it is a rendering finally of the author's own ignorance and nervous incapacity as a historian. "I was present at the opening of the Constituent; it was a terrific performance from beginning to end. About eight o'clock the delegates assembled and the air fairly crackled with excitement." In an interview at the recruiting office of the Women's Battalion, where patriotic women from all classes had enlisted to fight the Germans, she was told that some of them were in the Winter

Palace when it fell and were rumored to have been raped. Here Louise Bryant is more sympathetic and her conversational, quick-impression style is more suitable.

Interviews with Breshkovskaya and Spirodonova, two great women of the revolutionary period, are sketches of vivid personalities who, somewhat unfortunately for Louise Bryant, have political ideas outside her comprehension. Breshkovskaya, the Grandmother of the Revolution as she is called, was heroic and dramatic and old. She was also a right-wing socialist revolutionary and unwelcome after the fall of the Provisional Government. Louise Bryant writes: "History almost invariably proves that those who give wholly of themselves in their youth to some large idea cannot in their old age comprehend the very revolutionary spirit with which they themselves began; they are not only unsympathetic to it, but usually they offer real opposition. . . . It is a question of age."

The handsome, learned Spirodonova had in her youth killed the sadistic Lupjenovsky, governor of Tambov. For this act she spent an appalling eleven brutalizing years in prison in Siberia until she was released when the February Revolution broke out. "Spirodonova as a member of the Left Socialist Revolutionist Party is surrounded by a number of the finest young idealists in Russia. Hers is the only party that in a crisis rises above party for the benefit of the nation. It will have more and more to say as the revolution settles down."

The folly of this prediction is scarcely credible. When John Reed returned to Russia in 1919 to get recognition for the Communist Labor Party of America, Spirodonova, who opposed what she saw as the Bolshevik betrayal of the peasants, was again a "martyr," in and out of Soviet prisons. Because of her revolutionary fame she was perhaps the first to be incarcerated under the "nervous breakdown" euphemism. Emma Goldman tells of talking to Reed about the case and hearing his claim that the imprisonment was due to acute neurasthenia and hysteria. On this matter Emma Goldman's comment was brief and dismissing: "As to Reed, unfamiliar with the language and completely under the sway of the new faith, he took too much for granted."

Six Red Months in Russia sold fairly well and the author went about the country lecturing to large audiences. "Miss Bryant appears a demure and pretty girl, with a large hat, a stylish suit, and gray stockings. . . . In a burst of applause, the demure little speaker sits down." Thus was achieved the professional identity she very naturally wanted.

Her return to Russia to "rescue" Reed is not entirely the epical samaritanism of the film. She did not pass over the icy tundra, nor did she go to the prison in Finland where Reed had been held after his second Russian journey. She went to Russia by way of Murmansk and for various reasons, one of which was to be reunited with Reed, even though she was not fully aware, because of the difficulty of communication, of the suffering he had endured in solitary confinement. When she took off she was "bursting with guilt" over an affair she had been having with Andrew Dasburg, formerly Mabel Dodge's lover. She told Dasburg she wanted to continue her career as a journalist of the revolution, and also to dissuade Reed from coming home lest he go to prison on the indictments handed down for criminal anarchy and other charges during the Palmer Raids.

Her letter to Dasburg is interesting because of the remarkable persistence of her triadic confusions. "If J comes he will only go to prison and that will be horrible. Always to know he is there—more dependent than ever—it would destroy us, you can see that. It would destroy all three." *All three* is full of future intention to be worked out *somehow*. And "more dependent than ever" points to those midnight, untrammeled characterizations of the absent one, very much in tune with her telling Eugene O'Neill that Reed was impotent, which he was not. Reed's affairs, after he met Louise, are, at least in history, nameless phrases: "Jack romping around the house with a naked female" and "a desultory passion for a young Russian girl kept Jack too busy for sustained writing."

Three years after Reed's death, Louise Bryant had a sensational affair with William Bullitt, the rich Philadelphia diplomat who was later ambassador to Russia. He divorced his wife, married Louise, and they had a daughter. Bullitt was thirty-one and Louise was thirty-five, although keeping a bit ahead by being a bit behind she admitted only to being thirty. What seemed to the world a splendid social coup led to, or coincided with, one of those unpredictable, unaccountable swervings of human character. She began to drink heavily, spent time in sanitariums, and drove Bullitt to shame and fury. After seven years he sued for divorce and was awarded custody of the child. She returned to the Village, took up with a slippery younger man, brought him to court for stealing a valuable antique comb, and, oh the old chestnuts, the old songs, giving it to the famous Village restaurant owner, Romany Marie.

She left the Village for Paris and lived there a miserable life of drink and drugs. Janet Flanner's description: "When she came back to Paris she was in the lowest stage of degradation. One of the last times I saw her was on a rainy night when I was walking along Rue Vavin in Montparnasse. Literally out of the gutter rose a terrifying creature. Her face so warped I didn't recognize her."

The sudden meeting, the rainy night, the gutter—how like those endings in French novels of the sweet little tart or music hall singer, done in. Louise Bryant died in 1936 at the age of forty-nine, and if she ended in the manner of Balzac or Zola, she was in life, I think, more like Sister Carrie. Even her journalism might remind one of the theatrical success of Carrie, some aspect of performance that is not art and yet a public definition.

Reed called *Ten Days* "intensive history," and perhaps he meant history intensified by his feeling. Bolshevism came to be thought of as a magical phenomenon which not only consumed radical parties but embraced and erased all other radical political ideas. Power was a great part of this mystical inclusiveness and the mere fact of embodiment was an overwhelming, if irrational, magnification of value. The messianic mode and profound inexperience separated Reed from those who made the revolution, those whom Hannah Arendt in *On Revolution* called professional revolutionists who arrive on the scene from the "jail, the coffee house or the library."

But no matter what his "innocence" he is led as if he were merely another seeker of power into the simplications of propaganda. The intellectuals of the Menshevik Party, he asserts, by virtue of their education "instinctively reacted to their training, and took the side of the propertied classes." And "the only reason for Bolshevik success lay in their accomplishing the vast and simple desires of the most profound strata of the people." It is unthinkable that he could feel or write after a stirring speech by Trotsky anything close to what was written by the great diarist of the period, Sukhanov: "With an unusual feeling of oppression I looked on at this really magnificent show."

The revolution, the scene, drew Reed slowly into a degree of participation unusual for a foreign journalist, even for a radical one. Waiting for his transit visas at the end of the first trip, Reed attended the meeting of the Constituent Assembly and easily accepted the Bolsheviks' decision on dissolution after they failed to win a majority. The Constituent Assembly, providing for elected, representational government, was a sacred item on the agenda of the future and the Bolsheviks had bitterly condemned the Provisional Government set up after the overthrow of the

Tsar for failing to honor this hope. The Bolsheviks in electoral defeat decided the Assembly was a bit of "bourgeois counter-revolution," and Reed, according to Rosenstone's research, was "not disturbed."

In addition he spoke at the Congress of the Soviets to great applause and joined the Red Guards in patrolling the streets and worked for the Bureau of International Propaganda. In his efforts to get back to America with his notes intact, Reed thought of having himself appointed a Soviet courier and for a time Trotsky actually proposed that Reed be appointed Soviet consul to the United States. Fortunately that did not happen and he returned to write *Ten Days*, to become famous, and to enter radical political life as an *exalté* representative of his ideas, or rather of his experience *there*, at the very moment. A new vocabulary, pulled out of the sludge of militarism, would now need to direct his actions: tactics, strategy, maneuver.

He joined the Socialist Party in bad faith and participated with Louis Fraina in a left-wing split whose aim was to Bolshevize the party.* There was a further split between Reed and

---

* Louis Fraina: a life of one miserable opaque drama after another, all wonderfully told in Theodore Draper's *The Roots of American Communism*. Fraina cannot be summarized because his is a story of circular details, plots ever-returning to haunt as in nineteenth-century fiction. Under the shadow of a strange spy charge by a perjurer when he went to Russia with Reed, but exonerated after a "trial" by the Comintern, the Party felt he was, nevertheless, cloudy and chose Reed to be the member from America of the Executive Committee. Fraina was exiled to Mexico, given $50,000 for Party work, of which the sum of $4,200 would bring him into Party disrepute as an "embezzler." Returned to Europe, back once more in New York under the name of Charles Skala; went to work in a dry goods store for $12 a week, finally employed as a proofreader.

In his evenings he decided to write a review on corporate ownership which was published in *The New Republic*, under a new name which he gradually made distinguished, Lewis Corey. Corey wrote analytical books on capitalism, taking a Marxist view, became a professor of political economy at Antioch College even though he had never been to high school. His past, in and out of the graces of the Communist Party, caused him fantastical difficulties and, his anticommunist position notwithstanding, he was subjected to threats of deportation by the American government. As Draper writes, "The man who

Fraina and both went to Moscow in 1919 for the meeting of the Comintern, with Reed representing the Communist Labor Party and Fraina the Communist Party, composed mainly of many foreign-language radical groups. Reed's return seems to have rested upon his acknowledging himself as the American most known to the Soviet leaders and most likely to achieve recognition for his branch of the party. When he arrived the revolution had hardened like a footprint in cement and there was no way to avoid knowledge of the evident suppression of political opposition, the rule of the Communist Party bureaucracy, the consolidation of the power of the secret police, the Cheka. The knowledge could not be avoided, but there was—as always—interpretation.

Reed traveled about the demoralized, starving country, seeing and partly seeing. He brought hyperbolic greetings from the American workers and was received with great enthusiasm which seemed to testify to the endurance of the heroic phase. According to Rosenstone's research, he was prepared to see the repressions as necessity and to find the opposition of the peasants rooted in their petty-bourgeois mentality. He welcomed the threat of the hated conscription for the peasants to bring them out of isolation, into education so that each peasant "will return to his village a revolutionist and propagandist." The Cheka was not alarming since it was only acting against traitors and the shooting in one short period of 6,000 men was justified since "this is war." Coarseness enters the mind of the enthusiast as quietly as a faint, hardly noticeable cerebral accident.

It is necessary, it is necessary. Even the church bells are imagined to be ringing out this terrible refrain at the end of Victor

---

began as Louis C. Fraina and ended as Lewis Corey provided the complete symbol of the American radical in the first half of the twentieth century." (In the film Fraina speaks with an Italian accent, which perhaps serves a useful purpose for dramatic variety. The fact is that he came to the United States at the age of three.)

Serge's great, tragic novel about the betrayal of the revolution, *Conquered City*—his Petersburg where perhaps he brushed by Reed and Louise Bryant as they were rushing to the "great Smolny ablaze with light." And when Reed is going about the Russian countryside, the poet Tsvetaeva is writing about the soldiers:

> He was white and now he's red—
> The blood reddened him.
> He was red and now he's white—
> Death whitened him.

After the meetings with the executive committee of the Comintern the dispute about the American Party was settled by the decision to unite the factions and Reed was chosen for the committee. He prepares to leave for home, taking with him $14,000 in diamonds and $1,500 in currencies, "Moscow gold," to assist the Communist Party of the U.S. He was captured in White Finland, put in prison as a spy, where he stayed for almost three months in solitary confinement, before being returned to Petrograd and Moscow. In Moscow he waited for the summer meeting of the Comintern, made speeches, and was always a striking, admired, if singular, figure.

At this time he had the dispute with Zinoviev and Radek over the Party line about the AF of L. Reed felt strongly that the Soviets did not understand the labor situation in America and indeed it would be sticky for him, with his Wobbly history and convictions, to carry this autocratic, "united front" decision on his shoulders. He agitated, he resigned from the executive committee, and he gave in, withdrew his resignation, and the domination by the Soviets of the Communist Parties of the world became another necessity.

In the film, Zinoviev is the enemy, the symbol of autocratic rule and cynicism, and Reed is cast as a "dissident." In the role Jerzy Kosinski is in a sense an idealization of Zinoviev. His dramatic hawk nose, thin-lipped whine, and lemon-chewing precision are what Zinoviev might better have been for dramatic purposes, for style. In reality Zinoviev, who was executed in the first of the old Bolshevik purges of 1936, was a pudgy, jowly, irritating agitator, one of the original mesomorphs of the Politburo, a physiognomy of enduring replication.

At Baku, the mad gathering of Turks, Persians, Arabs, and others, to which Zinoviev took him, Reed was dismayed by the distorted translation of his speech and by the use of Islamic "holy war" rhetoric from Moscow. From these last months before his death arises the question of Reed's final attitudes toward the Soviet Union. To find this attractive person sunk at the end in the airless Communist Party provokes the salvaging instinct on the part of some such as Max Eastman, now on the other side and unwilling to surrender the corpse of this glorious friend of his youth. Late conversations described by Angelica Balabanoff indicate Reed's resentment of Zinoviev and a general sadness and depression about the Soviet scene. Louise Bryant gives testimony of a bitter disillusionment to Balabanoff and says that Reed died because he had lost the will to live. However, just after his death she had written Eastman that "he would have died days before but for the fight he made." Her testimony is erratic in the extreme, moving from disillusionment to some auditors, complete denial to others, and her record even includes an accusation that Reed was a secret agent for the United States. Louise Bryant returned to Russia after Reed's death and wrote the dispatches that appear in *Mirrors of Moscow*, published in 1923. At this time she, who had never been content to be The Wife, was The Widow, legendary. Her book shows no diminution of her passion for the revolution, which had become her *spécialité*. The secret police "were back again protecting now a revolutionary government as energetically as they once protected the Tsar!"

Emma Goldman believed that Reed had maintained belief in the revolution until the end. Louis Fraina, who was at the death scene, wrote, "As one of the two or three Americans who saw him before his death, I can affirm that Jack Reed kept all his loyalty to the Soviet Union and communism." There is a sympathetic and very interesting account of Reed's life and his relation to Soviet communism in Theodore Draper's *The Roots of American Communism*. Draper, a brilliant, fair-minded historian, does not give up Reed's possible disillusionment easily and he feels in the end that "Reed was probably as disillusioned as it was possible to be and still remain in the movement." Rosenstone disagrees with this more or less on the grounds of Reed's nature and temperament and while he sees distress he does not find that it would be sufficient cause, for Reed, to be rightly considered disillusioned at the time of his death.

John Reed was a morally attractive man marked by generosity and openness and for the most part unacquainted with the torments of ambivalence. Still he is not deep enough or reflective enough to be a moral hero and his life at the end shows the damage of a too-eager receptiveness. The curious last lines of Granville Hicks's biography tell of the funeral and the speeches by Party leaders. "For Bukharin and Radek and the others the death of John Reed was only an incident in the struggle for world revolution. He would have approved." A peculiar epitaph for one who was only thirty-three and whatever he may have been was never content to be only an incident.

part three

❖❖❖❖❖❖❖❖❖❖❖❖❖❖❖❖❖❖❖❖❖❖❖❖❖❖❖❖❖❖❖❖❖❖

After Going to the Theater

A Death at Lincoln Center

Danton's Death by Georg Büchner
Repertory Theater of Lincoln Center

Danton's Death is a lyric tragedy, a work of great and expressive beauty. True, on the surface it appears too calm in its development, too negligent in its shifts from private to public life; and yet in the end it is just this slow, careless moving toward death that is the very center of the peculiar power of the play. The paralysis, the static nihilism, the already ruined hopes, the fixed despair of Danton are the astonishingly moving and complicated results of his previous explosion of revolutionary energy. To have brought these two themes together is the glory of Büchner's conception. The French Revolution is the scenery in which an individual man, Danton, comes to his last act—the Revolution at that moment when idealism has frozen into corruption and the revolutionary victories are beginning to institutionalize themselves by the Terror and the destruction of revolutionaries. Ideology and Terror, as Hannah Arendt says, "one compelling men from within and the other compelling them from without," have been the fate of almost every country at one time or another. We see at present no relief from Terror in support of Ideology and so there was every clear civic, as well as artistic, reason to open our new "people's theater" with *Danton's Death*.

"I love you like the grave," Danton says at the very opening of the play. This is the announcement of his theme—death. Danton bears the fiercest scars of the Revolution and of his own violence. He had gone, as Carlyle writes, "through seas of blood to Equality, Frugality, worksome Blessedness, Fraternity, and the Republic of the virtues. Blessed shore, of such a sea of Aristocrat blood: but how to land on it? Through one last wave . . . " It is on the one last wave of blood that Danton himself is sinking—or almost the last. The meaning, or meanings, of this were what concerned Büchner when, in 1834 and he was only twenty-one, he wrote *Danton's Death*.

Narcissistic fatigue, a weakening of the will to resist have seized the hero of the Revolution. But it is not merely a peculiar, personal despair. It is despair about mankind, a sorrow fringed with carelessness and tolerance. Danton no longer loves the people, but he wants to leave them alone. The questions that had meant everything to him are now meaningless.

> Does it matter whether they die on the guillotine or from fever or from old age? The first is even preferable. They tread with supple limbs behind the scenes, and are able to gesticulate prettily as they go off, and hear the spectators clap.

Danton does not value life much now and for that reason he does not want to go on killing others. "I'd rather be guillotined than guillotine. I've had enough of it." The deeds of the Revolution have brought him to this point, that and a radical uncertainty about life itself. "A mistake was made in the creating of us; something's lacking in us. I don't know the name for it."

Neither lover nor sex subdues ennui. The Absurd and *le Néant* (a word used by both the historical and dramatic Danton) poison hope. A bitter rationalism alternates with a romantic, nostalgic weariness.

> How tedious it is always to have to put one's shirt on first and then pull up one's trousers; to spend the night in bed and then in the morning have to crawl out again and always place one foot in front of the other—and no one ever imagines it could be otherwise. It's very sad; millions have already done so and millions more are destined to do so; and besides that we consist of two halves, each doing the same thing, so everything happens twice—it's very sad.

After the revolutionary fervor, there is nothing left except sensuality, disillusionment, and death.

Perhaps this is the moment to face the disabled production of *Danton's Death* Herbert Blau has put on at Lincoln Center. That the Danton Büchner has imagined is of surpassing interest will come as a surprise to those who know the play only from this new rendering. Alan Bergmann, as Danton, is a mistake of the most thoroughgoing, the most devastating, order. From the moment he comes on the stage the production is doomed. He is charmless, monotonous, and boring from the first moment to the last. Carlyle calls Danton "a gigantic mass of valor, ostentation, fury, affectation and wild revolutionary force and manhood." Nothing of the historical person is suggested by Bergmann and nothing of Büchner's character, who is less robust and more romantic. The Danton of Büchner is coarse, but there is also about him a sweetness, mystery, and grace. The proper casting of this role is the first concern of the play—and what can one say of the present casting except that it was not necessary.

Still, what is the virtue in insulting actors? The injury done to a noble and complicated play was the grief of the evening. Many men of the press go to the classics all nude and fresh and seem to greet each play as if it were written yesterday on Central Park West. Many considered the banality of the evening to be equally shared by Blau and Büchner and one had the idea they were sending the heroic young genius, who died in 1837, back to some play-writing class at The New School. One reviewer remarked that it would help to know something about the French Revolution, but he did not explain what it was that held the knowledge at bay.

Danton's drama is to wait, with a cold sophistication and an elaborate self-consciousness, for his execution. He has himself been an executioner. He knows the nature of power and its readiness to destroy. A curious lassitude sweeps over him. He has learned the lessons of his own political experience. The famous "Ils n'oseraient" is merely a gesture. Of course they will dare and who knows better than he? Carlyle reminds us that Danton had every vice except cant. In his refusal to make a truly considered effort at self-defense he has our sympathy. Indeed Robespierre himself will soon show this same sweep of lassitude, the same collapse of the will as he gives a sort of consent to his own execution. We find, or rather we feel, some hint of *surrender*, also, in Stalin's first purge. Of course the power of the Terror speaks most clearly to those who have used it; others, the innocent and the weak, it takes by surprise. Yet, there is the possibility of some deeper root to the paralysis; it appears almost as an unconscious act of atonement. The careless manner in which Danton goes to his death is a comment upon all those other deaths. The blood of the revolutionaries atones for the blood they have shed in the service of Idea. The orderly sequence of nature seems to be, at least for a time, restored by their atoning deaths.

The crimes behind Danton's disillusionment are terrible. From Salvemini's *French Revolution* a few "minor" instances: " . . . the Princess of Lamballe was killed on the morning of the 3rd at the Force, and her body subjected to abominable abuse.

Her head, struck off and fixed upon a pike, was paraded by a howling mob beneath the Queen's window . . . Forty-three boys, aged from twelve to fourteen and detained at their parents' request, were put to death. 'The poor boys were dispatched with difficulty for at that age, life is tenacious . . . there was one who looked like a sleeping angel, but the others were horribly mutilated.' " We know from his letters that Büchner, young as he was, was tortured by the awful questions raised by the French Revolution. Danton's mood in the play is fascinating because every action, even love-making, or particularly love-making perhaps, is darkened by historical questions.

All critics have remarked upon the striking modernity of Büchner's ideas, his "alienation," and his "existentialism." This play and his other great work, *Wozzeck*, touch our lives at every point. The intellectual and poetic seriousness of the dialogue is the art of genius. In *Danton's Death*, Thomas Paine, a character, says, "One can deny evil but not pain; only the understanding can accept God, the feeling rebels against him . . . Why do I suffer? That is the rock of atheism. The least twinge of pain . . . rends your creation from top to bottom."

Power, political rhetoric in the service of tyranny, personal despair, sensual disillusionment, courage, neurotic weariness, the abyss, Nothingness: these themes, created in a natural and beautiful language, should have brought to our stage a great moment of enlightenment and beauty. "The stars are scattered through the night like glistening teardrops; what a terrible grief must be behind the eyes that dropped them." In the production, Blau did not seem to have any ideas of his own or to be solicitous about the abundance of ideas to be found in the text. A sort of tarpaulin fell over the whole enterprise, coarsely covering the poetry, the subtlety of characterization, the seriousness of the philosophical questions.

Take for instance the staging of the crowd scenes. Might we not have had something new from the mob, something of its cruel silence, its monumental forgetfulness of its own sufferings. Anything except the same old cackling, milling, and nudging. And Robespierre, that dry, unpleasant man, Carlyle's "sea-green formula": he was well-enough played by Robert Symonds, made up to look like McGeorge Bundy, but the interpretation was routine, conventional, and genuinely uninteresting. Or the speech made by Marian in the love scene with a Danton stripped to the waist, but who unfortunately achieves nothing of increased interest by the way of bare midriff and visible shoulder. This speech, off-hand, reflective, is delivered with a disintegrating rush of breathless intensity, the old Broadway "serious" manner.

Few of the actors have any sense of style, except Roscoe Lee Brown, who gives his scenes as Saint-Just an angular pace and authority. Most of all one regrets the sheer present in which the actors seem fated to live no matter what the role may be. The ability to look backward, whether it be learned in the study of the craft of acting, or gained by some individual gift of imagination, seems to be pitifully lost on our stage. The smothering contemporaneity is always there like the smog outside. It is this lack of historical feeling that makes our attempt to do the classics so often seem amateurish. They are indeed up there, dressed to the nines in period drag, but still themselves, today's waifs. And because of this inadequacy, the great guillotine trundles downstage, and, clump, clump, clump, go the heads of our tragic heroes and we feel no more than if a stapler had pierced a piece of paper.

The Theater of Grotowski

Akropolis, a production by Jerzy Grotowski for the Polish Laboratory Theatre, takes the concentration camp at Auschwitz for its setting, and, for its plot, the building by the prisoners of the gas chamber in which they will be consumed. This work is of a transcendent pity and terror and is the only work of art I know that is in some measure aesthetically commensurate with the Nazi history it springs from. *Akropolis* stands alone, a strange, classical moment of genius, lyrical, painful, of a sublime seriousness, rooted in our forgotten life, in the tatters of the Hellenistic and Biblical culture that trembled there before the darkness of extermination.

Grotowski's group performed in a beautiful rectangular space in Greenwich Village, the plain and serene auditorium of a Methodist Church. This was a dramatically useful setting for the Lab Theatre, giving as it did something Protestant—perhaps one could say wholesome—to the extraordinary Counter-Reformation brilliance of the performances. In the sudden blow of darkness that announced the end of each play, one could for a moment see the outside world filtered through the heavy reds and blues of the high, narrow church windows. And when abruptly the house lights came on, everything was erased forever: emptiness, no actors, only the silent audience moving out. For a number of reasons you cannot applaud the Laboratory Theatre. The mood is much too somber, and in addition applause seems to be the reward for a different sort of theatrical craft. It signifies the resolution of the story and returns the actors to themselves, separating them from their creation and commending them as artists and workers, craftsmen and performers.

Grotowski's works are too deep in suffering and death to be resolved. The actors, also, try for something beyond representation. They are not characters on the stage and therefore you are not quite sure what the self might be to which they are returning at the end of the performance. In the long run it is the bitterness and ruthlessness of the world of this theater that stays the hand. It is in many ways an obscure liturgy of scenes and sound, but I would not call it a ritual because of the difficulty of definition and because the word means a shared, often repeated ceremony, in which foreknowledge and the habitual are a great part of the hold the action and feeling have upon the imagination.

This is quite untrue of the work of Grotowski. You are lost in atonality from beginning to end, unable to predict the next note, to find the phrases, discover the structure. The assent one gives is of another kind: it is a surrender to the peculiar genius before you, to the fascination of the alien, to the triumph of conception, beauty of design even when mysterious, and to a powerful, original, and disturbing mode of performance. It is a poetic theater and the insights are those of poetry rather than drama. Still it is theater and I never once thought of it as dance, as so many people did.

Description and definition of the Grotowski Theatre are genuinely difficult and in the long run no doubt rest upon the unyielding hard ground of the works themselves. The ninety or so minutes of each performance were each one brilliant and intense and of such complexity one had not the time, at least for the purpose of a later description, to take in details. The acting asks for the very limits of endurance from the actors and verges on the inhumane; at the same time an inward concentration gives this endurance and strain an impressive otherworldliness and purity. The contrasts, a sort of Jesuitical union of ends and means, the intensities, the mood are strikingly new and also alien. The works are abstract and yet psychological—in the way a Bernini tomb sculpture is psychological. This psychology is generalized, historical, and meditative; it comes more from Jung than from Freud. The observation of life actors have always transmitted by their smiles, their accents, their gestures plays no part here. This is not the psychology of the mundane, of humble experience and habit, but of the soul, the race. It is death and transfiguration, historical memory, transformation (Christ-Apollo).

Voices are stretched to strange tones; in *The Constant Prince* the speed of the speech is so great, the pitch of the voices so unfamiliar that we are assured even Polish-speaking audiences cannot understand more than a few words. You feel you are listening to music and indeed every element of sound—the stomp of boots, the clap, clap of wooden soles, the sound of a hammer on iron, the high C of laughter—is utterly arresting and indescribable. Yet we do not feel the technique is one of formal gesture and symbolic movement that long acquaintance would decipher. There is no code, as in some Oriental theater. The faces, blond or brown, are masks, free of the usual emotions and particularly of the marks of "emoting"—and yet they are beautiful faces, untheatrical and still not quite real either. In the Grotowski Theatre there is no pathos, no tears, no real laughter, no friendliness, no love, no personal history, no disappointment, no victory. There is, instead, constant activity and pain, suffering, death, torment, fear, mockery, persecution, submission, ecstasy—and a sense of history.

The Polish Lab Theatre is not properly described by its negations. True it is, as Grotowski calls it, a "Poor Theater" and he has sought by the elimination of the normal intrusions of prop, costume, lighting, and set decoration to get at the heart of the theater. (For him it lies entirely in the actor, in his body and voice, and in his self-abandonment to truth—the "holy actor.") Still, the minimal props, the spotlights, the bits of costuming, the capes, the shoes, the glow of candles are always of a special inspiration and interest.

The group limits the number of spectators, never more than a hundred, and then again only forty. The audience is sometimes seated on a ramp up above the action, or around the wall, or in a square around the performing area: the arrangement is a part of the design of the work itself, a contrast with the usual practice of placing the spectators wherever the structure of the theater building has left space and rows for them. Perhaps it was the difficulty of understanding the works that led so many commentators to discuss the conditions under which they were presented. The limitation of the audience and its careful dispersal seem absolutely necessary and there is strong doubt that these works could be effectively seen in the usual auditorium, for they are intimate and concentrated to an extreme degree. Grotowski's regular theater is in the provincial capital of Wroclaw and perhaps there his restrictions can more easily fulfill the demand for these singular works. It is a "poor" theater but able to create special conditions—and like a monastic order it combines poverty with obedience, neither of which is very congenial to our nature.

How has this come to be in Communist Poland? The Grotowski Theatre does not merely survive, it is supported by the state. It is not only an assault on Socialist Realism, but on traditional realism as well. The intensity of intellectual life in Poland after the war and its long history of passionate avant-gardism explain in some measure the ability of an original talent like Grotowski to flower. His message is a mixed one also, expressing the romantic spirit of "Polish martyrdom" with certain contemporary austerities and despairing modes. In all of his works, the Polish experience is there for an audience who wished or needed to find it. This country has suffered humiliation at the hands of its tormentors and conquerors and has cruelly inflicted sufferings on its own people, its Jews and peasants. Perhaps "the constant prince," tortured, debased, with "no other weapons but his own human identity," passively doomed to suffering, but in endurance supreme—perhaps this is Poland itself.

Akropolis is based on a symbolist play written around the turn of the century by the great Polish poet-dramatist, Stanislaw Wyspianski. Czeslaw Milosz, in *The History of Polish Literature*, gives an account of Wyspianski's work and theories that shows them to bear a striking relation to Grotowski's ideas. Through this we can see the Polish strain that endures in spite of the modernity. Grotowski's aesthetic radicalism goes back beyond the Absurd and the Surrealist to earlier theatrical experiments.

Some ideas taken from Milosz's account of Wyspianski: First, a quotation from Brzozowski: "The thought of Wyspianski never expressed itself through words; he did not think in words, he thought with tensions of his will and with emotions expressed in color, movement, and sound. He thought in theatrical terms." Wyspianski's revolution was deeply rooted in the Polish past and in sadness over the provincialism of the country around 1900. He turned to Greek tragedy and to Wagner's theater for inspiration, and thought, with Mickiewicz, that "Slavic drama was called to continue the only valid theatrical line, begun in Greek tragedies and carried on in medieval mystery plays. The Slavic drama was to combine all the elements of national poetry—lyricism, discussion of current problems, historical images—into a blended unity. . . ." Wyspianski's plays were "librettos" for a stage director. Another quotation from Brzozowski: "Wyspianski does not know what the life of the new Poland will be, but he knows the death of the old Poland is death indeed. . . . The world that emerges in his work *negates itself*, undermines its own foundations. A structure of thought is erected, but only in order to be destroyed."

In Wyspianski's play *Akropolis*, the statues in the Royal Cathedral in Cracow come to life and enact scenes from history, from the Bible and Homer. Grotowski has had the daring notion of acting out this play and its "vision of Mediterranean culture" inside the concentration camp at Auschwitz, which is the contemporary "necropolis of the tribes," as the old Cracow castle was the necropolis of ancient Poland. *Akropolis* is a little more open, at least in the outlines of its action, than the other works shown here, but it would be misleading to think of it as "realistic." The inmates are dressed in torn burlap, skull caps, and wear heavy work shoes with wooden soles. They have a few rusty bits of pipe, the sections of an old tin flue. These are the materials of the gas oven. The other props are a tub, a kind of rag doll, a wheelbarrow. About these props, Ludwig Flazen, the literary advisor to Grotowski, has written, "Each object has multiple uses. The bathtub is a very pedestrian bathtub; on the other hand it is a symbolical bathtub; it represents all the bathtubs in which human bodies were processed for the making of soap and leather. Turned upside down, the same bathtub becomes an altar in front of which an inmate chants a prayer . . . One of the stove-pipes, transformed by Jacob's imagination, becomes his grotesque bride."

Here, between gestures of hard labor, the prisoners seem to fall into a daydream of history. Somehow the history of the race is projected, the memory of Isaac and Jacob, of Paris and Helen, of Western culture alternates with the clanging of the hammer on the pipes of the gas chamber. There is a lack of mere pathos—

and this is the genius of the work—and a sense of the death of the world instead. The work is lyrical throughout, with poetic lines not directly related to the Nazis or even to the twentieth century. The romantic words go whining through the fitting together of the pipes. As the furnace is completed, the text reads:

> *God, the living word descended on the graves.*
> *I honored him with a song.*
> *On the shattered stone of the castle*
> *God has inscribed his laws.*

The prisoners go into a big box in the center of the square. They pull the top over their heads. A voice says, "They are gone and the coils of smoke hover in the air." The audience leaves.

The last phrases are as close as the text comes to a representation of the extermination camps. And nothing has been acted out in the usual sense. When one reads, after the performance, that a piece of plastic is Rachel's wedding veil it is almost impossible to recall either the scene or the little bit of plastic. What you do recall is a lyrical tragic feeling, and the death of civilization as the players close the box. The text is a reverent one. Paris and Helen (two miserable male prisoners singing in unearthly voices), Laban and Jacob—the moments rush by. It is all pain, in the voices, in the arched feet, the stretched leg muscles. As you are going out you are urged to hurry on because the players are, all six of them, actually in the small airless box and cannot leave until the theater is empty. They suffer it—for what? For us, for themselves, as a witness?

The Constant Prince is based on a play by Calderón. Grotowski's production is very "Spanish" and suggests some great sympathy between the Spanish, before Franco, and Polish natures. The audience sits high up, looking down upon the scene, as you might look down upon an operating arena. The program notes mention Rembrandt's painting "The Anatomy Lesson of Dr. Tulp." And the two are similar in more than the "medical" arrangement; both the play, as Grotowski does it, and the Rembrandt picture are filled with religious iconography and intensity. In his book on Rembrandt, Sir Kenneth Clark says about the "Anatomy": ". . . he has given his central figure the pathos and solemnity of a pietà. Involuntarily we look for the stigmata on hands and feet. . . . Dr. Deyman rose above the corpse like the celebrant of some religious rite, and his assistant has the solicitude of an acolyte. Behind him the spectators sit and stand as if in the apse of a church and even the indecipherable emblem over Dr. Deyman's head is reminiscent of a crucifix." And this is precisely the feeling of *The Constant Prince*. The groupings, the furl of the capes, the blacks and reds and whites brought to mind also certain Spanish paintings of Zurbarán and Goya, and always the exquisitely suffering frame of the company's great actor, Ryszard Cieslak, recalls the baroque Descensions of Europe. Grotowski's work is full of painting memories, just as it is rich with the history and poetry of our tradition.

Apocalypsis cum Figuris is a powerful, episodic work, dealing with the transformations—or co-existence—of types: Simpleton-Christ, those "resemblances . . . toward the eternal figurations of myth." The work is harsh and disturbing, using candles and long white monk's capes, shifting from a sort of Inquisition feeling to a hard contemporary mood, like some of the figures in George Grosz's pre-war paintings. The text is taken from the Bible, from Dostoevsky, Eliot, and Simone Weil. The last line is "Go and come no more." Who is being turned away?

Problems of the Grotowski Theatre: Text: I would not consider this "non-verbal theater." First, the theater is soaked in literature and history, in a deep knowledge of the classical texts of the Bible, *Faust*, of poetry. A spectator without a good deal of literary knowledge would, it seems to me, lose tremendously. And the theater, the work, the entire enterprise could not exist without these constant references that deepen the conceptions, actually give them their impressive sense of history and their significance. Grotowski uses well-known texts, the common high culture of Europe, as the ground upon which he builds. A vulgar text would be a disaster and no text would, I believe, reduce the work to meaningless exertion, almost to pathology. In *Akropolis*, the very sound of the names of Jacob and Rachel and Helen gives coherence to the structure.

Grotowski has said, "Every producer must seek encounters which suit his own nature. For me this means the great Romantic poets of Poland. It also means Marlowe and Calderón. I should make quite clear that I am very fond of texts which belong to a great tradition. For me, these are like the voices of my ancestors and those voices which come to us from the sources of our European culture."

The use Grotowski makes of the text is another thing: this is not the Comédie Française. Plot and characterization are diminished, almost erased from the old texts, and what is left is the word, wrenched, re-arranged, but still supporting the conception. In spite of the brutality and cruelty, the concentration on suffering, this is a lyric theater.

Actors: There is no doubt about the greatness of the actors, but I do not think they are the center of Grotowski's Theatre. Grotowski himself is the center. It is the magnitude of his theatrical conceptions, the development of his theory of acting, the principles of training, the discovery and framing of his unique view of the past and the present that give his theater its overwhelming interest. I cannot conceive that the actors, for all their glory and dedication, could have within them the immense conceptual gifts of their director. Even as it is, the work is always threatened with disintegration because of the abstract nature of the embodiment of the ideas and the sense often of an arbitrary, almost mad, rigor, and of an inwardness beyond understanding.

Grotowski said about Artaud: "Artaud's misfortune is that his sickness, his paranoia, differed from the sickness of the times. Civilization is sick with schizophrenia, which is a rupture between intelligence and feeling, body and soul." This schizophrenia is at the heart of Grotowski's dramatic intention and reminds us of Nietzsche's warning that he who looks at monsters should beware lest he become a monster himself. Perhaps nothing can stand for the "rupture between intelligence and feeling, body and soul." There is no peace attained in these works, no resolution. They end invariably on an abrupt blackout and they tell us the torture continues unto death.

Technique: A grueling conditioning of the body and the voice make possible the effects achieved in the works. Somewhat mystical moods and pronouncements support the extraordinary demands Grotowski makes upon the actors.

The voice: "Special attention should be paid to the carrying power of the voice so that the spectator not only hears the voice of the actor perfectly, but is penetrated by it as if it were stereophonic. . . . The actor must exploit his voice in order to produce sounds and intonations that the spectator is incapable of reproducing or of imitating." There are, also, curious ideas about "eliminating the pause" and the belief it should be used parsimoniously, "only where it adds expressivity." The elimination of the usual pauses, the reaching for "stereophonic" expansion of sound explain the disorienting speed of the dialogue and the peculiar range of the vocal patterns. Grotowski says that it is the integrity of the sentence and the poetic line he is anxious to preserve, its rhythmical and logical integrity. This he does by "the single respiratory and melodic wave."

How can one make a judgment on the strangeness of the sound? The results have a beauty of an unexpected kind and yet if speed destroys intelligibility, as it does apparently in *The Constant Prince*, then dialogue is reduced to sensation, to an emotional rather than a cognitive function.

Training exercises: The physical exertions asked of the actors are extreme and yet these players are not acrobats, forever "practicing." They are working, as in yoga and other methods of attaining "truth" through the discipline of the body, to an "encounter." "Self-penetration, trance, excess, the formal discipline itself—all this can be realized provided one has given oneself fully, humbly, and without defense. This act culminates in a climax. It brings relief. None of the exercises in the various fields of the actor's training must be exercises in skill. They should develop a system of allusions which lead to the elusive and indescribable process of self-donation." These ideals defy analysis. The high achievement of the group bears witness to the strength of the dedication, to the discipline of the body. The language is that of the Catholic saints, struggling to find words for the effort that goes beyond, for the mystical joys at the end of the fasting and praying. It is one of the oddest developments in contemporary culture—that, at least.

Grotowski's fame and example have spread throughout the theater world. An original talent of this order confirms the art itself. Things can never be the same after the appearance of a genuine innovator and yet imitation does not seem likely. Grotowski's theater comes from a world and a private sensibility apart from ours. It is Catholic, authoritarian, pessimistic. Our theater is Jewish, humanistic, and optimistic. Accounts of Americans and Grotowski in an issue of *The Drama Review* bear on this. Americans, at a Grotowski seminar, were worried about "authoritarianism," about the lack of social content in his work, about the excessive austerity of his idea of the actor's life and purpose. (Grotowski was dismayed to find two American actors holding hands and fondling each other while waiting for their cues. He also complained that American actors were continually lying on the floor, relaxing!)

About the idea of social engagement Grotowski said, "I could indulge my ego by juggling with grand words such as 'humanism,' 'solidarity with the oppressed,' 'the rights of my own personality,' but this would serve nothing but my own sentimental and intellectual comfort."

To return to Grotowski as "Polish." Perhaps his protest, in a country from which so many artists and scholars have fled in order to breathe, is a formal and abstract one. His theater by its classical themes, its opaque detail, its circuitous methods of revelation keeps alive certain elements of the eternal and opposes them to the fleeting and contemporary. This is a possible art for the oppressed and particularly for the "censored." Everything in the works asks for deliverance, and without that, for discipline and concentration and purity, that which makes life and art orderly and victorious over destructiveness. People—like the Polish intelligentsia—who have been controlled, made helpless, and bound by the chains of an imposed political system, and who are at the same time the products of an elite, thorough European education, can see the revolutionary aspect of this artistic development. Or counterrevolutionary. There is not an element of the folk in Grotowski—at least as it appears to a foreign eye. His works are a translation of classical European themes, under extreme conditions. There is about them the feeling of a prison, both in the actual created works and in the theories surrounding them. Society breaks; the actor has only his body and the painful purity of his art. The works are a chorus without a plot. The only plot is suffering, blackness, desperation.

Grotowski is a bleak genius. The carnival anarchism of our own experimental theater is an expression of a totally different world view and history. We are a people disturbed, but still hopeful. The penitents of Wroclaw live in an eternal Holy Week, going through their exercises and remorseful re-enactments.

Auschwitz in New York

Peter Weiss has said about *The Investigation* that it could be recited or sung, but could not be acted. At one time, when the work was in progress, he called it "Auschwitz Oratorio," and actually the text is a sort of counterpoint of voices, uttering an inexpressibly cruel libretto. All except a few lines of the text is taken from the testimony in the 1964 trial, in Frankfurt, of the SS men attached to the Auschwitz concentration camp in Poland. No attempt has been made to shape the testimony dramatically, although certain things are included, such as the mention of German industrial firms, to support Weiss's idea that the camps were an economic advantage to Germany and were a product of capitalism and a possibility for every capitalist society. "The Camp is still here," one of the survivors says. It lives on, according to a recent interview with Weiss, in the prisons in Spain and Portugal, in the killing of hundreds of thousands of Communists in Indonesia, in Vietnam, in South Africa. For the most part, however, *The Investigation* is a recitation and remembrance of torture and murder and gas pellets and crematoria and individual acts of sadism. The stage is a bare courtroom. The witnesses and defendants face us. The witnesses produce their ghastly memories and then turn to point to the defendant, in his business clothes, who some twenty years before had done the dreadful acts.

What are we supposed to feel, there in the theater, listening to the unadorned recitation of horrors? The idea for such a work is more complex than it would seem on the surface. To whom is it addressed and for what purpose? And what is the reality of the theatrical fact? First of all, the limitations of the stage, or of any art form for that matter, are dramatically exposed when you attempt a realistic presentation of the crimes of the Nazis. The sheer magnitude of the crimes, the numbers, cannot be taken in. The case history—and that is what a trial inevitably is—seeks the general by way of the particular, the national in the individual, the many through the one. This is a way the imagination will try to cope with enormity and yet it will necessarily reduce, personalize. The spectator, watching the representation, will watch in sorrow, or guilt, or pain; and yet he will also feel sorrow, or guilt, or pain about the smallness of his own feelings, the abject insufficiency of his response. The limits of art and the limits of the private emotions meet suddenly as the testimony goes on.

The reality of Auschwitz is not on the stage. Nor are the criminals represented on the stage. Everything is not only once but twice or many times removed. When you see a representation, in the body of an actor, of the monstrous sadist, Boger, you experience only the sense of a faint shadow hinting at a receding corporeality. Were Boger himself present, as he was in Frankfurt, you would only be one step closer to the Auschwitz Boger, you would not truly have him before you. Boger can only be represented by his actions, not by his physical being later or by the *description* of his actions. And even if, to pursue the idea to the end, one saw an actual murder or two actual murders on the stage, that in turn would give only a suggestion of the mass extermination, the vast cruelties of the Nazis and the camps. The actors are only actors, innocent, acquainted not with death but at the most with words. And we, the audience?

What is expected of us? Birth or death? We are not, in this play, brought into the theater to receive essential information. The theater audiences of the great cities of the world are not in ignorance of the camps and the personal bestiality of those who ran them. (These persons as an idea have made their claim, their clear immortality, as "The Beast of Belsen" and other fast-selling titles in the pornography shops.) In the excerpts from the Frankfurt trials perhaps some bits of the horror are "new" to the audience, but these are only details. If one were to want the transcript of the Frankfurt trials he might better be sent to the publication of them in book form than to a rapid selection offered in a theater. Of course, we are probably meant to feel complicity and, no doubt, to hear a political warning about our own society. In Germany, where it was first performed, the intention may have been a more open one, a determination to try once more *to make them see.* (Absorbing, shattering, staggering, chilling: to quote a few words from the reviews, printed in advertisements for the play. These are *façons de parler*, with which one can only sympathize as an effort to have appropriate feelings about what is only *ostensibly* on the stage: the concentration camps.)

Peter Weiss is one of the most interesting dramatists writing now. He works in a very curious manner, almost as if he were reluctant to know what he is doing. He provides librettos, scenarios almost, and these he flings to the world, for each country, each production to do with as it will. To accept his work plain is to miss the whole point; he seems to want to put on the stage huge explosions of the instinctual life, instincts that have become politicized, but are not merely politics, in spite of his own preoccupation with that part of our current life. The camps were reality; the trial at Frankfurt was a sort of near-reality; but *The*

Investigation is a dream, a sublimation, a play. It is at one with Sade's play on the death of Marat.

Sade is in prison and cannot, as he did in life, torture live prostitutes. Through the theater, the sadistic impulses find expression, the impulses of the audience in particular. The audience is sly and cunning: History, truth if you will, reality, that which *really happened* serves the sadistic theater better than the simply concocted. For one thing one does not feel so guilty about a play on Charlotte Corday stabbing Marat, nude in his bath. Sade's imaginary *Justine*—we would not accept *that* acted out by the inmates; it is not *true*, we would say; it is merely deranged. We feel that Oedipus once, somehow, in the dawn of history really happened and that we are not readers of Oedipus but somehow descendants, as we are somehow descendants of Adam and Eve. The French Revolution happened, Sade himself happened; Auschwitz happened, Boger lived, indeed lives. *The Investigation* then is a play within a play. It is "The Prosecution of the SS as Performed by the Inmates of the Auschwitz Concentration Camp." And we are the audience, the benevolent director of the asylum. ("Coulmier incites the nurses to extreme violence . . . Patients are struck down . . . Sade stands upright on the chair, laughing triumphantly. In desperation Coulmier gives the signal to close the curtain.") Showers, death baths, inmates, the prison itself, sadists, the helpless . . . and above all history, in both plays. A one-to-one parallel is not suggested, and does not exist. Yet, in the theater, *The Investigation* is a theatrical event. If you accept it as reality itself you will feel defrauded and tricked, or unable to allow such feelings or unable to explain them. Appropriate, self-satisfying assertions of emotions one *believes* are asked for— that one *ought* to have—are then dredged up. In truth then, *The Investigation* is another cruel libretto. Perhaps its aim is self-hatred—to produce self-hatred, and not through an egregious or facile effort to identify with the beasts who are just pretending to be on the stage, but through circles and circles of gloom and false feeling to come at last down to the core, indifference.

The New York production is not "good." I have never seen another and yet I am convinced that this one is very bad. It is outrageously disappointing, and no joke is meant when one says that Uli Grosbard has directed *The Investigation* as though it were written by Arthur Miller. (If it *had* been assembled by Arthur Miller, it should not have been directed as his previous plays have been.) The play is not properly cast and is tonally dull and uninteresting. It is conceived only in the self-loving earnestness that is the curse of our stage. True, the play cannot be acted, but it must be staged, embodied. The art of doing nothing, of some suitable non-acting, has not even been attempted. The right people must be found and dressed and arranged. The creation of non-theater would be almost the opposite of what we have in this production—which is done in the *verismo* style and with the "real-life" sort of actor who functions so effectively in that law court serial on afternoon television.

What you see in the production of *The Investigation* is our fear of stylization, of "interpretation." Perhaps this clinging, adhesive didactic naturalism, year after year, play after play, had its roots in commercialism. But its development has been peculiar and complex. Stylization, where it is called for, is the work of a free imagination, of a confident spirit, following his inspiration. The imagination, the person, must be free and yet, by a paradox, stylization is the willingness to be rigid, to control and order, to interpret, even, at times, to wrench and distort in favor of some ruling design or idea. You must of course stand upon it, since it is clearly a decision, an idea. And in that, great risks are involved.

Stylization is too personal as an action, and too refined as a conception, apparently. How much safer to trust the simple flow of "real life," to fall back on sincerity at the expense of truth, to trust earnestness more than inspiration. (A comparison of *The Blacks* by Genet and *Blues for Mister Charlie* by James Baldwin comes to mind here. However, when I read the Baldwin play it hadn't occurred to me that it would *necessarily* have to be done as it was, in the old, dead, black town–white town sermonizing way. And what this did was to weaken the most interesting thing about the play: Baldwin's belief in the Negro's superior sexuality.) You must have inner freedom before you can trust design and form. And further, to turn one's back upon plain-dealing externalization, one must have some notions of the meaning of life, of the ambiguity of experience, of artistic possibility. Here in New York, every play from every period and of every sort turns out to be the same. They are all sprinkled with a tenderizing salt, and pork and beef and entrails turn out, comfortably, to taste just alike after all. Perhaps by this time, no power on earth could sever our actors from their "serious," eyes-glinting, next-door realism. The insufficiency, the falseness of this is never more pathetic than when you have a possibility, a hidden script like *The Investigation.*

Timon of Paris

Timons of Athens by William Shakespeare
French version by Jean-Claude Carrière, directed by Peter Brook
Théâtre des Bouffes-du-Nord (Paris)

Timon enters the space, a space as public and indiscriminate as a street. He is surrounded by people and yet without a setting. His claim to the space is scarcely greater than ours, the audience. Everything is bare and yet disorderly, not at all neat, not cool. Geometry is a statement, expensive; this space is a negligent, empty mess. There are sandbags, objects without character, defiant instead, merely useful to sit on, to form a circle for the dinner parties that are the peculiar and essential symbolic actions of Timon's life. The sandbags are not attractive; they are just sand, dirt and absence. The bareness and the omissions are not in themselves to be called interesting, unless their interest is to make us happy that the scenic hole, the theatrical blank, is not to be filled with Greek tunics, Shakespearean ruffles, and page boys carrying platters on their palms.

Nothing is clean, shapely, pure in its quiet. It might be a rehearsal—the periods without illusion when the actors seem locked in their imperfect private lives, their faltering selves. No, it is not a rehearsal. Everything trembles, becomes tense. The simplicity is not an experiment, a trick, educational. It would be a folly to look upon it in that way. The simplicity is real. When there is no money it is not necessary to simulate poverty.

The house is filled. It is a Sunday afternoon. The audience has waited outside in the cold drizzle for quite a while. We are in St. Denis, a working-class district in Paris. Communist posters and beautiful gray, worn stone buildings whose windows form a glimmering triangle as the streets narrow to meet a crossroad. Bouffes-du-Nord is the name of the theater and the place is a part of the manner in which this outstanding event, shaped by Peter Brook, seizes the public attention, defines itself. The building is a site, unredeemed, not stripped down but instead shaking in an ornate, interesting decay. It is a dingy, bankrupt, and splendid old structure with a dome of blackened, cracked glass. Its interior walls are flaky and stained; black grime and patches of white plaster melt into each other without renovation or restoration. It is a face in eruption and the holes cut into the walls so that the actors may appear and disappear from a height —these holes are like decayed teeth. The space itself, there, works on the spirits of the spectators as a teasing negative accepted. Necessity and the creative will meet; the encounter is an achievement and lack is, of course, almost natural, not to be considered. It is a question then of something else, beyond, further. Luxury and illusion give way; easily too.

Timon itself, Shakespeare's play, is in a state of reduction, at the least unrevised, thin in spots, late. It is perfectly served by the thrift of the staging, the challenging scantiness. Nothing would be worse than gold and silver, cloth from the ancient world, gilded sandals. The banquet scene with its Cupid, lutes, and Amazons is given by suggestion, without *luxe*. Instead a moody, hashish, blurred atmosphere, high, shrill sounds from the Arab quarter and mercifully no orgy or spot of nakedness standing out from the surface like a pimple upon which we are to gaze without pardon. The riches, the waste are all in the mind.

Shakespeare's *Timon of Athens* is about the philanthropy the rich confer upon each other. ("O! what a precious comfort 'tis, to have so many, like brothers, commanding one another's fortunes.") The parties, the gifts, the courtesies, the lavish impulses plainly gratified—all of these carefree gestures to be underwritten by painstaking, by obsession. Yes, one's whole life may be a benefaction distributed with no thought of necessity. With Timon, as with so many positioned thus by luck and inclination, it is the thing itself to some degree, the social contract also, and the aggressive planting of gnarled, complex roots of obligation. The generosity has in it a random, quite sharp competitiveness and it is by agile calculations that one keeps ahead. Timon is very much on the strain in this matter; he is watchful, quick, serious. "No gift to him / But breeds the giver a return exceeding / All use of quittance."

There is only the giving, the parties, and, of course, the previous consumption by the giver. One must buy a jewel in order to press it upon a friend who does not need it. This is all we know about Timon, nothing else. Generosity, or wastefulness, is his definition at the beginning and misanthropy is his definition at the end. He is an attitude and each comes to us in the midst of its flowering, without any preparation or backward glance. We accept it, if we do, because prodigality is indeed common, perhaps more common than greed, but certainly not more than selfishness. It is in no way contrary to selfishness, either, and the cynic sees the connection with a ready clarity.

Timon does not boast of his heavy habit of giving. He has style, the style that puts a glaze on his ruling passion. His social nature appears as truly his own as a pair of blue eyes. He is refined, offhand, and it is sometimes hard to discover where his true pleasure lies. In diversion or just in the satisfaction of an unaccountably strong impulse? The happy days of liberality pass in the purest courtesy; it is the misanthropy to come, when his friends prove stingy and indifferent to his run of bad luck, his shrunken fortunes, his classical reversal in the shape of bills come due—it is at this moment that Timon seems almost coarse. His insistent and intense hatred of the perfidy of man comes upon him suddenly, like an ugly drunkenness. This outrageous defensiveness baffles us. When he is still the giver rather than as he becomes, briefly, the suppliant, the petitioner, Timon is occupied with all the veiled and difficult reticences of the interesting host.

Flattery: in constructing the moral air of the play we are reminded that prodigality and flattery are instant friends. This is the way things go in society. "He that loves to be flattered is worthy of the flatterer." Yet one of the striking ways of Timon is his need to treat extravagant praise and attention as if they were the dreaded reciprocity his nature and his enterprise are so set against. The jeweler, showing a fine gem, remarks that Timon would enhance the beauty of the stone in the wearing of it. This is quickly dismissed by "Well mocked."

Flattery is a challenge. The proper turning away from it, undercutting, diminishing it without offense or vehemence, is a social grace sweeter even than the swift determination to keep ahead in the race of hospitality. Ventidius, who has been made rich by the death of his father, tries to repay a debt to Timon. The repayment is refused along with praise for the refusal. Timon draws back, fastidiously, abruptly from the compliments. "Nay, my lords, ceremony was but devised at first/To set a gloss on faint deeds."

Timon in Paris: he is young, thin, not tall. His presence is
such that it is not out of order to speak of him as beautiful. An
unflawed face. He is wearing a white linen suit. It is the romantic gaze that surprises, dominates the space, draws you toward him, as if toward an inward young man of the nineteenth
century, found on a soft, lazy afternoon, approaching his sorrow.
It is said early that through Timon one may "drink the free air."
This is more than his ruling liberality, his obsessive bestowing;
it speaks also of the atmosphere of an ineffable, unattainable
wish, a memory of the golden age. Timon seems to move in a
sunlight very clear and fragile. The senators, the painters and
poets, the strangely conceived Apemantus ("a churlish philosopher") all have a good deal of lead in their natures. The leaden
breathe Timon's free air—in sloth and a bit of suspicion.

But who is the Timon in St. Denis? He is not an Athenian
and although he speaks his lines in French he is not a French-
man. He is not Shakespearean; still he is Timon, or *a* Timon.
The world is waiting for him as the play opens. He appears to
be the only person in Athens with imagination. He is on everyone's mind—jewelers, merchants, soldiers, "friends." They form
a gathering that gives him his substance but none of them is
quite real. They simply trail this curious young man through his
moods.

His gaze is graceful, and the faint smile, the pleasingly self-
absorbed lightness of his gestures, are suitable to the mono-
chromatic drama, the slow and insistently peculiar single theme.
Timon, the splendid young actor (François Marthouret) in
Peter Brook's production, greets the world in the manner of a
young prince, an heir, but a prince with the gentle, strangely
caressing and careless charm of a flawed inheritance, an irregular
line. Yes, he is a rich and pleasing prince—but, we wildly imagine, one whose mother was an actress or an artist's model. Thus

he lacks, we think, the ingrained prudence, the caution, the patience of the pure line with its marbleized suet of inherited economies and thrifts.

Timon is dreaming, like the Prince von Homburg, who also had his temper tantrums, his indiscreet princely impulses, his lovely forgetfulness of the rules. Timon is a romantic, a spend-thrift, full of longings for something perfect, if only the perfect gift, the dazzling charity. Jewels and horses, dowries and fanci-ful favors take up his time, but through it all he maintains, for himself, a kind of chastity, as if he were too young for lust. Or perhaps something warns him even at the first that the acute, burning misanthropy lies waiting for the exhausted innocent and the weary aesthete.

The play is an exceedingly cold one but there is a tropicality in the Paris scene, the tropicality of the desert perhaps. Athens is corrupt; it is a city of solid usurers and fat hypocrites. You can think of it as the Greece of the colonels if you like, or so the comments made by Brook on the text suggest. But the real stage makes of the play a pastoral, a dreamlike, empty, poor place, filled with ragged "senators" and unlikely "lords" and black com-panions, and a small, brown, beautiful, weasel-faced *"putain"* and another, large, tall, screeching. It is an arid playground with luxurious words and real dust on the sleeve of the master mis-anthrope. The final Timon is a raving, wounded lover of life who falls into reality with a cry of "No!" and who, betrayed, prepares for a ritual suicide. "A madman so long, now a fool."

Money is merely an idea, an ornament to Timon. Gold is a joke and in the end all it can give you is a lesson. Timon has no family, no history. We are surprised that even the foolish sena-tors, facing defeat by Alcibiades, should urge Timon to return from his bitter exile to "take/The captainship, thou shalt be met with thanks,/Allowed absolute power, and thy good name/ Live with authority." This is madness. The young man digging his grave by the sea has never had the slightest use for affairs of state, is no more honest than his creditors, and is so moody in his swings from courtesy to abuse that his "heroism" can only be that of the romantic, the personal. Even when his creditors are at the door in search of his "desperate debts"—desperate because a "mad man owes them"—even when he descends to acknowledge his unbearable change from giver to beggar, Timon is a hurt and weary youth, his love rebuked. He can only act, not as a leader of Athenian society, but as an *actor*, on the stage.

His plan is not to create money, but a dramatic impression. The invitation goes out for the last banquet. He who is now "naked as a gull" invites the old heavy feeders to open pots filled only with water. It is a gesture and the young man, poised like a dancer, flashes his eyes and splashes the water around the circle of sandbags for the "dogs," as he now sees his friends, "to lap." The guests make off, hardly caring, looking for their hats, pulling themselves together. It is all over for Timon. The gesture was not sufficient.

Early we had been warned that when fortune changes there will not be one of the former friends "accompanying his declining foot." And so it proved to be, although the servants are loyal. Timon leaps into misanthropy, without a delaying moment of study. He is quick to assume his role, his place in history: he is a misanthrope, high, special, complete. Plutarch says he "embraced with kisses and the greatest show of affection, Alcibiades, then in his youth." But it was a show, a performance even in the earliest recording. His reason—the hovering paranoia of the stabbed romantic. He embraced Alcibiades because he knew that the soldier would "one day do infinite mischief to the Athenians." And then, near the grave, Timon will live by his most successful turn as an actor—his invitation to any Athenian who wishes to come and hang himself on the fig tree before it is cut down.

Timon is an attitude and in the end he is drowned by words. He does not speak of aches and hunger and loneliness; he speaks of his attitudes, of what he has in a flash learned about the squalid nature of human beings. He invites the most terrible sufferings for mankind and councils children, "To general filths / Convert o' th' instant, green virginity! / Do 't in your parents' eyes!" Humanity has not harmed Timon. The ingratitude was local, limited, and we had not expected him to keep such a deep accounting or to extend his demands so widely. He and Apemantus have a dialogue extreme in its pettiness. The Paris Apemantus is black and has a lilting accent, perhaps that of a North African. He is a wanderer and carries a burlap bag on his back, along with the disillusionment that Timon sees not as philosophy but as *ressentiment*. Timon, having betrayed his own fortune in the manic spending, reminds Apemantus that his long melancholy is not disinterested. Apemantus has never clasped "fortune's tender arm," and so he mistrusts the world merely because he was "bred a dog." Here the snob passes the day. "Dog" as a word is everywhere in the play. The lowly dog, outcast, ignored, hunting for the scraps of life, seems to fill a place in the dreaming mind; the image is firmly locked behind the eyes.

Timon is a parable or a fable, but what is its instruction? "Here lie I, Timon, who, alive, all living men did hate." An odd idea. The lottery money is spent, but it is not the loss, the deprivation and decline, that turn the heart to rage. To understand Timon is to imagine his own false memory of a garden of love greater than life, his own dreaming of a plenitude so greatly flowering that he himself seemed to direct it, command it. But it was not Eden after all. It was only another Saturday night with one's own set; and at the end the dishes, the ashes, the quarrels, the squeezing pain of repetition, the hope that was a lie to ourselves more than to others. "One day he gives us diamonds, next day stones." This is a comment from the outside, but it is the understanding of the host also. All those evenings he had been writing his epitaph, breaking the stones of the grave with his teeth.

part four

❖❮❮

Memories

Simone Weil

Simone Weil, one of the most brilliant and original minds of twentieth-century France, died at the age of thirty-four in a nursing home near London. The coroner issued a verdict of suicide, due to voluntary starvation—an action undertaken at least in part out of a wish not to eat more than the rations given her compatriots in France under the German occupation. The year of her death was 1943.

The willed deprivation of her last period was not new; indeed refusal seems to have been a part of her character since infancy. What sets her apart from our current ascetics with their practice of transcendental meditation, diet, vegetarianism, ashram simplicities, yoga, is that with them the deprivations and rigors are undergone for the payoff—for tranquillity, for thinness, for the hope of a long life—or frequently, it seems, to fill the hole of emptiness so painful to the narcissist. With Simone Weil it was entirely the opposite.

It was her wish, or her need, to undergo miserly affliction and deprivation because such had been the lot of mankind throughout history. Her wish was not to feel better, but to honor the sufferings of the lowest. Thus around 1935, when she was twenty-five years old, this woman of transcendent intellectual

gifts and the widest learning, already very frail and suffering
from severe headaches, was determined to undertake a year of
work in a factory. The factories, the assembly lines, were then
the modern equivalent of "slavery," and she survived in her own
words as "forever a slave." What she went through at the factory
"marked me in so lasting a manner that still today when any
human being, whoever he may be and in whatever circumstances, speaks to me without brutality, I cannot help having
the impression that there must be a mistake. . . ."

For those of us here in America who have known Simone
Weil from the incomplete translation of her work and from the
dramatically reduced and vivid moments of her thought and
life, she has taken on the clarity of the very reduction itself.
There the life was as if given in panels of stained glass, each
frame underlined by a quotation from her writings, quotations
unforgettably beautiful and quite unlike any others of our
time. It is only in quotation, not in paraphrase, that the extraordinary quality of her concerns shines through. ("The intelligent
man who is proud of his intelligence is like the condemned man
who is proud of his large cell.")

This "life,"* written by her friend, Simone Petrement, is a
work of the most serious kind of affection and the most serious
dedication. And yet the result of it all is to obscure and blur by
detail and by a wish, no doubt unconscious, to retain memories
and moments of the normal and natural in a character of spectacular and in many ways exemplary abnormality. Those who
live with a breaking intensity and who die young have a peculiar
hold upon the world's imagination. The present fashion of biography, with the scrupulous accounting of time, makes a long
life of a short one. It is not the careful gathering of facts or the
mere length—a year is a long book—but the way the habit and

* *Simone Weil*, by Simone Petrement, translated from the French by Raymond Rosenthal (New York: Pantheon Books, 1977).

practice work upon the grand design, turning form into bricks. Short lives that sum themselves up in final explosions of work and action are especially vulnerable to amiability, discretion, and accumulation. (Sylvia Plath is another example of reduction by expansion—high school, tennis lessons, dates.)

Simone Weil was born in 1909 into a Jewish family with little interest in Jewish religion or Jewish culture. The parents were unusually attractive because of their elevated traits of mind and patient sympathies. Both Simone and her brother, André, a distinguished mathematician, were clearly gifted from the beginning, having talents that revealed themselves in inspired concentration. The family was a close one and Simone's frail intensity and her ingrained refusals—luxuries of all kinds, personal comfort in the manner of living, acceptance of girlish ways—caused the parents anxiety which did not, however, take the form of denunciation. Throughout her life, her parents are to be found urging people to give her decent food without her knowing it, worrying about the unheated rooms she invariably discovered, taking her for vacations, visiting her in factory towns, tracking her down among the dangers of Spain during the Civil War, where she had gone as a volunteer and where she had suffered a terrible burn on her leg which they were anxious to have properly treated. The daughter's letters to her parents are noble, loving, and real. The cover of *Seventy Letters* reproduces an envelope addressed to these now uprooted Europeans, then living at 549 Riverside Drive, coming from the daughter in London and written during her last week of life; it is extraordinarily moving.

Simone Weil was a student of the philosopher Alain (Emile Chartier). Alain was a special figure as a writer and teacher in Paris in the 1920s—one of those arresting French academic stars who throw the light of their ideas and the style of their thinking over young intellectuals and have a dramatic fame quite unusual here. His *Propos*, essays on many aspects of culture, very likely confirmed Simone Weil's own genius as a philosopher working in the form of passionate essays rather than in theoretical explication of positions and arguments.

Alain's attention was given to morality, good deeds, the exercise of will by which one becomes free, to pacifism and to suspicion of the need to exercise power over others. In many ways these thoughts prefigure the great themes of Simone Weil's writings. Her own nature was, of course, much more extreme; that is, she was determined to live out truth, not as an example which would have involved the vanities and impositions of leadership, but as a dedication marked by obsessive discipline.

She appeared odd and, to some, rigid and forbidding, giving "the impression that some element of common humanity was missing in her, the very thickness of nature, so to speak." In her revolutionary youth she was a striking, intransigent, awkward figure. Simone de Beauvoir tells of meeting her when they were preparing for examinations to enter the Normale. "She intrigued me because of her great reputation for intelligence and her bizarre outfits. . . . A great famine had broken out in China, and I was told that when she heard the news she had wept. . . . I envied her for having a heart that could beat round the world." When the results of the examination in general philosophy were posted, de Beauvoir says, "Simone Weil headed the list, followed by me."

The "saintly" shape of Simone Weil's life grew amidst the unbelievable density of left-wing politics in the Europe of the 1930s. The various parties, the strikes, the violent factionalism in unions, the eschatological intensity of theoretical disputes, Russia under Stalin, the challenge of Trotsky, the nature of Marxism, the ruthlessness of colonial rule, and the anguished clinging to pacifism with its horror of conscription as a central theme of radical thought—all of this Simone Weil took part in, writing a prodigious number of pamphlets and political letters, giving speeches, organizing meetings.

Trotsky had been allowed asylum in Paris under the Daladier Government, with the condition that he refrain from political activities of all kinds. Nevertheless, Simone Weil convinced her parents to allow a meeting to be held with Trotsky in their apartment house. Trotsky arrived with his family and armed bodyguards, all of them entering "with their hats pulled down over their eyes and their coat collars raised to their noses," looking exactly like what they had wished to disguise, like conspirators. Simone took advantage of the chance to have a discussion with Trotsky. "The discussion quickly turned into a quarrel; in the adjoining room, where they were seated, the Weils heard a series of loud shouts."

This period, with its organizations and counterorganizations, its cells and splits, is almost impossible to return to its genuine context because of the simplifications of thought and possibility finally brought about by Nazism, the war, the atomic bomb, the cold war, and the devastation of serious left-wing hopes in Europe and America under the power realities of postwar existence.

For Simone Weil, peculiar and "eternal" as her profound concerns were, it is impossible to imagine that she would have remained on the outside, quietist, contemplative, unpolitical. Oppression, exploitation, liberty, national prestige, force, dignity, history, faith: in her reflections upon these conditions rest her claims upon our minds and feelings. Without the common political life of her time surrounding her writings with its urgencies, her essays would be different. They would be literature rather than prophecy, a tone they clearly have and by means of which her language achieves its beauty and uniqueness.

Her reading of history and her culture were enormous. But she read history without objectivity, meaning that she read the past in a mood of violent, agitating partisanship, believing that it mattered not in the sense that an educated person must know the past but with the conviction that the legacy of the past was as much a part of life as airplanes, automobiles or armaments. Thus her dislike of the Romans and the Hebrew tradition of the Old Testament and her love of the Greeks and the Gospels.

"The Great Beast: Some Reflections on the Origins of Hitlerism" maintains that the Roman Empire was the model upon which the iniquitous, militarized, centralized states of Europe developed their totalitarian policies. Louis XIV lacked the true spirit of legitimacy, she thinks.

> The miseries of his childhood, encompassed by the terrors of the Fronde, had induced in him something of the state of mind of those modern dictators, sprung from nothing and humiliated in their youth, who have thought that their peoples must be tamed before they can be led. . . . The degradation of hearts and minds in the second part of his reign, when Saint-Simon was writing, is as sad as a phenomenon as anything of the kind that has been seen since. . . . Domestic propaganda . . . reached an almost unsurpassable degree of perfection. . . . base flattery . . . or cruel persecutions and the silence that surrounded them, foreign policy conducted in the same spirit as Hitler's, with the same ruthless arrogance, the same skill in inflicting humiliation, the same bad faith. . . . Louis XIV took Strasbourg in exactly the same way as Hitler took Prague, in time of peace, amid the tears of its helpless inhabitants.

About the Romans: the sacking of Epirus, the destruction of Carthage, Caesar's "bad faith" in his negotiations with Ariovistus, Cartagena, Numantia, on and on. The sacrificing of peoples to the concerns of Roman prestige. "They knew how to undermine by terror the very souls of their adversaries, or how to lull them with hopes before enslaving them by force of arms." She connects the uprooting of peasants in her own day with the lines from Virgil's first "Eclogue": "We are leaving our country's bounds and our loved fields . . . We go to parched Africa." Elsewhere she says, in comparing the *Aeneid* to the *Iliad*: "God would be unjust if the 'Aeneid,' which was composed under these conditions, were worth as much as the 'Iliad.'"

Her attitude about Hebrew history in the Old Testament rested upon the same ferocious objections. Yahweh, "the god of armies"; God's rejection of Saul because he did not exterminate the Amalekites down to the last man; Elisha dismembering forty-two children who had called him "Baldhead"; subjugation of the people of Canaan. In answer to the objections that the Canaanites themselves were immoral, she would have answered that we were not brought up to honor them. Also, in her feeling about "historical perspective" and its tendency to understand cruelties of the past as part of the sanctions of earlier cultures, she seemed to believe that morality did not improve and to hold with Plato that all people, at all times, had knowledge of the ideal "good."

Catholicism was attractive to her spirit, although in her dealings with priests and Catholic friends she was contentious, vehement about certain doctrines such as no salvation outside the Church and, as always, inclined to look upon history as alive. "What frightens me is the Church as a social structure. . . . I am afraid of the Church patriotism that exists in Catholic circles. . . . There are some saints who approved of the Crusades or the Inquisition. I cannot help thinking that they were in the wrong." In any case, she was never baptized.

The 1945 publication of Simone Weil's essay, "The Iliad, or The Poem of Force," in Dwight Macdonald's magazine *Politics*, in a translation by Mary McCarthy, was, it is no exaggeration to say, an event of great importance to those of us who read it. This is one of the most moving and original literary essays ever written. "For those dreamers who considered that force, thanks to progress, would soon be a thing of the past, the 'Iliad' could appear as an historical document; for others, whose powers of recognition are more acute and who perceive force, today as yesterday, at the very center of human history, the 'Iliad' is the purest and loveliest of mirrors."

In the *Iliad* the afflictions of force grow and grow, and each side weaves back and forth under the dominion of suffering. "At the end of the first day of combat . . . the victorious Greeks were in a position to obtain the object of all their efforts, i.e., Helen and her riches . . . That evening the Greeks are no longer interested in her or her possessions: (*For the present, let us not accept the riches of Paris; nor Helen; . . . He spoke, and all the Achaeans acclaimed him.*) What they (the Greeks) want, is, in fact, everything. For booty, all the riches of Troy; for their bonfires, all the palaces, temples, houses; for slaves, all the women and children; for corpses, all the men." The losses fall upon everyone, without mitigation and finally without meaning. "The death of Hector would be but a brief joy to Achilles, and the death of Achilles but a brief joy to the Trojans, and the destruction of Troy but a brief joy to the Achaeans."

In 1942, Simone Weil came to New York with her parents. Her whole mind was taken up with returning to Europe, with ideas for getting back into France to participate in the suffering and the resistance of her country. That was her mind at least insofar as action was concerned. Otherwise this was a period of intense religious contemplation. She did succeed in making her way back to London at the end of the year, saying as she left her grieving parents: "If I had several lives, I would have devoted one of them to you, but I have only one life."

Her will to undertake dangerous missions in France was frustrated. Instead she wrote her celebrated *The Need for Roots*, a group of very personal and typical essays that must have bewildered the Free French who had asked for a sort of government report, filled with the usual bureaucratic "recommendations." Instead Simone Weil addresses herself to "the needs of the soul."

In this work and in others, the peculiarity of her vocabulary arises from the fact that she is occupied with the expression of distinctions, with definitions not of much interest to most thinkers. The difference between affliction and misery, for instance. Affliction is the suffering that separates one from others, causes in them dread and repulsion. "It is the mark of slaves." It is "anonymous" and does not arouse the emotion of pity. "The same incapacity for paying attention to affliction that inhibits compassion in someone who sees an afflicted man also inhibits gratitude in an afflicted man who is helped. Gratitude presupposes the ability to get inside oneself and to contemplate one's own affliction, from outside, in all its hideousness. This is too horrible."

In London her health vanished, even though the great amount of writing she did right up to the time she went to the hospital must have come from those energies of the dying we do not understand—the energies of certain chosen dying ones, that is. Her behavior in the hospital, her refusal and by now her inability to eat, annoyed and bewildered the staff. Her sense of personal accountability to the world's suffering had reached farther than sense could follow. She died young, like so many of the wretched in history whose misery had haunted her throughout her rare and noble life.

Svetlana

I am not quite sure why the passing months make one feel less and less interested in Svetlana. Perhaps it is that everything she has experienced and remembered is now hard news, mercilessly distributed in every capital and hamlet. When you come now to the reading of her actual book there is, about some of it at least, the staleness of yesterday's headlines; it is the eleven o'clock news telling you just as the seven o'clock news told you that when Stalin's son failed in a suicide attempt the great leader said, "Even this he cannot do right." More importantly, a resistance grows in our fertilized soil quite as naturally as that freedom of expression Svetlana came here to enjoy. This is our defense, for we have so often seen expression turn into unwanted evangelism and have discovered that he who tries, publicly, to find himself also finds the engulfing temptation, almost the necessity, of self-exploitation. Tragedy and courage, so profoundly covered for our information and pleasure, so exuberantly donated to the indifferent and interested alike, turn, the next dawn, into Pop. This is one of the oddities of our abundance.

Originally published under the title "The Crown Jewels: Letters by Stalin's Daughter, Svetlana."

Svetlana is a worthy and attractive person. Her memoirs have a great deal of interest and her general ideas none at all. Her first appearance on television was singularly calm, a triumph of virtuous determination and steady articulation. Those reassuring freckles, her aura of a sort of Soviet-induced moral rearmament could immediately be seen as readily adaptable to our own morality and purpose. For had not our own Virtue and Suffering, like hers, had its origin in the resistance to the same Soviet? She shares our urgent impulse to counterrevolution. She had, clarity, will, and all, been nurtured in the Kremlin, but she had chosen freedom. It was natural that she should flee to us. Still, that alone would be a bit spare and ideological. In addition she had buried her Indian lover, she had meditated on the Ganges, she had left her grown children, she had written it all down, she had found God. She arrived here, a capable messenger from the underworld, Pluto's daughter, seeking light.

It is easy to make fun of her, to forget what she has suffered, and to be casual about her need for a new life and for freedom. It is perfectly right that she should come here if she wanted to do so. She did not trust the future in Russia, and had little reason to feel otherwise. The stupidity and the meanness of the bureaucracy die for a day, only to be reborn the next.

Svetlana could not have made it without her book. These pages are her crown jewels. And they are, for her purposes, enormously negotiable. She has considerable literary talent and has organized her book with great skill. The letter form is miraculously right, allowing her to move in and out of different periods of her life without formal strain. She is a good reporter of the actual events of her life and recreates the atmosphere of her childhood with a pleasant and convincing naturalness. Her Kremlin is not political—it is, instead, the great house in which the poor, lonely little heroine lives. There she had everything

Soviet society could confer, even the death, suicides, and disappearances. Stalin demanded this of his immediate family just as of the Soviet people as a whole.

Svetlana had private tutors, nurses, summer houses, home movies, pocket money—all turned a bit gloomy and morose in keeping with the character of her father's reign, but interesting nevertheless. She says that her father was austere in his habits and private life, and the atmosphere about him does represent the style of the new class he created—created, destroyed, and created again, with a compulsive attachment to bureaucratic structure and a fear and hatred of the bureaucrats who ran it. Dachas were built and seldom used, gardens planned and left to ruin because there was no time for them; servants and bodyguards and ugly, dark halls. Stalin had known real poverty and there is in the life he made for himself and the style he allowed the bureaucracy to enjoy no attempt to imitate the wild, frenzied luxury one finds nowadays in the suddenly elevated leaders of poor countries. There is instead something suburban and just barely middle-class in the luxuries of the Soviet elite. But the privileges are real, if not inspiring.

Stalin demanded, in Bukharin's phrase, a "corpse-like obedience," but his daughter is not a corpse. She has a high conception of possibility and that curious, somewhat heavy self-confidence of those who have known hereditary advantage. She tends to fall in love with commoners (Jews) and the monarch threatens, but in all this there is, or so I read it, again that sturdy, grinding sense of self and the self's rights that sustains her to a remarkable degree. There is in the daughter if not coldness, at least coolness, about family members and she has just enough necessary blindness: the blindness necessary to survive in the Stalin household. Blood ties were dangerous and in the end Svetlana had only her old nurse. And what a prophetic curiosity it is that she first knew of her mother's suicide when she read it in an old copy of *Life* in 1942, when she was seventeen years old, and ten years after her mother's death.

Stalin did not, apparently, have the ability to love and it is hard to feel Svetlana meant much to him even though she naturally longs to believe in his love and treasures whatever meager, affectionate memories she can call upon. His letters, quoted in the book, are written to a very young girl, but even allowing for that, they are brief, general, and read like those dutiful, very short notes children, rather than parents, are required to produce. Stalin's children were always reminders of his painful experiences with their mothers: he treated them as he treated "his people," with caprice, vindictiveness, suspicion, and extinction. Svetlana's half-brother, by Stalin's first wife, was a casualty of his father's great cruelty and finally, in a German prison camp where he had been captured, killed himself by rushing onto an electrified fence. Stalin had refused to intervene on his behalf and indeed took the position that captured Russians were traitors and punished them and also their surviving Russian relatives.

Vasily, the other son and Svetlana's full brother, came to a miserable end. His story is a terrible one and in its particular squalor and waste has its counterpart in American experience. Vasily was a spoiled, foolish, greedy alcoholic, corrupted by his position as Stalin's son and corrupting everything about him. He shared, in full measure, his father's violent, hateful nature. Svetlana tells his story with supreme candor—and a sympathy that is only "technical." (She feels he was "ill" and needed "treatment.") When Vasily was brought to his father's deathbed, "he was drunk, as he often was by then, and he soon left. He went on drinking and raising cain in the servant's quarters. He gave the doctors hell and shouted that they had killed or were killing our father." He was made chief of aviation of the

Moscow Military District when he was so far gone "he could no longer fly his own plane." In Svetlana's list of the misdeeds and dishonesties practiced by Vasily, many are surprisingly familiar to us. "He was surrounded by shady characters from the sports world, masseurs, and soccer players, trainers and 'promoters' who put him up to all kinds of 'deals,' such as tampering with hockey and soccer teams and having swimming pools and Palaces of Culture and Sport put up at public expense." What is this except the very worm in the Capitalist apple? Svetlana says that throughout the period before Stalin's funeral, Vasily was in "a dreadful state and his behavior was appalling." Later, after arrests and jail and wanderings and squalid decline he died. "He'd been on a strenuous drinking bout with some Georgians and never regained consciousness. The autopsy showed that his body was completely destroyed by alcohol. He was only forty-one years old."

Just as Stalin does not come through as much of a father, so Svetlana finds her real strength in defiance of her father and in the elaborate revenge upon him which her defection represents. Her analysis of his crimes is not complete, and sympathetic persons will say that she really did not know the extent of his guilt. Actually, there is probably very little she didn't know about her father and one could even suppose that her late discovery of her mother's suicide was not quite genuine and that she had guessed something much earlier. Still, it would not be especially edifying for her, a daughter, to make the final gruesome accounting, and she puts much of the blame on Beria, seeing him as an evil force manipulating Stalin's natural suspiciousness. It was more likely that the truth was just the opposite: that Beria's cruel, opportunistic nature was used by Stalin. Also, Svetlana feels that the "system" was really at the bottom of the terrible suffering in Russia. The whole Party apparatus oppressed the people and destroyed the goodness of life. She feels doubtful that the accomplishments of the Revolution have been worth the price. She identifies with *Doctor Zhivago* in her sorrow over the destructiveness of the Revolution.

Yet all that makes one feel much less spiritual elation about Svetlana than about Pasternak is very much to the point. It is not her "position" or her failure to show the full horrors that stops us. We could hardly demand more of her in the rejection of her country, her hatred of Communism and enthusiasm for her new life. In the end, it is the quality of her mind, the lack of genuine intellectual and imaginative force that causes one unease. A passionate simplification characterizes her observations whenever she departs from the concrete, remembered detail. She appears as an ambitious, disciplined person, very determined in the pursuit of self-realization, clinging to the grand and the abstract rationalizing emotions, simple and yet self-righteous, profoundly—"naturally," if you will—conservative.

Her great themes are extreme simplifications: she begins her book with a hymn to Nature. The woods, the little villages where they "still draw their water from wells and do their cooking on kerosene stoves." Over and over in her memoirs, nature descriptions hang in the wings, to be brought forth like a good character to sweeten a sordid plot. Nature is innocence, beauty, and goodness. It is Peace. "After such cruel bereavements, after so many disappointments and losses, after thirty-seven years of a foolish, pointless, hopeless double life, I see you shining, my beloved, chaotic, all-knowing heartless Russia. You comfort me and light the way. Nothing will ever blacken you in my eyes. If your goodness and truth hadn't lit my way, I'd have given up long ago . . ." (A note is appended to this, saying that at the time it was written she had no thought of leaving Russia, and instead had hope for real improvement and democracy.) What is so off-putting about this rhetorical, contrived counterpoint of nature is that it prevents her from saying what she really feels. She doesn't love her father and she doesn't love Russia and she took her ultimate revenge on them by escaping to the enemy. America is not just another place, a refuge; it is a land many believe to be seized with a phobic fear and hatred of her native land.

Her second theme is the presence of a universalist, non-denominational God commenting upon and making bearable the horrors of reality. After a moving, courageous description of her father's death, which she rightly saw as a deliverance for her and for the people of Russia, she writes, "My father died a difficult and terrible death. It was the first and so far the only time I have seen somebody die. God grants an easy death only to the just." Svetlana does not seem to be well acquainted with His ways.

She left Russia and came into an outside world of revolutionary violence. She does not have much to say to that world because she shares what seems to be the political exhaustion of her country, the draining away in their long inward and outward civil war with Stalinism of all revolutionary hope and interest. Her fatigue, her nostalgia for simpler times tell us the one thing Americans do not want to hear, since they believe the Russians to be filled with a menacing revolutionary zeal. What is most interesting about Svetlana is not her revelations about the perfidy of Communism, which are more fully given elsewhere, but her personal strength, that sense of an amazing integrated self she and other favored Russians who have visited the West seem to have. Perhaps the little people are less strong and show all the ill effects and personal diminishment of a life without political freedom.

Part of her strength and that of other Russians comes from the consolation of the Russian past. Stalin could not—or did not—destroy Russian culture. Literature seems to be the Soviet citizen's hold on sanity. Literature keeps alive his sense of what is true and valuable, the knowledge of human feelings. The great modern tradition of the Russian novel and Russian poetry fortunately concerned itself with just those questions of suffering and morality and the place of man in society that Stalin made a most awful day-to-day anguish. There seems to be no reason to doubt that starving prisoners lived on the poetry of Blok, that Tolstoy and Dostoevsky filled the emptiness inside. Perhaps a more perfect industrialization will do away with all that, as it has here.

It is hard to know what lessons America is trying to learn or teach through the story of Svetlana. There is something sad and something absurd in the amplitude of our exposure to her thoughts. All those names popping off the pages of the Bangor or the Louisville daily: Kirov and Bukharin and Nadya Alliluyeva, all dead and all so suddenly resurrected, shadowy, somehow Americanized. As for Svetlana herself we can only hope that she will not, as Pasternak said of the Soviet exploitation of Mayakovsky, be propagated here "like potatoes at the time of Catherine the Great."

Thomas Mann at 100

If Thomas Mann were alive today, 1975, he would be 100 years old. That is very old indeed and yet it is not at all impossible to imagine Mann reaching the age of 100, celebrating the year in the rather stiff, worldwide, panegyrical manner of the Supreme Instance, great and long-lived. He combined the purest gifts with the earthbound consent, of a distinguished old dray horse, to pull heavy loads. Mann lived to be eighty—and the irony was noted that these were a considerable sequence of years for an artist who connected inspiration with disease and early death.

He was never young. Youth fascinated him as the acute, fateful moment, not only the moment of sexuality but of revelation of the threatening shape of personal destiny. Youth announces the drama of differences, complementarities, dissents; the leap into the anxiety of swirling and life-giving ambivalences. The over-sensitive may not last. Typhoid, lung disease and malicious fevers are like the temptations of Eros—they kill the special.

One could almost speak of Thomas Mann's life as without incident, except for his works. He is a superb family chronicler and yet, in the most real sense, he himself does not have a biography. Nothing happens except his genius and the setting of wife and children that supports him who needs little support. It is a *career*, profound, engulfing. He is a little cold and far-away as a man; in person short, neat and with a fading countenance.

Mann married when he was thirty years old, four years after the extraordinary achievement of his youth, *Buddenbrooks*. And immediately things fell into line, assumed their first and lasting shape. Books, public statements, great and dignified success, marriage and children, exile for political reasons, honors, more books, lectures, lots of mail, many importunings, return to Europe, death. There are apparently no love affairs or break-downs, none of the ever-returning indiscretions of his idol, Goethe, none of the madness of Nietzsche, the folly of Wagner, never the bruising, angry loneliness of Schopenhauer. Always, Mann was steady, an artist of the highest and most excruciatingly faithful ambitions—a condition for which his genius and his nature served perfectly. His books are difficult—at least many of them are. He had, in his settled, concentrated existence, time for the bizarre accretion of classical and curious learning that is the material of his fiction quite as fortunately as the material from psychological and social scrutiny.

His wife, Katia Mann, is still living and has published a small memoir about herself and her husband: *Unwritten Memories*. Most of the incidents and memories relate to the works, the writings of the husband. The happiness and charm of Frau Mann are very pleasing and the great novelist, unlike so many others, knew what he was about when he made his choice. We, his readers, his heirs so to speak, are not surprised at this con-stancy needed, sought and found.

Mann's letters to Erich Kahler, Hermann Hesse, and Karl Kerényi, many of which appeared in the 1971 *Letters of Thomas Mann*, are now printed in the centennial year with the corres-ponding letters of the recipients. These are all interesting exchanges, even if the writers have fallen into a Mann-like tone of address and comment. With Hesse and Mann, separated in their fictions by an oceanic gap, it is often only the signatures that indicate authorship. The spell of the occasion is overwhelming. There is friendship, particularly with "dear friend Kahler," but somehow the dots and dashes, the humors and jokes and groans and ellipses of life cannot scratch the fine grain of a gracious impersonality, seriousness and appropriateness.

There is not much biography in the letters either. Mann's need to control the disruptive, the intolerably hurting, extends even into his family life. A letter to Hesse about the suicide of Mann's son, Klaus: "The thought of this life cut short fills me with grief. My relations with him were difficult and I often had a sense of guilt, for from the very start my existence cast a shadow over his. As a young man in Munich he was quite the rambunctious prince and much of what he did was offensive. Later, in exile, he became more serious and moral; he worked hard, but too quickly and with too much facility. . . . Despite all the love and help he was given, he persisted in destroying himself; in the end he became incapable of any thought of loyalty, consideration, or gratitude."

In Mann's fiction, a deep psychology of symbol and wound moves beyond family life, gossip, and the dramaturgy of personal relations, into a bold, secret life of repression, erotic fatality and a driven, complicated denial. His attraction to opposites shows the need for a frame to contain the chaos of consciousness and to explain the inexplicable balancings in one soul of heredity, historical moment, character and choice. The practical, calculating North and the impulsive, careless South; illness and health, love and death, humanism and demonology, ordinary love and denying dedication: in the contraries, in the opposites, the art and thought of Europe bear down upon the individual destiny.

All of his life Mann studied to understand the great artist—himself, more in fear than in pride—and where he came from and at what cost the art was produced. At the beginning of his work, the opposites are somewhat simple and arbitrary. In the story *Tonio Kröger*: "My father, you know, had the temperament of the North: solid, reflective, puritanically correct, with a tendency to melancholia. My mother, of indeterminate blood, was beautiful, sensuous, naive, passionate and careless at once, and, I think, irregular by nature." The attraction of the alienated artist to the blond, the normal, the healthy—Kröger's friend Hans—is also simplified in the early writings. As Mann's career goes on it will turn out that the demonic, the forbidden, the shameful are tragically at work also in the bourgeois artist, dazed by his wound of understanding. Still, some things will never change in life. Kröger will never be able to make the agreeable, lively Hans turn his attention to Schiller's *Don Carlos*; and later, in *Doctor Faustus*, it is quite unlikely that the healthy and happy will attend Leverkühn's radical musical composition, "Apocalypsis cum figuris."

Alienation survives irony, but alienation has its temptations to the monstrous. The underside of life, cruel and destructive, also imparts its mighty knowledge. When the great composer, Leverkühn—deliberately following the appalling sadness of Nietzsche's life—infects himself with syphilis, the action is one of hubristic violence against the self. Illness, infections, sufferings are the price paid; by way of isolation a creative life is possible. Flaubert's "fits" and Proust's neurasthenia are visionary hindrances. When Leverkühn pursues the infected prostitute, Esmeralda, to Hungary in order to achieve the fated union with her, he will also go to hear the first European performance of Strauss's *Salome*. In the conjunction of a real event in European art, the parallel with Nietzsche, the opaque, mythical and exhausting Faust legend, the peculiarly baroque, original quality of Mann's art is revealed. *Doctor Faustus*, his next to last work, is a kind of apotheosis; lifelong themes, prodigious scholarship, spendthrift imagination. It is very slow, hard, and yet it has the power to move the feelings in the odd way of something dense, muddy, thick and grandly real. It is very European, one of those moments of the fabulous, written one imagines in a heavy overcoat, amidst the cold stone and marble of the great libraries.

The career of Leverkühn, his final madness and collapse into death, take place in historical, recent time: the rise of Nazism, the sweep of the German army through Europe; at the time of Leverkühn's death in 1940, "Germany [was] reeling at the height of her dissolute triumphs." There is a disaster ahead for this lowest and cruelest historical insolence, but Leverkühn is not Nazism; he is perhaps to be thought of as Germany, as the health destroyed by the demonic cells within its own being.

One of the outstanding things, amidst the Teutonic obstinacy of the challenge of the Faust theme, is the creation of Leverkühn himself, a complex, alive man who is credible at what he is asserted to be—an important avant-garde composer. His learning, his coldness—of the hypnotic sort that draws disciples, biographers, students and landladies deeply into a respectful infatuation—his pride and his impressive perversities are individualized by the brilliance of his mind, the fascination of the discourse, the travels, the musical learning, the weaving of obsessions and withholdings. The intellectual and bohemian life of the Weimar Republic is created by a heightened dazzle of mimicry and memory, and yet all of the persons are lifelike, sad, full of waste, loss, moral and social devastations.

The Rodde sisters, for example, Clarissa and Inez, with their strained "hybrid" nerves—hybrid because of the mixture in their circumstances of a diminished hereditary middle class and the social unsteadiness of a world created by their widowed mother, with her mild pleasure-seeking and inchoate unfulfillment—are creatures of the purest novelistic mastery. Clarissa fails as an actress, bungles by chance and weakness the possibility of a genuine love marriage, and ends by taking poison. Inez marries conventionally, then falls in love with the violinist, Rudi, and with the feeling that "pain is an indignity" sinks into morphine addiction and at last shoots her lover in a tramcar. Obsessions, unrestrained by firmness of character, are part of a deteriorating social and political stability. They are a counterpart to Leverkühn's own tainted, afflicted heights of inspiration and his final collapse into dementia, "with woeful open mouth and vacant eyes."

Mann has the rare gift of creating characters out of ideas, prejudices and cultural affectations. In *Doctor Faustus* Dr. Chaim Breisacher, an insinuating intellectual, stretches the accepted cultural conservatism of Munich society to a far, fantastical historical scorn for the unfortunate results of the discovery of the laws of perspective, scorn for the "modernist disintegration" of Palestrina and Bach. King David and King Solomon are "debased representatives of an exploded late theology." "Prayer," finishes Dr. Breisacher relentlessly, "is the vulgarized and rationalistically watered-down late form of something very vital, active and strong: the magic invocation, the coercion of God."

Mann's artists and thinkers are marked by a sense of separateness, but they are also attacked from time to time by the rash of envy. Their great loneliness is a calling, and in solitude they honor that part of themselves Goethe called his "sacred earnestness." Nevertheless the exalted person will be brought down to envy the easy and unreflecting sexuality of the "normal." Mann's characters are cut off from love by illness, by a chastity that is either circumstantial or temperamental, by an overwhelming sublimation.

The appeal of *The Magic Mountain* lies partly in the attraction of chastity and denial, in the paradox of the solitary-communal—conditions that have some roots in almost everyone. The monastery, the college, the shipboard, the hospital, grand hotel and even the imaginary prison are aesthetic satisfactions to some part of the troubled spirit. Here one is solitary, one's real life having been lived or to be lived elsewhere, and yet one's solitude is joined with the solitude of others enclosed in the same space. Remember that the hero, Hans Castorp, is an orphan and so he has early on lived a life without a good deal of the usual luggage. When he enters the Berghof, healthy, he is assigned to a bed in which an American woman patient had died just a few days before.

Tuberculosis, high up in the snow of Switzerland, is a vocation with its hours and rituals and its strange unctions. Illness imposes passivity as a consolation. In this book, life is conversation and since there is little action it is conversation surrounded by silence. Explosions of activity are a defiance; one leaves only to return. The arguments of Naphta and Settembrini finally become violent, as they must; words must be given life. In the stillness of diseases ideas must stand for living, and so the Humanist and the Catholic-Marxist end up with their duelling pistols.

"All disease is only love transformed," Dr. Krokowski tells the patients. Homoerotic currents are very strong in Mann's writing. Extraordinary displacements occur in memory and in dreams. Hans Castorp remembers his "admiration" for a schoolmate, Hippe, remembers the vibrating drama that can accompany unacknowledged love. "He loved the emotions it brought in its train, the suspense as to whether he was likely to meet him that day . . . loved the subtle and wordless satisfaction imparted by his secret, loved even the disappointments inseparable from it. . . ." The scene of the "pencil" is as peculiar as any in literature. Hans finally approaches his schoolboy love when he must borrow and return a drawing pencil from him. In the beautiful Walpurgisnacht scene with Frau Chauchat the scene is repeated. Her last words to Hans Castorp are *"N'oubliez pas de me rendre mon crayon,"* don't forget to return my pencil.

The description of the young boy Tadzio in *Death in Venice* surpasses in tenderness and lyricism anything in Mann's work. "No scissors had been put to the lovely hair that . . . curled about his brows, above his ears, longer still in the neck. He wore an English sailor suit, with quilted sleeves that narrowed round the delicate wrists of his long and slender though still childish hands. . . . His facial tint was ivory-white against the golden darkness of his cluttering locks." When Tadzio smiles, Aschenbach, the aging writer, in a seizure of intense misery and feeling, falls onto a bench in the garden and whispers the "ridiculous enough, yet sacred too . . . 'I love you!' " The catastrophic onset of love is the same damage to the soul that disease is to the body. And of course, stricken, infected, poor Aschenbach will die there in Venice of the plague that has come down upon the city and upon him.

The artist as a subject has suffered a sea-change in our time. His drunkenness, infidelities, vanities, madness are looked at with a ruthless, acerbic intimacy—looked at thus even by himself. His suffering is kept at a distance by distortion and parody. Lest he appear too self-aggrandizing, too much in love with his pity or revenge, a satiric diminishment is offered by a relaxed, mimicking style. Mann's elaborate heroes have by comparison a statuesque quality; they are, even in minor parts, figures from history, already cast in their own bronze. Yet what ties them to our time is their demonism, their hidden passions, seeping out in a symbolic mist, their obvious failure to reach the wholeness of the bourgeois, whose health they must have in order to work, but whose happiness they must surrender because of their violent consciousness and vulnerability. Mann's sense of

vulnerability modifies his temptation to abstraction; his awareness of the tawdry and shameful humanizes his concentration
on the very act of art. He is saved by the perverse, by the knowledge that comes from having looked at the lost. For this his
greatness, threatened by its own energy, still inspires awe and
love.

Wives and Mistresses

> For who are we, and where from,
> If after all these years
> Gossip alone still lives on
> While we no longer live?
> Pasternak, *Zhivago Poems*

I

The famous carry about with them a great weight of patriarchal baggage—the footnotes of their lives. Footnotes worry a lot. They, loved or unloved, seem to feel the winds of the future always at their back. The graves of the greatly known ones are a challenge to private history; the silence is filled with riddles and arcane messages.

These "attendants" are real people: mistresses and wives, sometimes but not often husbands; friends and enemies, partners in sudden assignations. Some have been the inspiration for poems or have seen themselves expropriated for the transformations of fiction. They have written and received letters, been lied to, embezzled, abandoned, honored, or slandered. But there they are, entering history with *them*, with the celebrated artists, generals, prime ministers, Presidents, tycoons.

The future may be an enemy. Time can turn happy days and nights into nothing. It can uncover secrets that impugn experience. Children in old age struggle to remember games on the lawn, agreeable picnics once shared with the infamous old tyrant whose photograph keeps appearing in the newspapers as yet another drudge of information and interpretation offers the assertive intimacy of long study in a tone that would surpass all life acquaintance.

The maligned see their quarrels with the famed one as a battle which can have no ending, see themselves squirming in an eternity of calumny which they would contest with document, affidavit, witness—right up to their own death. The determination of footnotes cries to Heaven. Lady Byron vindicated!

"On his marriage-night, Byron suddenly started out of his sleep; a paper, which burned in the room, was casting a ruddy glare through the crimson curtains of the bed; and he could not help exclaiming, in a voice so loud it wakened Lady B., 'Good God, I am surely in hell!' "

Where are all my years, my thirteen confinements, my seven copyings of *War and Peace*, Sofia Behrs Tolstoy asked again and again. Forty-eight years and, of course, one quarrel will be the last and all is too late. She is kept away from the bedside in the stationmaster's house. Distraught, accused, excluded beyond endurance, the Countess wanders about begging for reassurance, repeating, explaining her devotion, her understanding, her care. The young Pasternak, rushing with his father to the amazing, outstanding death scene, wrote in *I Remember*: "Good Lord, I thought, to what state can a human being be reduced, and a wife of Tolstoy at that!"

The Tolstoys knew all there was to be known about marriage and therefore all to be known about each other. More indeed than one is put on earth to understand. More than could be endured but certainly not more than could be recorded by one or the other. "Immense happiness . . . It is impossible that this should end except with life itself."* And soon, quarrels, and he will be found writing: "I arrive in the morning, full of joy and gladness, and I find the Countess in a tantrum. . . . She will wake up absolutely convinced that I am wrong and she is the most unfortunate woman alive!" She writes: "How can one love a fly that will not stop tormenting one?"

How real the Countess and her inflamed nerves are. There is no question of authenticity and she cannot maneuver with any more design than a trapped bat. With her mangled intelligence, her operatic, intolerable frenzies of distress, she comes forth still with an almost menacing aliveness, saying it all like a bell always on the alert. Years and years, threats of suicide, collapse, hysterias, and the swiftest remorse as defeat hits her at the most passionate moment of declaration. Weeping reunions: "The bonds uniting me to him are so close! . . . He is a weak child, delicate, and so sweet-tempered." Again jealousies and plots. He feels a horrible "disgust and outrage" as he finds her creeping into his room when she imagines him asleep. She is looking for the will, or for the diary; always looking for herself in history, the self the pious, pedantic Tolstoyans would disinherit and deny, looking, too, to find the way to remain the inspiration, the adviser, the considered one whom the hated disciple, Chertkov, would supplant.

Problems of life and often the distorting, defacing mirror of his work, which sent forth its scarred images of home into the public view: when *The Kreutzer Sonata* was published with its murderous rages against carnal passion and marriage—"two convicts serving a life sentence of hard labor welded to the same chain"—the Countess felt herself mocked all over Russia, pitied even by the Emperor, gossiped about in the street.

* The quotations from the Tolstoys are from Henri Troyat's biography, *Tolstoy* (New York: Doubleday, 1967).

She recorded her feelings: "I always felt the book was directed against me, mutilated and humiliated me in the eyes of the whole world, and was destroying everything we had preserved of love for one another. And yet never once in my marriage have I made a single gesture or given a single glance for which I need feel guilty toward my husband."

Also after the publication of *The Kreutzer Sonata* there were comic consequences for *him*, who had after all "stigmatized all fornicators." Suppose his wife were to become pregnant again? "How ashamed I would be . . . ," he wrote. "They will compare the date of conception with the date of publication."

It was, of course, impossible for the Countess to bring her will, her great temperament, and her devotion to Tolstoy into a harmony that could survive more than a few sundowns. The overwhelming scene, the tremendous importance of the union and its dismaying, squalid complications of feeling, Yasnaya Polyana, the children, the novels, the opinions. The programs for transcendence and her thought: "This vegetarian diet means that two menus have to be prepared instead of one, which adds to the cost and makes twice as much work."

It is not quite clear how they found the time for the *record*—the fascinating, violently expressive record, like some strange oral history which catches the rises and falls of the voice, the impatience, the motive, the love itself heard in a sigh as sleep comes down—when it mercifully sometimes does. Every quarrel, every remorse, moments of calm and hope and memory. Diaries, rightly called voluminous, letters, great in number, sent back and forth. Longing for peace and the provocation of discord. "Until five in the morning he sighed, wept, and inveighed against his wife, while she, exhausted, momentarily contemplated suicide." *Momentarily*.

The cross the Countess hung upon was not inadequacy or even that crucifixion of mismating, common enough in all conditions of life. It may be said of her that one cannot imagine anyone else as the wife of Tolstoy. Their struggles always have about them the character of fate. He is as vehemently occupied with her as she is with him. The record alone, each in so great a hurry to say what the day had brought, indicates a peculiar obsession, one of those obsessions often punitive and yet inescapable. She had energy and mind of an extraordinary sort and so she moved back and forth one can only say *naturally*, calling upon the word so often used to describe the greatness of Tolstoy's art. She lived out a penalizing contradiction, devoted one minute, embattled the next. An adjutant, wracked by drama, brilliant in her *arias*; and then awakening to uncertainty, shame.

The Countess Tolstoy herself is a character in a great Russian novel, perhaps one by Dostoevsky rather than Tolstoy. Tatyana Tolstoy in her recently translated memoir, *Tolstoy Remembered*, writes about the more or less "serene" survival of her mother for nine years after Tolstoy's death. Serene, perhaps, "but she retained one weakness: she was still afraid of what people would say and write about her when she had gone, she feared for her reputation. As a result she never let slip the slightest opportunity for justifying her words and actions. There was no weapon she would not use in her campaign of self-defense. . . ."

The Countess Tolstoy had no more need for self-defense than a barking dog. But the eminence of Tolstoy brought the very existence of her frazzled nerves into question. The dazzling scrutiny they directed upon their marriage left behind a rich dustheap of experience, but the documentation was not a court of judgment, as she imagined. It was simply their life itself.

In his beautiful reminiscence of Tolstoy, Gorky tells of walking along the beach with the "old magician," watching the tides roll over the stones. "He, too, seemed to me like an old stone come to life, who knows the beginnings and the ends of things. . . . I felt something fateful, magical, something that went down into the darkness beneath him . . . as though it were he, his concentrated will, which was drawing the waves and repelling them." No doubt the Countess felt also that Tolstoy controlled the tides. What she often could not do was to flow and ebb in the certainty of nature, like a wave.

Lady Byron: from her short union with Byron she got her name and a lifetime of poisonous preoccupation. In her bad faith, deceits, and, above all, in her veiled intentions, so veiled indeed that gazing about with her intrepid glance she could not find the purpose of her intense lookings, there is nothing of the tragic exhaustion of the Countess Tolstoy. Lady Byron is unaccountable. She is self-directed, dangerously serious, and became a sort of Tartuffe in petticoats. "Marry Tartuffe and mortify your flesh!"

Lady Byron's industry produced only one genuine product: the *hoard* of dissension, the swollen archives, the blurred messages of the letters, the unbalancing record of meetings, the confidences, the statements drawn up, and always the hints with their cold and glassy fascination. The hinter, Lady Byron, was in a drama upon which the curtain never came down, and never will. An eternity of first acts. Her marriage lasted one year, ending in 1816; Byron, the *perpetrator*, as the police now refer to the accused, died in 1824, a century and a half ago. But the story of the marriage and the separation knows no diminishment. Instead it accelerates, develops, metamorphoses: all of it kept bright by its original opacity, all enduring forever out of the brevity.

No doubt, Byron, hard up, capriciously married Annabella Milbanke for her money and for the weary interest aroused by her first rejection of him. (When she at last accepted his offer, he is supposed to have said: "It never rains but it pours.") She married Byron for the fame of his notoriety and because of its engaging unsuitability to her own nature. But most of all they seemed to have married in order to create the Separation.

The story is well known, but the details, told and retold so many times, are unknowable. "So here we must beware of ignoring the sharp incompatibility of Lady Byron's original attitude and that which so suddenly took its place." Or "Compare that with Lady Byron's statement in 1830: the discrepancy, already observed by Drinkwater (1,54) is highly significant." (These tangles quoted in G. Wilson Knight's *Lord Byron's Marriage* are but a few among hundreds in his book, and cannot indicate the manifold puzzlements in the huge number of important Byron studies, each with its dazed laborings to cope with the hoard.)

As for Byron, "On the sixth Byron cheerfully assured Lady Melbourne that 'Annabella and I go on extremely well.'" However, "His opinion changed completely during the following week as he wrote to Lady Melbourne on the thirteenth: Do you know I have grave doubts if this will be a marriage now; her disposition is the very reverse of *our* imaginings" (*Lord Byron's Wife* by Malcolm Elwin). Marry they did, allowing Hobhouse to make his famous remark, "I felt as if I had buried a friend."

The Separation—often called The Campaign—followed the next year, after the birth of a daughter, Ada. The legal inferiority of women and wives gave a good start to the rise of Lady Byron's litigious temperature and to the onset of symptoms of "proof." She also wanted custody of the child, even though most scholars think she greatly "overused" this point since it was hard to imagine Byron assuming the care. (He had once written his half-sister Augusta Leigh that the sound of her squalling children gave him "a great respect for Herod.")

Byron had been throwing bottles of soda water on the ceiling (stains never found), posing with his pistols and bottle of laudanum by the bedside, and speaking of "crimes unimagin-able." Murder, sodomy, incest? None of these? All of these?

So began the vivacity of the separation months, the deliriums of dissimulation, the doctors consulted, the families, the meetings and the refusal of meetings, the solicitors and their huge bills, the advice of friends, the decisions taken and rescinded, the demands countermanded. All of this gave witness to the resonant incompatibility of the two persons, even though each might sometimes pretend for purposes of the "case" to warmer emotions drifting in and out.

The incongruity of Lady Byron was to have devoted a long life to a short marriage that ended in her youth. She had, at the church, taken an injection of poison into her veins. To Byron's fame and uncertain character, to the charm and scandal of it, she would oppose her rectitude, her virtue, her injuries. But she did this in the most complicated, insinuating way, finding as she did that the achievement of a virtuous appearance in the midst of her accusations of horrors is to ground oneself on ice. She slipped and slid, tottered and regained her balance with an almost admirable audacity and endurance.

The incest of Byron and his half-sister, Augusta: Lady Byron brought to her suspicious concentration on this an imagination in flame, a motive of the left and right, like the blinders worn by a horse, and behavior so shadowed with contradiction that it is only her pursuit of the theme that can be counted on. She was determined to prove the incest and yet was not quite sure when she preferred it to have taken place—the problem being an uncertainty about the usefulness of its continuing during her marriage.

"Now, she had two objects in view: one, to establish the fact absolutely, preferably by getting Augusta to confess, and thus to know for certain whether Byron had ever persuaded her to repeat the crime after his marriage (that was important to her). . . . The jealousy which her principles would not allow her to acknowledge found sublimation in a truly sadistic zeal to extract the sin from Augusta's life and save her" (*Byron: A Biography*, by Leslie A. Marchand). Lady Byron was also sliding about on the wish to discover a secret and to insist she would not divulge what she had discovered. An insane complexity of effort went into divulging while not divulging. Byron thought her purpose was to "sanction the most infamous calumnies by silence."

Lady Byron maintained a careful "friendship" with Augusta, broken only for a period late in life and even then mended. She was driven by a curiosity deeper than she knew and also by fear of losing control over any of the large cast of actors. Augusta experienced for years the most painful dilemmas of confusion. "Lady Byron presumably wants a confession of incest: Augusta, still not seeing the point, assumes she is merely being accused of some kind of disloyalty" (G. Wilson Knight).

Lady Byron had so many confidantes, advisers, doctors, and lawyers that of course the accusation was known to everyone—and, in any case, it had been spread about by Lady Caroline Lamb. Still, Lady Byron, talking and insinuating with a violent energy that left no gap, took moral refuge in the legalistic balm of never having *publicly* stated or "confirmed" what she had spent so much time proving.

Toward the end of her life, she had her operatic encounter with Mrs. Harriet Beecher Stowe. One could play a scene and the other could write it. They sequestered themselves after a luncheon in 1856, now forty years after the Separation. The "silent widow" spoke: "The great fact upon which all turned was stated in words that were unmistakable: 'Mrs. Stowe, he was guilty of incest with his sister!'"

Lady Byron was "deathly pale." HBS nodded, saying, yes, she had heard as much. Lady Byron went through her drama once more, starting with her childhood to set the stage. At one point she was asked by her American sympathizer whether Augusta was beautiful. Lady Byron answered, "No, my dear, she was plain."

All of this appeared in Mrs. Stowe's *Lady Byron Vindicated*, published after the death of the subject. There had been a *Lord Byron Vindicated* published the year before.

Lady Byron suffered in her calculations from the promptings of an outlandish pride. Her dilemma was that she took pride in the marriage to Lord Byron and pride in the Separation. In the various positions she assumed, many deforming conditions were working against one another. No sooner was she secure in her virtuous behavior than she was thrown from the ladder by the shakings of Byron's fame, which could turn every scandal into an attraction. She had always to be wary and wariness wore down her command of strategy. "Public outcry against Byron" could be punishing to him but it could not be depended upon. She understood this from the surest knowledge: her own peculiar attraction to and pursuit of him, a man she deeply disapproved of.

Lady Byron, an arrogant, intelligent heiress, appears to have needed a daily, yearly exercise of power and to need it in union with moral superiority. She feared no one, unless it may be said that she feared the shade of Byron. Byron's *Memoirs*, his account of the marriage and separation, was destroyed by a murky alliance of his own friends and Lady Byron's supporters. In life it cannot be said that she feared Byron. When asked if she were not afraid of the madman, she said, "My eyes can stare down his" (G. Wilson Knight).

It was her own life rather than history Lady Byron was most zealous to conceal and color—and a good thing too. She, voluble, alert, devious, has been looked at subsequently with a devastating alertness to motive, wish, contradiction that rather resembles her own deep archival diggings for "proof." In Doris Langley Moore's new biography of the daughter, Ada, Lady Byron is standing naked under an avalanche of falling rock. Her ill-health, her charities, her friendship with Augusta, her resistance to publicity, her jealousy of kind servants, her devotion to her daughter, her truthfulness: every noun except jealousy must from Mrs. Moore's researches be put within impugning quotation marks.

Lady Byron brought up her daughter, in relation to Byron, with a dreary contrariness, always displaying the will to retain and the will to renounce at the same time. Thus, a portrait of Byron hung in the house "perpetually covered by a green cloth." Ada was made to know she was the daughter of a renowned poet, "but all specimens of his handwriting were locked away from her."

Ada, an interesting result of the cynical union, was a good deal like her mother. She inherited from her mother—"the princess of parallelograms" as Byron called her—a genuine gift for mathematics. She had ambitions, too, and studied with the distinguished Professor Babbage, who was working on ideas later developed into computer mathematics. Ada married an agreeable, suitable man, who fell under the insistent domination of her mother.

There was much that was promising in the girl's beginnings, but she began somehow to sink into the mud of maneuver, manipulation, and her own marked self-satisfaction. Her mathematical skill turned toward the race track and she soon lost money, went into lying and debt, and squirmed around miserably in the pit of blackmail. From badly diagnosed illness, and the for-once inattention of her mother, who was intent upon her own notorious hypochondria, Ada went to larger and larger doses of morphine, to glittering eyes and vague drug elations and depressions. She suffered an excruciating death from cancer, dying when she was thirty-six and leaving Lady Byron to carry on for eight more years. To persevere with new problems of denial and blame, new ruptures, as Ada's gambling debts were revealed.

Both Ada and Lady Byron were afflicted with the wrinkles of class arrogance. Ada's belief in her own "phenomenal brain" inhibited the progress of her learning. Mother and daughter loved themselves too ardently. Mrs. Moore writes that Ada had a strong "desire to collaborate with Babbage in developing the intricate machinery to bring the computer to a state of practical usefulness, which would have been an unprecedented triumph for a woman." But Ada was often high-handed with the great Babbage and wrote him letters in "an air of conceit which is not to be found in any claim her father ever made, even in his artless boyhood." Riches, flattery for every cleverness, the oppression of her mother's rule, cut Ada off from serious work while leaving her the comfort of a boastful superiority.

What was Lady Byron's wish? If she was a victim, she was a most active one, responding long to Byron's fame and her short connection with it. Byron, of course, fared better in the time he had to live after the separation. He soon produced an illegitimate child elsewhere, he traveled, wrote poems, occupied himself with ideas and certainly with life. He had other affairs, also "historic," and also remembered and "published." The Countess Guiccioli, "the last alliance" as Iris Origo calls her, wrote her own recollections for the world. After she was widowed, she married the Marquis de Boissy who, the report went, used to introduce her as *"La Marquise de Boissy ma femme, ancienne maîtresse de Byron."*

Katherine Mansfield wrote in a letter to Middleton Murry:

"Did you read in *The Times* that Shelley left on his table a bit of paper with a blot on it and a flung down quill? Mary S. *had a glass case* put over same and carried it all the way to London on her knees. Did you ever hear such rubbish!"

Tolstoy, after a miserable time, said about his wife: "She offers a striking example of the grave danger of placing one's life in any service but that of God." True—not that he meant it.

II

The loved ones—what a sinking it is from the high-flying insistence of the miserable to the slow, steady hum of affirmation. Egotists of affirmation have problems of form spared the truculent and the misrepresented, who carry their injuries about on their persons like a glass eye. In the pastoral mode, the drama will often come from without, from the obstructions of others, from the recalcitrance bred into the very nature of things, from bad reviews, the envy of rivals, tyrannies of the social order.

My Years With ———— are likely to form a part of the title. Blank must be one whose years with are of interest to others besides oneself. For compositions in the pastoral mode, friends perform more felicitously than family members or lovers: the gloss need not be so radiant. In love memoirs, psychological inquiry is either missing or inadvertent; one does not usually loiter over the question of why he might be loved. It is the loss of love that arouses the speculative faculty and its rich inventions.

Anna Dostoevsky and Nadezhda Mandelstam are in no way similar, except that both by character and intelligence survived marriage and devotion to great writers without loss of common sense. The diary kept by Anna Dostoevsky is a plain reminiscence of a life of singular shape. The gambling in German towns, the epileptic attacks, the composition of the great novels, the bitter contest with debts, greedy relations, thieving publishers, the raising of children: all of this survives in her modest intelligence and truthfulness. One cannot leave a record of another without leaving a record of oneself.

Nadezhda Mandelstam's two large volumes, *Hope Against Hope* and *Hope Abandoned*, are of such brilliance and passion they cannot rightfully be called "memoirs." Her books are a battle against tyranny and death. The poet, Mandelstam, was extinguished in the flesh during the Stalin purges. It was his widow's determination to keep his poetry from extinction, to discover the awful circumstances of his murder in a prison camp, to write the history of the tyranny as she lived it, and still lives it, to analyze the circle in which they lived and Russia itself. In doing this, she has produced her own monument, one of the outstanding literary and moral achievements of her time.

Olga Ivinskaya, the mistress of Boris Pasternak, has written her book. It is called *A Captive of Time: My Years with Pasternak.* A florid, obsequious composition, issuing from an uncertain and harsh life. Her love memoir of her fourteen years as the mistress of Pasternak brings to mind that "fat brute of a word" —*poshlust*—as Nabokov examines it in his book on Gogol. "What the Russians call *poshlust* is beautifully timeless and so cleverly painted over with protective tints that its presence (in a book, in a soul, in an institution, in a thousand other places) often escapes detection." Gogol tells the story of a German gallant, trying to conquer the heart of his Gretchen. "Every evening he would take off his clothes, plunge into the lake and, as he swam there, right under the eyes of his beloved, he would keep embracing a couple of swans which had been specially prepared for him for that purpose." Here, as Nabokov has it, "you have *poshlust* in its ideal form and it is clear that the terms trivial, trashy, smug and so on do not cover the aspect it takes in this epic of the blond swimmer and the two swans he fondled."

Pasternak met Olga Ivinskaya in 1946. He was fifty-six and

she was thirty-four. The writer who, as Tsvetaeva remarked, "looked like an Arab and his horse," was a revered, romantic figure. His beautiful work attracted to him the positive radiance that shines around the poet in Russian society, an effulgence matched by the negative reverence of the state, which displays itself in constant surveillance and oppression such as other countries would think a waste of time.

All young girls may have been in love with Pasternak, and many not so young. In any case, when Olga first attended a Pasternak reading she went home with her book and greeted an interruption by her mother with, "Leave me alone, I've just been talking to God!" They met, they met once more, fell in love, and ushered in, like a reign in history, the fourteen years.

It settled into a triangle, in which all suffered—he the least. Pasternak had been married to his second wife, Zinaida, for ten years. This second marriage took place from materials near at hand, perhaps one could call them, since Zinaida's first husband was Pasternak's friend, the pianist Neigaus. That indeed was a "move." The first Pasternak wife was a painter and they had one son. So there was his life—choices, consequences, things settled in the past.

Olga herself had a daughter by her first marriage. The husband committed suicide: her second husband died. When Olga and Pasternak met, the marriage with Zinaida was a "mess"— but it had that paradoxical quality of marriages in being a *solid* mess. Ivinskaya's habit is to put memories of conversations uttered long ago into direct quotations and, thus, dialogue of a doleful reduction sounds throughout her account. She quotes Paternak on the state of things: "It was just my fate . . . and I realized my mistake during my first year together with Zinaida Nikolayevna. The fact is that it was not her I really liked, but Garrik [Neigaus] because I was so captivated by the way he played the piano. At first he wanted to kill me, the strange fellow, after she left him. But later on he was very grateful to me!" He explains that "in this hell" he had been living for ten years— and so on and so on.

Pasternak did not leave Zinaida and in a deep hidden way that fact is the occasion for this book. Ivinskaya's love-haunted spirit wanders in the shades without rest, needing always proof of love from him and proof offered to the world. This is a curiosity since she is a good deal better known to the world than the wife and even appears in the 1975 *Columbia Encyclopedia* as an "intimate friend and collaborator," in the entry on Pasternak. She was an openly acknowledged, beloved mistress.

Still the memory of his hesitations troubled. From the beginning she reports her mother's nagging: "They were always harping on the need for BL [Pasternak] to make a clean break and leave his family, if he really loved me." Her mother rang up, made scenes, which Pasternak tried to "fend off," assuring everyone that he loved Olga more than life, but that one couldn't change things so quickly. Even when Olga is in the prison camp her mother renews the theme in a letter to her: "He lives in a fantastic world which he says consists entirely of you—yet he imagines this need not mean any upheaval in his family life, or in anything else. Then what does he think it means?" (There may be something Russian in all this. A marvelous scene in Madame Mandelstam's book: Mandelstam for a time also had his Olga. At one point her mother came to the house and in the wife's presence urged Mandelstam to take the daughter off to the Crimea. When Nadia objected, the mother told her to shut up, that "she was here to talk business with her old friend Mandelstam.")

Of the fourteen years with Pasternak, Olga spent four in a prison camp, entering in 1949 and coming out in 1953. The caprice of Stalin's imprisonments and murders leaves each one under a question mark of motivation. To look for provocation, however insignificant, is to imagine a lingering legality, or appearance of legality, even in the heart of the most anarchic criminal whim. The immediate prelude to her arrest had to do with dealings about her desperate need for an apartment where she could meet with Pasternak. The woman involved in this turned out to be engaged in dishonest bribes and was arrested. Ivinskaya's arrest followed immediately. However, in so far as one can tell, the true reason for the arrest was her relation to Pasternak. In a letter written some years later he says: "She was put in jail on my account, as the person considered by the secret police closest to me, and they hoped that by means of grueling interrogation and threat they could extract enough evidence from her to put me on trial. I owe my life and the fact that they did not touch me in these years to her heroism and endurance."

The strangeness of Olga's arrest to inform on Pasternak is equaled by the caprice of Pasternak's escape from arrest during the most brutal years of Stalinism. Everyone who writes about him ponders his lucky fate, just as the ill fate of so many was the subject of tragic speculation. "Do not touch this cloud dweller," Stalin is rumored to have said when Pasternak's name came up for arrest. But that is only a rumor, a suggestion of some benign fascination with Pasternak on the part of Stalin— a peculiar quirk that may have been true in fact.

Ilya Ehrenburg wrote, "I can see no logic in it," and wondered why "Stalin did not touch Pasternak, who maintained his independence, while he destroyed Koltsov, who dutifully did everything he was asked to do." In his introduction to Alexander Gladkov's *Meetings with Pasternak*, Max Hayward recounts various complicated hypotheses for the relative immunity of the free-spirited Pasternak. Perhaps Stalin did not want the squalor of the Mandelstam case repeated; or it has been noted that Pasternak's refusal to sign the abominable hyperbole of the letter sent to Stalin on the death of his wife, whom some think he murdered and others believe committed suicide, while sending instead a courteous, reserved note of his own, may have moved Stalin by its "sincerity." The most appalling theory of all is Gladkov's bitter view that they had decided to "make do with Meyerhold and Babel," both of whom lost their lives.

Pasternak was indeed persecuted in the literary and spiritual sense, and in spending most of the 1930s doing translations experienced an "inner migration"—the refuge of gifted writers. He was expelled from the Writers Union, harassed and denounced over the Nobel Prize, and yet he kept his treasured house in Peredelkino and his work, with the exception of *Doctor Zhivago* and some of the religious poems, is not only published but "canonized."

During Olga's prison years Pasternak supported her family, who otherwise would have starved. In 1950, he had his first heart attack, soon after her arrest; in 1952, he had a second attack, a year before she was released in 1953. At this time he wrote to Olga's mother, saying that his wife had saved him. "I owe my life to her. All this, and everything else as well—everything I have seen and gone through—is so good and simple. How great are life and death and how insignificant the man who does not know it."

Just before Olga's release he seemed to fall into a kind of panic, perhaps a dream of retreat. A message was sent to her daughter, saying that perhaps "change might come about in our relationship," meaning that it would not fall back into the previous fixed and settled intimacy. As always, Olga, writing in retrospect, skates around this rock as if it were a pebble. And indeed she must, having set for herself two mind-numbing conditions: first, an idealized human being, Pasternak, and second, an idealized love, without pause, for herself. His hestitation on the doorstep of reunion is described as "candor, guileless charm and undeniable heartlessness." Olga's words, in moments of dis-

tress, always war with each other, although it is a rhetorical
slaughter beween dummies on horseback. And always the nouns
and adjectives of a sunny armistice prevail. They reunite: "In
short, our life, after being torn apart by sudden separation, all
at once bestowed an unexpected gift on him—so once more
nothing mattered except the 'living sorcery of hot embraces,'
the triumph of two people alone in the bacchanalia of the
world." Bacchanalia?

There is nothing she will not write. "While I was with him
it was not given to him to grow old." She presses us to read
between the lines to find any of the reality of this now ill man,
with the desperate personal and financial conditions of his life,
with his devotion above all to finding peace in which to work,
with his past, his age, his love for her which like any love, especially an additional one, brings along the moonbeams of guilt
and confusion with its happiness. Other tarred statements of his
on the subject of his wife offered in direct quotations: "Let
us not look ahead, or complicate matters, or hurt other people's
feelings. . . . Would you want to be in the place of that unfortunate woman?" Indeed, yes, she would.

He reassures: "For years now we have been deaf to each other
. . . and of course she is only to be pitied—she has been deaf all
her life—the dove tapped at her window in vain . . . And now
she is angry because something real has come to me—but so late
in life!" Olga's own thoughts sum up: "Happy as I felt at being
his chosen one, I had to listen to narrow-minded reproaches and
expressions of sympathy, and this upset me. . . . I suppose I
longed for recognition and wanted people to envy me."

Ivinskaya speaks of her book as one he wanted her to write. Pasternak, with the miraculous purity and lyricism of his own style in
poems and in prose, with his brilliant portrait in *Safe Conduct* of
Mayakovsky and the "black velvet" of his talent, and the magical
sweep of *Doctor Zhivago* ("her book"), did not catch her ear. As

a reminder of his own way with a sliver of imagined speech, his thoughts on the suicide of the gifted, corrupt Fadeyev, head of the Writers Union:

> And it seems to me that Fadeyev, with that guilty smile which he managed to preserve through all the cunning intricacies of politics, could bid farewell to himself at the last moment before pulling the trigger with, I should imagine, words like these: "Well, it's all over! Goodbye, Sasha!"
> [I Remember]

Olga's jealousy of Mrs. Pasternak is not mitigated by her own reports of Pasternak's discreditable animadversions on Zinaida, who died in 1966 and thus was not an impediment to discourteous description. A meeting between the two women is left for "history" by Olga and here she admits that she was ill and perhaps hasn't got it quite straight. "I no longer remember exactly what passed between me and this heavily built, strong-minded woman, who kept repeating how she didn't give a damn for our love and that, although she no longer loved BL [Pasternak] herself, she would not allow her family to be broken up." There is no reason this scene should be credited literally, especially since the notion that a rival does not love, but is instead moved only by the slyest attention to self-interest, is a provincial vulgarity.

Zinaida Pasternak does not get a good "press" from any account readily at hand, unless it may be considered that Pasternak's legal, "semi"-fidelity is a sort of remote credit. In *Hope Abandoned*, Madame Mandelstam tells of a visit to Peredelkino: "He told us he thought his wife was baking a cake down in the kitchen. He went to tell of our arrival, but came back looking glum; she clearly wanted to have nothing to do with us." A few years later, during a time of their great suffering, Zinaida said on the telephone to the Mandelstams: "Please don't come out here to Peredelkino." Worst of all, the scandal of the wife of Pasternak saying, "My children love Stalin most of all, and me only second."

A scene for which research turned up two versions: Toward the end of his life, Pasternak went with his wife for a visit to the Caucasus: as Olga puts it, Zinaida "took him off to Tiflis with her." Olga was wounded and angry and Pasternak begs her not to talk like a bad novel. She went off to Leningrad and refused to answer his sad, lonely letters—but of course soon she is remorseful. "To this very day the misery of this last quarrel in our life still gnaws at me."

An account of the visit is given in the introduction Lydia Pasternak wrote for her translation of an English selection of her brother's poems. "This short visit to the Caucasus had a wonderful effect on my brother. The wild majestic scenery, the universal love and admiration for him of the Georgians, the freedom and the recollections of the happy days they had both spent in the same surroundings in the Thirties, before their marriage—all of this gave Pasternak new strength and a feeling of peace and fulfillment. He returned to Peredelkino happy and rejuvenated. . . ." Who can say? Sisters often incline toward the status quo.

Lara in *Doctor Zhivago*—when a friend from abroad meets Olga: "She said we were exactly as she had imagined us—BL and me." Pasternak wrote in a letter to a Swedish correspondent: "Lara, the heroine of the novel, is someone in real life. She is a woman very close to me." Zinaida is also, he says, somewhere in the conception of Tonia, Zhivago's wife. In a letter Pasternak wrote of "my wife's passionate love of work, her eager skill in everything—in washing, cooking, cleaning, bringing up the children—has created domestic comfort, a garden, a way of life and daily routine, the calm and quiet needed for work."

In *A Captive of Time*, the dilemmas of Pasternak's career are examined with the fullest compassion: his survival, his lean-ings toward Christianity, the famous telephone conversation with Stalin when Mandelstam was arrested, his response to the desperation of Tsvetaeva just before her suicide, the cringing letter to Khrushchev renouncing the Nobel Prize, a letter Ivinskaya says she wrote herself and urged upon Pasternak. There is much of interest in all of this even if it comes, also, under the disaster of Ivinskaya's style and the hallucinated folly of the transformation of life and history into questions of their love.

What is the intention of her book and to whom is it addressed? All we know is that it has been sent out to the West, to us, and in some odd fashion sent back to herself, her memories. "My love! I now come to the end of the book you wanted me to write. . . . The greater part of my conscious life has been devoted to you—and what is left of it will also be devoted to you." What is the meaning of *conscious*?

After Pasternak's death, Ivinskaya and her daughter were arrested on the claim, or pretext, of dealing with rubles smuggled into the country by way of the Feltrinelli firm, Italian publishers of *Doctor Zhivago*. She served another four years. The misery of this life seemed to have no ending. It must be said of Ivinskaya that she can take a cold, icy bullet into her flesh, pull it out with a wince, sugar it and offer it to the world, to herself mostly, as a marshmallow. Out of prison once more, she speaks of the "total lack of sympathy for me in influential Soviet circles." Here she is not speaking only of party hacks, but of the hostility of such persons as the courageous novelist, Lidia Chukovskaya, who even at this moment is being persecuted in the Soviet Union as a defender of human rights. Another puzzle.

Ivinskaya is now old, poor, and bereft. Pasternak's death certainly left her quite undefended, without, as she says somewhere, "the protection of his name." She has occupied herself with this book, a success in the West. There is much awry in her character and understanding, and thus Pasternak, one of the great writers of the century and a man who seemed to have no enemies, is much reduced. But that is the turn of the wheel of history for *him*. Her own apotheosis, so beautifully accomplished in Pasternak's poems to her and in the novel, in the many hundreds of letters in her keeping, might better have been left to stand alone.

At the end of *Hope Abandoned*, Madame Mandelstam prints a letter she wrote to Mandelstam just before she learned of his death. It was never sent, was put away, retrieved thirty years later. She speaks of her love in a way that her quirky, thorny nature might not have allowed years before. It is one of the most beautiful letters we have:

> You came to me every night in my sleep, and I kept asking what had happened, but you did not reply. In my last dream I was buying food for you in a filthy hotel restaurant. . . . When I had bought it, I realized I did not know where to take it, because I do not know where you are. When I woke up, I said to Shura, "Osia is dead."

The letter ends: "It's me, Nadia. Where are you? Farewell."

Postscript: Husbands

From *Close to Colette*, by Maurice Goudeket:

> There is great temptation to consider that the intimate hours of a person or a couple, whatever their public position may be, belong to themselves alone. But when a wave of fervor such as has rarely been seen irradiated the last years of Colette . . . would it be fair not to offer in exchange the most precious thing one has kept?

Mmmmm. So, a modest memoir, not very interesting. Houses, gardens, animals, food, journeys in motor cars, holidays on handsome yachts, writing, the German occupation, death. "Suddenly there was silence and Colette's head bent slowly to one side, with a movement of infinite grace."

Katherine Mansfield, Letters and Journals, edited by C. K. Stead. From the introduction by Stead:

Murry's promotion of his wife's literary remains brought him royalties and opprobrium and increased her fame. The good and the bad seem inextricably mixed in his work on her behalf. He transcribed, edited, and wrote commentaries tirelessly but in a way which encouraged a sentimental, and sometimes a falsely mystical interest in her talent. He could not keep himself out of the picture either, seeing the development of her art always in relation to the development of her feeling for him.

Nabokov: Master Class

When Vladimir Nabokov died in Switzerland in 1977, a life chronically challenged by history ended in the felicity of a large, intrepid, creative achievement. Nabokov left Russia with his family in 1919, took a degree at Cambridge University and in 1922 settled among the Russian colony in Berlin, where he began his work as a poet and novelist in the Russian language. In 1937, after fifteen or so un-Teutonic years "among strangers, spectral Germans," he pushed on to France for three years, to those "more or less illusory cities" that form the émigré's past. In 1940, with his wife and son, he arrived in the United States, "a new and beloved world," as he calls it in his autobiography *Speak, Memory* where, among other adaptations, he patriotically stopped "barring my sevens."

To America, Nabokov brought his supreme literary gifts and wide learning and a great accumulation of losses: childhood landscape devastated, gravestones blurred, armies in the wrong countries, and his father murdered, hit by a bullet intended for another on the stage of one of those intense political debates among the Russian exiles in Berlin.

From 1940 to 1960, here he is among us, cheerful it seems, and unpredictable in opinion. Not a bohemian, not at all, and not a White Russian dinner partner, but always dramatic and incorruptible. On the present occasion he is standing before his classes at Cornell University in Ithaca, New York, delivering the now published first volume of *Lectures on Literature*. He is forty-nine years old, an outstanding modern novelist in the Russian language, and still in need of money. During the next ten years, the Ithacan afternoons and evenings will be spent writing in English: *Pnin*, the memoir *Speak, Memory*, and his uncompromised masterpiece, *Lolita*, a financial success that released him from one of the cares of the literary life. When he goes back to Europe, to settle with his wife in an old, interesting hotel in Montreux, Switzerland, he will be one of the great twentieth-century novelists in English.

Not much happened during the American years that escaped transformation to the mosaic of the Nabokov page, with its undaunted English words glittering in their classical, rather imperial plentitude, a plentitude that is never a superfluity. Although Nabokov himself was unassimilable, his imagination is astonishingly porous. It is rather in the mood of Marco Polo in China that he meets the (to us) exhausted artifacts of the American scene. Motels, advertisements, chewing-gum smiles, academics with their projects like pillows stuffed under an actor's tunic, turns of speech advancing like a train on his amplifying ear— for Nabokov it is all a dawn, alpine freshness. His is a romantic, prodigal imagination, with inexhaustible ores of memory buried in the ground of an unprovincial history. "And one day we shall recall all this—the lindens, and the shadows on the wall, and a poodle's unclipped claws tapping over the flagstones of the night. And the star, the star."

As a teacher, Nabokov had, before Cornell, spent a good deal of time at Wellesley College, and not much time at Harvard. His misadventures with the Comparative Literature Department at Harvard, told in Andrew Field's biography, *Nabokov: His Life in Part,* have the comic "Russianness" of some old head-scratching tale of serf and master. Nabokov lectured at Harvard in 1952. There the exile's brightly confident dimming of a long list of classic authors and works shed its blackening attention upon Cervantes. Professor Harry Levin, on behalf of the old Spaniard, said: Harvard thinks otherwise. The remark, put into Professor Levin's pocket like a handkerchief, has the scent of Nabokov's own wicked perfume on it . . . but no matter. And all to the good indeed. Cambridge, Massachusetts, was not the proper setting for the touching derangements of Nabokov's created Professor Pnin and Dr. Kinbote—and not the right New England village in which Humbert Humbert would marry Lolita's mother. So, it was to be Cornell.

The published lectures are, apart from everything else, dutiful, even professorial. They are concrete, efficient, not the wanderings of an imported star who takes off early by way of discussion periods. We are told by Andrew Field that Nabokov's scientific work on butterflies was "painstaking" and marked by a "scale by scale meticulousness." There is something of this also in the approach to the performance before as many as 400 students and the acceptance of certain ever-returning weekends with 150 examination papers to read.

The young audience is there to hear him, even if he does not know what they may have brought with them. Nabokov stands aside in the beginning, perturbed, it may be imagined, not only by the rarity of literature but by the rarity of reading, true reading. He solicits rather poignantly from the students the ineffable "tingling spine" and "shiver" of the esthetic response, all that cannot be written down in notebooks and which is as hopeless of definition as the act of composition itself.

The first of Nabokov's Cornell lectures, as printed here, was given to Jane Austen's *Mansfield Park.* This author and this particular novel had been urged upon Nabokov by Edmund

Wilson. Wilson was dismayed by Nabokov's cast-offs, those universally admired works that seemed to be resting in overflowing boxes in the Nabokov vestibule, as if waiting to be picked up by the Salvation Army. A lot of it appears to be mischievous teasing by Nabokov, good-humored, even *winking*, if such a word may be used. ("Henry James is a pale porpoise.") Satire is one of Nabokov's gifts, and nearly all of his novels are appliquéd with little rosette-asides of impertinent literary opinion.

In any case, *Mansfield Park* finds Nabokov laying out the plot with a draftsman's care, patiently showing that one parson must die so that another can, so to speak, wear the dead man's shoes. And Sir Bertram must be sent off to the West Indies so that his household can relax into the "mild orgy" of the theatrical presentation of a sentimental play called "Lovers' Vows."

Here there is a curious intermission in which Nabokov tells the class about the old play, summarizing it from the original text. And again when Fanny cries out against a plan to cut down an avenue of trees, "What a pity! Does it not make you think of Cowper? 'Ye fallen avenues, once more I mourn your fate unmerited,'" Nabokov takes time out for a reading of the long, dull poem, "The Sofa" by William Cowper. It is true that Nabokov liked to remember the charm of vanished popular works of the sort that slowly made their way over land and sea to the Russian household of his youth. Still, the diversion to these texts is strikingly unlike the microscopic adhesion to the matters at hand in other lectures. There are brushings of condescension in the Jane Austen chapter, delicate little streakings, like a marbleizing effect. She is "dimpled" and "pert," a master of this dimpled pertness.

"Style is not a tool, it is not a method, it is not a choice of words alone. Being much more than all this, style constitutes an intrinsic component or characteristic of the author's personality." Nabokov's method in these carefully prepared lectures is somewhat less impressionistic and darting that one might have expected from his irreplaceable book on Gogol and the fantastical commentaries to *Eugene Onegin*. Words and phrases, even the words of Joyce, Proust, or Dickens, are not themselves often the direct object of inquiry. Plots, with their subterranean themes, are the objects, plots to be dug up tenderly so as not to injure the intention of the author by too gleeful an excavation.

Nabokov goes along the plot, step by step, telling us where we are now and what is happening there; and the steps are not mere excavations but attended by readings aloud from the texts. About Joyce's *Ulysses*: "Demented Farrell now walks westward on Clare Street, where the blind youth is walking eastward on the same street, still unaware that he has left his tuning fork in the Ormond Hotel. Opposite number 8, the office of the dentist. . . ."

Flaubert's punctuation and syntax most interestingly command Nabokov's attention. "I want to draw attention first of all to Flaubert's use of the word *and* preceded by a semicolon." And the use of the imperfect form of the past tense in *Madame Bovary*. Translators are rebuked for not seeing, in Emma's musings about the dreariness of her life, the difference between "She would find [correct translation] again in the same places the foxgloves and wallflowers," as against the simple "she found." These moments are the grandeur of Nabokov in the act of reading a novel. And when he speaks in the voice we know from his own novels, "Notice the elaboration of the moonlight in Proust, the shadows that come out of the light like the drawers of a chest. . . ."

Madame Bovary, Mansfield Park, Swann's Way, Bleak House, Ulysses, The Metamorphosis—two in French, one from the German, two from English—and to these a third from English, *Dr. Jekyll and Mr. Hyde*, a Nabokov surprise, so as not to confound expectations. The mad pseudo-science of "Dr. Jekyll" appeals to Nabokov, who in his discussion of *Bleak House* lingered lovingly on the "spontaneous combustion" of the gin-soaked Mr. Krook. He likes the "winey taste" of Stevenson's novel, and "the appetizing tang of the chill morning in London." "Appetizing" is the word most often used about the fable. The plan of Dr. Jekyll's house is the back and front of the man himself. Not too little and not too much is made of the work, "a minor masterpiece on its own conventional terms" and far from "The Metamorphosis," with its "five or six" tragic dimensions.

Kafka is "the greatest German writer of our times." Yes, yes —pause—"such poets as Rilke or such novelists as Thomas Mann are dwarfs and plaster saints in comparison to him." So, proceed. "The Metamorphosis," an exceedingly painful tale about Gregor Samsa waking up one morning to find that he has turned into an insect, arouses in Nabokov the most passionate and emotional moments in the lecture series. As an entomologist, he pronounces Gregor a large beetle, the lowly cockroach being just that, too lowly, for the largeness of Kafka's descriptive inventions. The doors, the poor beetle's legs or teeth or whatever finally turning the lock, the family theme, the "Greek chorus" of the visit of the clerk from Gregor's office, the "coleopteran's" food slipped under the door, the appalling suffering: all of this is tragically affecting once more as the lecturer puts it before us.

Nabokov judges Gregor's world with great feeling, even with indignation. The Samsa relatives are "parasites" exploiting Gregor, eating him "out from the inside." His beetle carapace is the "pathetic urge to find some protection from betrayal, cruelty." But it is no protection and he remains as a beetle as vulnerable as his "sick human flesh and spirit had been." Gregor's sister, in the beginning the only one to acknowledge the metamorphosis and to act with kindness, becomes his worst enemy at last. Gregor is extinguished so that the family can go out in the sunlight once again. "The parasites have fattened themselves on Gregor," Nabokov wrote in the margins of his copy.

If it were not the trade name of a commercial series, Nabokov's lectures might be called "Monarch Notes," in honor of their stately, unfatigued progress through the crowd of words, styles, and plots. What is most unexpected is the patience. *Bleak House*: "Now let us go back to the very first paragraph in the book." *Madame Bovary*: "Let us go back to the time when Charles was still married to Héloïse Dubuc." *Ulysses*: "Bloom's breakfast that she is to make for him that morning continues to fill her thoughts. . . ."

Following these lectures with their determined clinging to detail, and with the insistent foot on each rung of the scaffolding of the plot, is to be asked to experience the novel itself in a kind of thoughtfully assisted rereading, without interpretation. There is very little ripe, plump appreciative language. "Beautiful" turns are acknowledged by "note" and "mark." In *Madame Bovary* "note the long fine sunrays through the chinks in the closed shutters" and "mark the insidious daylight that made velvet of the soot at the back of the fireplace and touched with livid blue the cold cinders." A novel is a rare object. Look at it with a magnifying glass and the earphones turned off. And curiously each work is alone, not milling about among its siblings, *Emma*, *Our Mutual Friend*, *Portrait of an Artist*, and so on and so on.

Novels are fairy tales; *Madame Bovary* yet another fairy tale. Of course, with Nabokov a thing is asserted to counter a repellent, philistine opposition. A novel becomes a fairy tale so that it will not be thought to be a sociological study or a bit of the author's psycho-history, two ideas he may rightly have believed to be running like a low fever among the student body.

Nabokov's own novels very often end, and no matter what the plot, in a rhapsodic call to literature itself. "I am thinking of aurochs and angels, the secret of durable pigments, prophetic sonnets, the refuge of art. And this is the only immortality you and I may share, my Lolita." Also in his novels there are books within books and literature is almost a character. About *The Gift*, Nabokov said, "Its hero is not Zina, but Russian literature." The brilliant *Pale Fire* is entirely a deranged annotation of a dreadful poem.

Perhaps in the end it is not surprising that this writer who has walked every step of the way in two languages should look upon style as the self in all its being and the novel as a slow, patient construction of a gleaming fairy tale. "Let us look at the web and not the spider," he writes about Dickens. The web, the inimitable web, is what these lectures are about.

part five

Readings

Bartleby in Manhattan

While preparing some lectures on the subject of New York City, that is, the present landscape in which an astonishing number of people still live, sustaining as they do the numerical sensationalism that qualifies New York as *one* of the great cities of the world, if not the *greatest*, the orotund *greatest* being reserved with an almost Biblical authority for our country as a whole; and also on "old New York," with its intimidating claim to vanished manners and social dominion, its hereditary furnishings of aggressive simplicity and shy opulence which would prove an unsteady bulwark against the flooding of the *nouveau riche*—during this reading I thought to look again at Melville's story, "Bartleby, the Scrivener," because it carried the subtitle: "A Story of Wall Street."

There did not appear to be much of Wall Street in this troubling composition of 1853 about a peculiar "copyist" who is hired by a "snug" little legal firm in the Wall Street district. No, nothing of the daunting, hungry "Manhattanism" of Whitman: "O an intense life, full to repletion and varied! / The life of the theatre, bar-room, huge hotel, for me!" Nothing of railroad schemes, cornering the gold market, or of that tense exclusion to be brought about by mistakes and follies in the private life which were to be the drama of "old New York" in Edith Wharton's novels. Bartleby seemed to me to be not its subtitle, but most of all an example of the superior uses of dialogue in fiction, here a strange, bone-thin dialogue that nevertheless serves to reveal a profoundly moving tragedy.

(Melville's brothers were lawyers, with offices at 10 Wall Street; a close friend was employed in a law office and seems to have been worn down by "incessant writing." About the story itself, some critics have thought of "Bartleby" as a masterly presentation of schizophrenic deterioration; others have seen the story as coming out of the rejection of Melville by the reading public and his own inability to be a popular "copyist." Some have found in the story the life of Wall Street, "walling in" the creative American spirit. All of these ideas are convincing and important. "Bartleby" may be one or all of these. My own reading is largely concerned with the nature of Bartleby's short sentences.)

Out of some sixteen thousand words, Bartleby, the cadaverous and yet blazing center of all our attention, speaks only thirty-seven short lines, more than a third of which are a repetition of a single line, the celebrated, the "famous," I think one might call it, retort: *I would prefer not to.* No, "retort" will not do, representing as it does too great a degree of active mutuality for Bartleby—*reply* perhaps.

Bartleby's reduction of language is of an expressiveness literally limitless. Few characters in fiction, if indeed any exist, have been able to say all they wish in so striking, so nearly speechless a manner. The work is, of course, a sort of fable of inanition, and returning to it, as I did, mindful of the old stone historical downtown and the new, insatiable necropolis of steel and glass, lying on the vegetation of the participial *declining* this and that, I found it possible to wish that "Bartleby, the Scrivener" were just itself, a masterpiece without the challenge of its setting, Wall

Street. Still, the setting does not flee the mind, even if it does not quite bind itself either, the way unloaded furniture seems immediately bound to its doors and floors.

Melville has written his story in a cheerful, confident, rather optimistic, Dickensian manner. Or at least that is the manner in which it begins. In the law office, for instance, the copyists and errand-boy are introduced with their Dickensian *tics* and their tic-names: Nippers, Turkey, and Ginger Nut. An atmosphere of comedy, of small, amusing, busy particulars, surrounds Bartleby and his large, unofficial (not suited to an office) articulations, which are nevertheless clerkly and even, perhaps, clerical.

The narrator, a mild man of the law with a mild Wall Street business, is a "rather elderly man," as he says of himself at the time of putting down his remembrances of Bartleby. On the edge of retirement, the lawyer begins to think about that "singular set of men," the law-copyists or scriveners he has known in his thirty years of practice. He notes that he has seen nothing of these men in print and, were it not for the dominating memory of Bartleby, he might have told lighthearted professional anecdotes, something perhaps like the anecdotes of servants come and gone, such as we find in the letters of Jane Carlyle, girls from the country who are not always unlike the Turkeys, Nippers, and Ginger Nuts.

The lawyer understands that no biography of Bartleby is possible because "no materials exist," and indeed the work is not a character sketch and not a section of a "life," even though it ends in death. Yet the device of memory is not quite the way it works out, because each of Bartleby's thirty-seven lines, with their riveting variations, so slight as to be almost painful to the mind taking note of them, must be produced at the right pace and accompanied by the requests that occasion them. At a certain point, Bartleby must "gently disappear behind the screen," which, in a way, is a present rather than a past. In the end, Melville's structure is magical because the lawyer creates Bartleby by *allowing* him to be, a decision of nicely unprofessional impracticality. The competent, but scarcely strenuous, office allows Bartleby, although truly the allowance arises out of the fact that the lawyer is a far better man than he knows himself to be. And he is taken by surprise to learn of his tireless curiosity about the incurious ghost, Bartleby.

The lawyer has a "snug business among rich men's bonds and mortgages and title deeds," rather than the more dramatic actions before juries (a choice that would not be defining today). He has his public sinecures and when they are officially abolished he feels a bit of chagrin, but no vehemence. He recognizes the little vanities he has accumulated along the way, one of which is that he has done business with John Jacob Astor. And he likes to utter the name "for it hath a rounded and orbicular sound to it and rings like unto bullion." These are the thoughts of a man touched by the comic spirit, the one who will be touched for the first time in his life, and by way of his dealings with Bartleby, by "overpowering, stinging melancholy . . . a fraternal melancholy."

A flurry of copying demand had led the lawyer to run an advertisement which brought to his door a young man, Bartleby, a person sedate, "pallidly neat, pitiably respectable." Bartleby is taken on and placed at a desk which "originally had afforded a lateral view of certain grimy backyards and bricks, but which owing to subsequent erections, commanded at present no view at all." This is a suitable place for Bartleby, who does not require views of the outside world and who has no "views" of the other kind, that is, no opinions beyond his adamantine assertion of his own feelings, if feelings they are; he has, as soon becomes clear, his hard pebbles of response with their sumptuous, taciturn resonance.

Bartleby begins to copy without pause, as if "long famishing for something to copy." This is observed by the lawyer who also observes that he himself feels no pleasure in it since it is done "silently, palely, mechanically." On the third day of employment, Bartleby appears, the genuine Bartleby, the one who gives utterance. His first utterance is like the soul escaping from the body, as in medieval drawings.

The tedious proofreading of the clerk's copy is for accuracy done in collaboration with another person, and it is the lawyer himself who calls out to Bartleby for assistance in the task. The laconic, implacable signature is at hand, the mysterious signature that cannot be interpreted and cannot be misunderstood. Bartley replies, *I would prefer not to.*

The pretense of disbelief provides the occasion for *I would prefer not to* soon to be repeated three times and "with no uneasiness, anger, impatience or impertinence." By the singularity of refusal, the absence of "because" or of the opening up of some possibly alternating circumstance, this negative domination seizes the story like a sudden ambush in the streets.

Bartleby's "I" is of such a completeness that it does not require support. He possesses his "I" as if it were a visible part of the body, the way ordinary men possess a thumb. In his sentence he encloses his past, present, and future, himself, all there is. His statement is positive indeed and the *not* is less important than the "I," because the "not" refers to the presence of others, to the world, inevitably making suggestions the "I" does not encompass.

Bartleby would prefer not to read proof with his employer, a little later he would prefer not to examine his own quadruplicate copyings with the help of the other clerks, he would prefer not to answer or to consider that this communal proofreading is labor-saving and customary. About his "mulish vagary"—no answer.

As we read the story we are certain that, insofar as Bartleby himself is concerned, there is nothing to be thought of as "interesting" in his statement. There is no coquetry; it is merely candid, final, inflexible. Above all it is not "personal"; that is, his objection is not to the collaborators themselves and not to the activity of proofreading, indeed no more repetitive than daylong copying. The reply is not personal and it is not invested with "personality." And this the kind and now violently curious and enduring lawyer cannot believe. He will struggle throughout the tale to fill up the hole, to wonder greatly, to prod as he can, in search of "personality." And the hole, the chasm, or better the "cistern," one of the lawyer's words for the view outside Bartleby's desk, will not be filled.

What began as a comedy, a bit of genre actually, ends as tragedy. But like Bartleby himself it is difficult for the reader to supply adjectives. Is Bartleby mysterious; is his nature dark, angular, subterranean? You are deterred by Bartleby's mastery from competing with him by your command of the adjective. He is overwhelmingly affecting to the emotions of the lawyer and the reader, but there is no hint that he is occupied with lack, disuse, failure, inadequacy. If one tries to imagine Bartleby alone, without the office, what is to be imagined? True, he is always alone, in an utter loneliness that pierces the lawyer's heart when he soon finds that Bartleby has no home at all but is living in the office at night.

(No home, living in the office day and night. Here, having exempted this story from my study of Manhattanism because of its inspired occupation with an ultimate condition and its stepping aside from the garbage and shards of Manhattan history, I was stopped by this turn in the exposition. Yes, the undomesticity of a great city like New York, undomestic in the ways other cities are not—then, and still now. Bartleby, the extreme, the icon of the extreme, is not exactly living in the office. Instead he just does not leave it at the end of the day. But it is very easy to imagine from history where the clerks, Nippers and Turkey, are of an evening. They are living in lodging houses, where half of New York's population lived as late as 1841: newlyweds, families, single persons. Whitman did a lot of "boarding round," as he called it, and observed, without rebuke, or mostly without rebuke, that the boarding house led the unfamilied men to rush out after dinner to the saloon or brothel, away from the unprivate private, to the streets which are the spirit of the city, which are the lively blackmail that makes city citizens abide.

Lodgings then, and later the "divided space" of the apartment house, both expressing Manhattanism as a life lived in transition. And lived in a space that is not biography, but is to be fluent and changeable, an escape from the hometown and the homestead, an escape from the given. The rotting tenements of today are only metaphysical apartments and in deterioration take on the burdensome aspect of "homes" because they remind, in the absence of purchased maintenance, that something "homelike" may be asked of oneself and at the same time denied by the devastations coming from above, below, and next door. Manhattan, the release from the home, which is the leaking roof, the flooded basement, the garbage, and most of all the grounds, that is, surrounding nature. "After I learned about electricity I lost interest in nature. Not up-to-date enough." Mayakovsky, the poet of urbanism.)

So Bartleby is found to be living in the office day and night. But Bartleby is not a true creature of Manhattan because he shuns the streets and is unmoved by the moral, religious, acute, obsessive, beautiful ideal of Consumption. Consumption is what one leaves one's "divided space" to honor, as the Muslim stops in his standing and moving to say his prayers five times a day, or is it six? But Bartleby eats only ginger-nuts and is starving himself to death. In that way he passes across one's mind like a feather, calling forth the vague Hinduism of Thoreau and the outer-world meditations of Emerson. (Thoreau, who disliked the city, any city, thought deeply about it, so deeply that in

Walden he composed the city's most startling consummations, one of which is: "Of a life of luxury, the fruit is luxury.")

To return, what is Bartleby "thinking" about when he is alone? It is part of the perfect completeness of his presentation of himself, although he does not present himself, that one would be foolhardy to give him thoughts. They would dishonor him. So, Bartleby is not "thinking" or experiencing or longing or remembering. All one can say is that he is a master of language, of perfect expressiveness. He is style. This is shown when the lawyer tries to revise him.

On an occasion, the lawyer asks Bartleby to go on an errand to the post office. Bartleby replies that he would prefer not to. The lawyer, seeing a possibility for an entropic, involuntary movement in this mastery of meaning, proposes an italicized emendation. He is answered with an italicized insistence.

"You *will* not?"

"I *prefer* not."

What is the difference between *will not* and *prefer* not? There is no difference insofar as Bartleby's actions will be altered, but he seems to be pointing out by the italics that his preference is not under the rule of the conditional or the future tense. He does not mean to say that he prefers not, but will if he must, or if it is wished. His "I" that prefers not, will not. I do not think he has chosen the verb "prefer" in some emblematic way. That is his language and his language is what he is.

Prefer has its power, however. The nipping clerks who have been muttering that they would like to "black his eyes" or "kick him out of the office" begin, without sarcasm or mimicry, involuntarily, as it were, to say to the lawyer, "If you would prefer, Sir," and so on.

Bartleby's language reveals the all of him, but what is revealed? Character? Bartleby is not a character in the manner of the usual, imaginative, fictional construction. And he is not a character as we know them in life, with their bundling bustle of details, their suits and ties and felt hats, their love affairs surreptitious or binding, family albums, psychological justifications dragging like a little wagon along the highway of experience. We might say he is a destiny, without interruptions, revisions, second chances. But what is a destiny that is not endured by a "character"? Bartleby has no plot in his present existence, and we would not wish to imagine subplots for his already lived years. He is indeed only words, wonderful words, and very few of them. One might for a moment sink into the abyss and imagine that instead of *prefer not* he had said, "I don't want to" or "I don't feel like it." No, it is unthinkable, a vulgarization, adding truculence, idleness, foolishness, adding indeed "character" and altering a sublimity of definition.

Bartleby, the scrivener, "standing at the dead-wall window" announces that he will do no more copying. *No more.* The lawyer, marooned in the law of cause and effect, notices the appearance of eyestrain and that there is a possibility Bartleby is going blind. This is never clearly established—Melville's genius would not want at any part of the story to enter the region of sure reasons and causality.

In the midst of these peculiar colloquies, the lawyer asks Bartleby if he cannot indeed be a little reasonable here and there.

" 'At present I would prefer not to be a little reasonable,' was his mildly cadaverous reply."

There is no imagining what the sudden intrusion of "at present" may signify and it seems to be just an appendage to the "I," without calling up the nonpresent, the future. From the moment of first refusal it had passed through the lawyer's mind that he might calmly and without resentment dismiss Bartleby, but he cannot, not even after "no more copying." He thinks: "I should have as soon thought of turning my pale, plaster-of-paris bust of Cicero out of doors." Ah. The "wondrous ascendancy" perhaps begins at that point, with the notion that Bartleby is a representation of life, a visage, but not the life itself.

The lawyer, overcome by pity, by troubling thoughts of human diversity, by self-analysis, goes so far as to take down from the shelf certain theological works which give him the idea that he is predestined to "have Bartleby." Since he is a merely social visitor to Trinity Church, this idea does not last and indeed is too abstract because the lawyer has slowly been moving into a therapeutic role, a role in which he persists in the notion of "personality" that may be modified by patience, by suggestion, by reason.

Still, at last, it is clear that Bartleby must go, must be offered a generous bonus, every sort of accommodation and good wish. This done, the lawyer leaves in a pleasant agitation of mind, thinking of the laws of chance represented by his overhearing some betting going on in the street. Will Bartleby be there in the morning or will he at last be gone? Of course, he has remained and the offered money has not been picked up.

"Will you not quit me?"

"I would prefer *not* to quit you."

The "quitting" is to be accomplished by the lawyer's decision to "quit" himself, that is, to quit his offices for larger quarters. A new tenant is found, the boxes are packed and sent off, and Bartleby is bid good-bye. But no, the new tenants, who are not therapists, rush around to complain that he is still there and that he is not a part of their lease. They turn him out of the offices.

The lawyer goes back to the building and finds Bartleby still present, that is, sitting on the banister of the stairway in the entrance hallway.

"What are you doing here, Bartleby?"

"Sitting upon the banister."

The lawyer had meant to ask what will you do with your life, where will you go, and not, where is your body at this moment. But with Bartleby body and statement are one. Indeed the bewitching qualities, the concentrated seriousness, the genius of Bartleby's "dialogue" had long ago affected the style of the lawyer, but in the opposite direction, that is, to metaphor, arrived at by feeling. His head is full of images about the clerk and he thinks of him as "the last column of some ruined temple" and "a bit of wreck in the mid-Atlantic." And from these metaphors there can be no severance.

There with Bartleby sitting on the banister for life, as it were, the lawyer soars into the kindest of deliriums. The therapeutic wish, the beating of the wings of angels above the heads of the harassed and affectionate, unhinges his sense of the possible, the suitable, the imaginable. He begins to think of new occupations for Bartleby and it is so like the frenzied and loving moments in family life: would the pudgy, homely daughter like to comb her hair, neaten up a bit, and apply for a position as a model?—and why not, others have, and so on and so on.

The angel wings tremble and the lawyer says: "Would you like a clerkship in a dry-goods store?"

Bartleby, the unimaginable promoter of goods for sale, replies with his rapid deliberation. Slow deliberation is not necessary for one who knows the interior of his mind, as if that mind were the interior of a small, square box containing a single pair of cuff links.

To the idea of clerking in a store Bartleby at last appends a reason, one indeed of great puzzlement.

"There is too much confinement about that. No, I would not like a clerkship; but I am not particular."

Agitated rebuttal of "too much confinement" for one who keeps himself "confined all the time"!

Now, in gentle, coaxing hysteria, the lawyer wonders if the

bartender's business would suit Bartleby and adds that "there is no trying of the eye-sight in that."

No, Bartleby would not like that at all, even though he repeats that he is not particular.

Would Bartleby like to go about collecting bills for merchants? It would take him outdoors and be good for his health. The answer: "No, I would prefer to be doing something else."

Doing something else? That is, sitting on the banister, rather than selling dry goods, bartending, and bill collecting.

Here the lawyer seems to experience a sudden blindness, the blindness of a bright light from an oncoming car on a dark road. The bright light is the terrible clarity of Bartleby.

So, in a blind panic: "How then would be going as a companion to Europe, to entertain some young gentleman with your conversation—how would that suit you?"

"Not at all. It does not strike me that there is anything definite about that. I like to be stationary. But I am not particular."

Definite? Conversation is not definite owing to its details of style, opinion, observation, humor, pause, and resumption; and it would not be at all pleasing to Bartleby's mathematical candor. Bartleby is *definite;* conversation is not. He has said it all.

But I am not particular? This slight addition has entered Bartleby at the moment the lawyer opens his fantastical employment agency. The phrase wishes to extend the lawyer's knowledge of his client, Bartleby, and to keep him from the tedium of error. Bartleby himself is particular, in that he is indeed a thing distinguished from another. But he is not particular in being fastidious, choosey. He would like the lawyer to understand that he is not concerned with the congenial. It is not suitability he pursues; it is essence, essence beyond detail.

The new tenants have Bartleby arrested as a vagrant and sent to the Tombs. The same idea had previously occurred to the

lawyer in a moment of despair, but he could not see that the im-
mobile, unbegging Bartleby could logically be declared a vagrant.
"What! He a vagrant, a wanderer that refuses to budge?"

No matter, the lawyer cannot surrender this "case," this
recalcitrant object of social service, this demand made upon his
heart to provide benefit, this being now in an institution, the
Tombs, but not yet locked away from the salvaging sentiments
of one who remembers. A prison visit is made and in his ineffable
therapeutic endurance the lawyer insists there is no reason to
despair, the charge is not a disgrace, and even in prison one may
sometimes see the sky and a patch of green.

Bartleby, with the final sigh of one who would instruct the
uninstructable, says: *I know where I am.*

In a last urging, on his knees as it were, the lawyer desires
to purchase extra food to add to the prison fare.

Bartleby: "I would prefer not to dine today. It would disagree
with me; I am unused to dinners." And thus he dies.

Not quite the end for the lawyer with his compassion, his
need to unearth some scrap of buried "personality," or private
history. We have the beautiful coda Melville has written, a
marvelous moment of composition, but perhaps too symbolical,
too poetically signifying to be the epitaph of Bartleby. Yet he
must be run down, if only to honor the graceful curiosity and the
insatiable charity of the lawyer. He reports a rumor:

The report was this: that Bartleby had been a subordinate clerk
in the Dead Letter Office at Washington, from which he had
been suddenly removed by a change in administration. . . . Dead
letters! Does it not sound like dead men? Conceive a man by
nature and misfortune prone to a pallid hopelessness, can any
business seem more fitted to heighten it than that of continually
handling these dead letters, and assorting them for the flames? . . .
On errands of life, these letters sped to death. . . . Ah, Bartleby!
Ah, humanity!

Bartleby in a sense is the underside of Billy Budd, but they are not opposites. Billy, the Handsome Sailor, the "Apollo with a portmanteau," the angel, "our beauty," the sunny day, and the unaccountable goodness, which is with him a sort of beautiful "innate disorder," such as the "innate, incurable disorder" represented by Bartleby. Neither of these curious creations knows resentment or grievance; they know nothing of pride, envy, or greed. There is a transcendent harmony in Billy Budd, and a terrifying, pure harmony in the tides of negation that define Bartleby. Billy, the lovely product of nature and, of course, not a perfection of ongoing citizen life, has a "vocal defect," the tendency to stutter at times of stress. By way of this defect, he goes to his death by hanging. Bartleby in no way has a vocal defect; indeed the claim this remarkable creation of American literature makes on our feelings lies entirely in his incomparable self-expression.

So, this bit of old New York, the sepia, horsecar Manhattan, Wall Street. Bartleby and the god-blessed lawyer. They were created by Melville before the Civil War and were coeval with John Jacob Astor's old age and the prime of Cornelius Vanderbilt. And yet here they are, strange apparitions in the metonymic Wall Street district where the exertions, as described by Mark Twain, were, "A year ago I didn't have a penny, and now I owe you a million dollars."

Looking down, or looking up, today at the sulky twin towers of the World Trade Center, "all shaft," the architects say, thinking of those towers as great sightless Brahmins brooding upon the absolute and the all-embracing spirit, it seemed to me that down below there is something of Manhattan in Bartleby and especially in his resistance to amelioration. His being stirs the water of pity, and we can imagine that the little boats that row about him throwing out ropes of personal charity or bureaucratic provision for his "case" may grow weary and move back to the shore in a mood of frustration and, finally, forgetfulness.

There is Manhattanism in the bafflement Bartleby represents to the alive and steady conscience of the lawyer who keeps going on and on in his old democratic, consecrated endurance— going on, even down to the Tombs, and at last to the tomb. If Bartleby is unsaveable, at least the lawyer's soul may be said to have been saved by the freeze of "fraternal melancholy" that swept over him from the fate he had placed at the desk beside him in a little corner of Wall Street. It is not thought that many "downtown" today would wish to profit from, oh, such a chill.

Sue and Arabella

Sue and Arabella, in Hardy's *Jude the Obsure*, are like a Pre-Raphaelite painting of Sacred and Profane Love. There they stand—assuming the absent man, the abashed, overwhelmed Jude. Sue is thin, pretty, with a light, abstracted, questioning gaze; Arabella is round, sly-eyed, sleepy, with the dreaming torpor of a destitute girl pondering an exchange of sexual coin. It is scarcely worth noting that they are different, almost opposites. The sources of feeling could not be more reflective than they are in Sue, or more immediate and formless than they are in Arabella. Experience, with them, is not merely the sum of events gone through; it is the response of their differing understanding of love, want, greed, or renunciation.

In the novel, Sue and Arabella are *connected* as women with Jude Fawley. But he does not initiate or control. Instead, he is identified by them and his situation is dominated by what they offer or withhold. In youth he comes under the sexual domination of Arabella, a surrender rather casual that immediately becomes a trap very steely. With Sue, a miserable life is redeemed by the joys of enlightenment and by the special importance that is given to a love or to an attachment by one who cares to think about it in a deep way.

There is every kind of suffering and failure in *Jude the Obscure*. This is its great glory as a novel—the passion, the complexity, the completeness, if you will, of petty, mean, bitter failure. Waste, oppression, injustice, indifference have soaked into the very soil of life, washing away all of the yearnings and rights of those with unlucky natures or unfortunate birth. Social and spiritual deprivation bears down on these modest persons who have asked only the lightest measure of possibility. Every single character fails and falls, in great pain, each one. The children, the lovers, the married, the ignorant, the intellectual. The only moments of happiness are the innocence of early hope and perhaps those instances of love and respect Sue Bridehead, a singular, deep creation, brings to the lives about her. Love and respect—or is it, instead, affection and sympathy, emotions a little more distant.

Sue is an original, mingled being. The outlines of her nature waver and flow. She is as we find it often in our lives one of these striking, haunting persons who endlessly talk, act, and analyze and yet never quite form a whole as a simpler and more rigid character would. Too many parts and each with its quality and interest; the design is there but it fades suddenly. Sue *thinks* and that is her mystery. It is not at all the usual mystery. The most fascinating and startling complications of her character have to do with sex and with the power of abstract ideas upon a truly superior female mind.

Sue Bridehead is frail, delicately balanced. She is a radical skeptic and it is her custom to ponder and question the arrangements and tyrannies of society. She is intense, "all nervous motion," and yet "artless" and "natural." Sue is more or less self-educated and has encountered avant-garde ideas about religion, art, and Biblical interpretation. When we first see her she is reading the chapter in Gibbon on Julian the Apostate. Somehow her involvement with critical, radical thought, the cluster of aesthetic and social attitudes, forms a frame for her disappointments and for the rebukes of society. It is the common thing of an intellectual alienation that gives an assurance to one's character and even a measure of tranquillity and resignation to balance the shatterings and shakings of psychological intensity.

In quite a different way, the pained, stumbling efforts of Jude to gain knowledge have about them a despondent, almost imprisoning aspect. His books, his noble, baffled yearnings create in us a great pity for him, but it is as if a necessary sense had been denied him along with the cruel denials of society. Jude's hopes for education are linked with the natural hopes for a profession, whereas with Sue ideas and learning have a gratuitous, spontaneous, altogether unprofessional character, that of the deepest inclination. When Jude is brutally turned down in his dream to enter Christminster (Oxford):

> . . . and, judging from your description of yourself as a working man, I venture to think that you will have a much better chance of success in life by remaining in your own sphere and sticking to your trade than by adopting any other course. . . .

he adjusts his hopes and plans to study theology, with the idea of making his life in the Church. He is astonished by Sue's lighthearted dismissal of much of religion and by, for instance, her contempt for the Church's efforts to deny the erotic meanings of the Song of Solomon. He cries out several times that she is a "perfect Voltairian."

In the end what is so poignant is that Sue's brightness and will to freedom cannot save her. She goes down into despair with Jude and, finally, under the strain of life, sinks into a punishing denial of her own principles about marriage and religion. She has not, through ideas and strong personal lean-ings, been able to break out of poverty and defeat and the undermining force of an accumulation of disasters. Life simply will not open itself to her frail, unsupported brightness. In despair she tries to name the mystery of implacable barriers. "There is something exterior to us which says, 'You shan't!' First it said, 'You shan't learn.' Then it said, 'You shan't labour!' Now it says, 'You shan't love!' "

Jude the Obscure is about poverty and the crushing of the spirit that goes along with it like a multiplying tumor. It is also about sex and marriage. Marriage is, as the plot develops, an experience violated by need, by the drastic workings of chance, and by the limitations of choice. It is also seen as an idea, an institution, open to the "higher criticism" in the same manner as religion and scriptural problems. At best it is a thunderclap, the sky lights up, and then a storm of entrapment, manipulation, and bad feeling rains down. Wholeness and freedom are violated and, for Sue at least, these qualities are of the first value. In putting this value upon them she creates a violent uneasiness in what would otherwise have been a more usual plotting of forces and resolutions.

The price of sex is a destruction for every fulfillment, and often a destruction without fulfillment. Love exhausts itself as a spur to action, in any case, and its claim upon the soul is not greater than the claim of pity—even less at times. Part of the peculiar quality of this suffering, tragic novel is that the relationships, worn down as they are by life, have, nevertheless, a kind of loveliness. Perhaps it is the glow spread by Sue's complicated candor and by her patient, analytical effort to understand her feelings and convictions. Only Arabella, limited, greedy, "normal" at least in her lack of the fastidious scrupulosities of Sue—only she is outside a certain grace and sweetness.

Arabella is as much a convention in the history of the novel as Sue is an original. It is the rule of conventions to ask us to accept as given a certain gathering of traits and motives. Arabella represents the classical entrapment by sex: the entrapment of an "innocent" sensual man by a hard, needy, shackling woman. Arabella's coarseness is a mirror of Jude's weakness. Her qualities are a force of a negative kind; their bad effects upon others are far more devastating than any advantages she may reap for herself. Advantage is forever in her mind and in many ways the failure of dishonest sex to bring about anything prosperous is always interesting. The person exploited by dishonest sex is weakened, distracted, and a falling off of personal and worldly fortune is likely to be observed. This is true for both the men and the women and especially striking if both are poor since, in that case, the entrapment has not found its proper object. In Arabella, sexual exploitation is combined with other deceits. Indeed the deceits are inevitable since she has no plan, conviction, or order that could give her relations with men a genuineness. What is absent in Arabella is love. Her compulsions arise from the survival struggle and not from obsessional passion. All of these exigencies are meant to signal that she is "bad" in some intrinsic way.

Arabella begins with the physical charms of youth, a bosomy air of possibility. But this is presented as a fraud. Her tendency is to face life as a desperate improvisation and she will naturally lack the discipline that might protect her small, early capital of beauty. Arabella's driven poverty, the crude urgings of an unenlightened family, the scheming habit of the other poor girls in the village have severely limited her vision. Hardy's presentation of her ignoble struggle scarcely hints at the numbness inside.

And her sullenness: only this has the shape of a deeply personal and meaningful condition of Arabella's feeling. It is a sullenness shrouded in peasant melancholy. The sullenness is her own comment on her deceitfulness and is some always dawning awareness of its futility. Even deceit needs a more nourishing soil than society has allowed Arabella. Her efforts are the traditional ones the novelist will give her: she works as a barmaid and early unsettles Jude with her knowledge of malts and hops. In the course of the novel she will move on to Australia; she will marry for the second time without unmarrying the first. She always ends up without money or help. She has a pitiful child whom she looks upon as one would look upon a mongrel dog loosely and accidentally attached to one's life.

For a poor and lonely young man like Jude, pleasure is not to be taken without cost. He is not hard enough for his encounter with Arabella—that is the way it has been designed. In the same way he is not gifted enough for the life of scholarship and learning his heart is set upon. Jude's longings have falsely come to rest in his dream of Christminster. He is a man who would sacrifice everything for the journey and yet takes the wrong road. Arabella's offering of sex is seen as a menace to learning and ambition and that does not prove to be wrong. There is a heavy consequence, a large bill to be paid for the perfunctory surrender. Latin and Greek are not accommodating. After he has been with Arabella he comes home to the accusing books.

> There lay his book open, just as he had left it, and the capital letters on the title-page regarded him with fixed reproach in the grey starlight, like the unclosed eyes of a dead man.

We are given Jude's collision with Arabella as a weakness, but one of those weaknesses most persons believe make men human, real. Arabella is deeply in tune with the consequential. By asserting cause and effect the weak avenge themselves and, of course, not always upon the strong. They avenge themselves as they must and can. They demand, they imprison. When

Jude thinks of ending his affair with Arabella, she deceives him about pregnancy and they marry, in hopelessness, without any joy or understanding of each other. Jude must sell his books "to buy saucepans."

The misery of this marriage is so great that Hardy has dipped the courtship and early days in the slow, filthy waters of the pig sty. Arabella and Jude undertake to kill a pig they have raised. Jude hears the animal scream and wishes to get it over quickly; but Arabella has a country knowledge of pigs and their killing. She cries out in anger against the idea of a quick passage to death. "You must not! The meat must be well bled and to do that he must die slow. . . . I was brought up to it and I know. Every good butcher keeps un bleeding long. He ought to be up to eight or ten minutes dying, at least." The connection with Jude hastily comes to mind. His life is to be a long-drawn-out suffering and pain. The gentler tones of nature surround the brute factuality of a hard existence only as an accompaniment, an aside. "A robin peered down at the preparations from the nearest tree, and not liking the sinister look of the scene, flew away, though hungry."

"Married is married," Arabella says when the child does not appear in due time. She grows tired of Jude and mercifully moves on, to Australia. It cannot be the end, for there is no end to consequence, connection. "But she's sure to come back—they always do," Jude says. It is hard to tell what has real power over Arabella except the depressed, sullen downhill slide based on flirtations, marriages, alliances made and dropped, hopes grabbed and abandoned, listless enterprises, absence of plans. These liabilities and follies are not in the real sense her own. They are part of the *given* and also of the absences of her life. She is destitute, anxious, brutalized by the blanks in the tradition, the only one she knows, a tradition she has to live out in the lowest, rural, most diminished terms. It is in no way softened as it is in more fortunate women, such as Eustacia Vye, who live also by manipulation and deceit.

Arabella is harshly treated by Hardy because she is so great a part of Jude's paralysis and despondency. In his other novels there is usually a great insistence upon the virtues of the poor folk who are hemmed in by nature and custom. The furze-cutters, the reddlemen, the country mothers are heroic in their simplicity, authenticity, and constancy of feeling. Restlessness—Eustacia Vye, Lucetta, Mrs. Charmond—is inclination to spoil, to appropriate, to introduce a worldliness and standard that corrupt. The waste of talents is condemned by Hardy with a strong class feeling in a doctor like Fitzpiers in *The Woodlanders*, who neglects his work; in an engineer, such as Wildeve in *The Return of the Native*, who out of sloth and distraction ends up running a tavern. There is a repetitiveness in this rural life that Eustacia Vye is overwhelmed by. It is the same repetitiveness Arabella is doomed to, although, in her, it is stripped of its romantic, dark, and arresting aspects.

Arabella is the bad side of the ignorance and pain of the country, just as Tess is the good aspect of rural courage and beauty and naturalness. The thing that finally seeps through the story is that a "sensual" risk like Arabella is really as abstract about life as Sue, as much a creature of skeptical reaction if not of thought. In her relentless trudging after the relief of love affairs, Arabella looks for the hopeless ideal. The numbing disappointments, the raging need for the means of survival, make the ignorant Arabella finally show the same lack of reverence for conformity, for the legalities of things, the same vaulting of the stony fences of convention that are found in Sue's fascination with ideas. Of course there is nothing critical or reforming in Arabella's delinquencies. She is blackness in action, and yet she is as miserable with Jude as he with her. Her tricking

him into marriage, her lies, her abandonment of him on his
deathbed are the deepest betrayals that follow on the first betrayal, their lack of real meaning for each other.

Arabella finds Jude's goodness and yearnings boring; it is her
habit to consider them as a rebuke to herself. Jude's exacerbated
sensitivity, his bouts of drunken frustration, his passion for the
refined and the gentle in life—these can scarcely be offered for
Arabella's realistic approval. Her sense of things is different.
Pigs have to be killed and the robin's dismay is not to the point.
Arabella's flaws are traditional; she is harsh, but comprehensible.
A contrast indeed to Sue Bridehead.

Bridehead: it is curious that Hardy should have chosen this
name for Sue. It is a curiosity and something of an embarrassment because the plot of Sue's life circles around two great
reservations—refusal of sex and grave misgivings about marriage. Is "maiden-head" to be thought of? Is the idea of attaching
"bride" to the name of a young woman genuinely questioning
about marriage meant as a telling incongruity? Yet there is a
sound to the name that does not impugn the high tone of Sue's
discourse or the ambivalences that are the very skin of her being.

Sex and marriage—of the two, marriage is the easiest surrender and Sue thoughtlessly submits to it with the unsuitable Mr.
Phillotson, the schoolmaster. He is confused to learn that the
other submission is not forthcoming. Sue asserts her right to
chastity as one would, without shame, assert any other inclination. Chastity—how embarrassing it is in a love story. And how
odd that it is faced so candidly and childishly rather than as a
distortion and disguise, a great, devouring secret, veiled in sub-
terfuge and duplicity. Sue is very unsettling in the prodigal
openness with which she greets these dark holes of withdrawal.
She tells Jude of the most important experience of her youth, her
meeting with a young undergraduate at Christminster.

He asked me to live with him, and I agreed to by letter. But when I joined him in London I found he meant a different thing from what I meant. He wanted to be my lover, in fact, but I wasn't in love with him; and on my saying I should go away if he didn't agree to my plan, he did so. We shared a sitting-room for fifteen months; and he became a leader-writer for one of the great London dailies; till he was taken ill, and had to go abroad. He said I was breaking his heart by holding out against him so long at such close quarters. . . . I might play that game once too often he said. . . . I hope he died of consumption, and not of me entirely. I went down to Sandbourne to his funeral, and was his only mourner. He left me a little money—because I broke his heart, I suppose. That's how men are—so much better than women!

Jude is distressed and cannot understand her "curious unconsciousness of gender." And yet Sue is all charm and sympathy. Jude and Mr. Phillotson are in no way graceful or inspired enough to be her companions but it would never occur to us that some "better" man would alter the curious course of Sue's character. We might say that the brute reduction of her prospects, the bleaching rural impoverishment, the rootless, unprotected strangeness of her life with Jude are a terrible burden upon her great intelligence and upon her wandering, artless courage. Those calamities do indeed push her to the edge, but there is the *essential* Sue, mixed and misty as it is, that is not in any way circumstantial.

Sue's marriage to Mr. Phillotson is the baldest inconsistency. She has a sort of unworldliness and caprice that allows her to undertake this union. The schoolmaster has none of the stirring pathos of Jude. He has early been overwhelmed by the hypocrisy and deadness of the small educational institutions of his time. He sees the lightness of Sue, her indifference to advantage, and he believes that he might appropriate some of her wayward magic to relieve his own heavy spirits. Sue, as it turns out, feels a profound aversion to Mr. Phillotson. She is aware of it—awareness of feeling is, as Irving Howe says in his brilliant portrait of Sue, part of her *modernity*, her fascination—aware not as an idea, but as an emotion completely personal and pressing. She hides in a dismal closet rather than enter the bedroom. Once, dreaming that he was approaching her, she jumped out of the window.

Is this neurasthenia and hysteria? To look at it in that way is to impose a late abstraction of definition upon a soul, one might almost say a new kind of human being, struggling to take form in history. The personal, the analytical, the passion for self-knowledge that raise *authenticity* above everything, and certainly above duty and submission, come so naturally to Sue that she is almost childlike. Hypocrisy, especially in matters of feeling, is to her a sacrilege. At one point, Jude asks her if she would like to join him in evening prayers and she says, "Oh, no, no! . . . I should feel such a hyprocrite."

After she has been married to Phillotson for eight weeks, Sue tries to voice her feelings. "Perhaps you have seen what it is I want to say—that though I like Mr. Phillotson as a friend, I don't like him—it is a torture to me to live with him as a husband!" She goes on to say in despair that she has been told women can "shake down to it," and yet "that is much like saying that the amputation of a limb is no affliction, since a person gets comfortably accustomed to the use of a wooden leg or arm in the course of time." In addition to aversion, she laments "the sordid contract of marriage and "the dreadful contract to feel in a particular way in a matter whose essence is its voluntariness."

Authenticity, chastity, renunciation. Of course, Sue is not able to live out completely the deep stirrings of her nature. She feels a sympathy for Jude that is a transcendent friendship as profound and rare as love. It is sanctified by their sufferings and by the ever-spreading insecurity of their existence, by the unreality of themselves as a plan of life. In the absence of *surroundings*—they are like itinerants with no articles to offer as they wander in a circle from town to town—in the way their need has no more claim upon society than the perching of birds in the evening, they come to fall more and more under the domination of the mere attempt to describe themselves. They live under the protection of *conversation*, as many love affairs without a fixed meaning, without emotional space to occupy, come to rest in words. Their drama is one of trembling inner feeling and of the work to name the feeling.

Sue does have children—an inauthenticity for her. The children come under the doom of thought, of analysis. They die in the nihilistic suicide *decision* of Little Father Time, the watchful, brooding son of Arabella and Jude. Nothing seems more sadly consequent than that the tragedy should finally come to Sue, after the pain of it, as a challenge to principle, a blinding new condition in her struggle to give shape to her sense of things and of herself. She begins to go to church and gradually moves away from her old self to the decision that her original marriage to Phillotson has a remaining churchly validity and therefore the highest claim on her. She returns to him and also at last submits in every sense. An immolation. In this ending Sue is faithful to her passion for an examined life; for indeed religion is at least an idea for her, not a mere drifting. The necessity for this is pitiful and even if it seems to have a psychological truthfulness as the end of the road for one who has been utterly rejected by destiny, religion and the bed of Phillotson are for her a sort of coma that destroys the life of a living mind. The defeat of Sue is total.

Sad Brazil

Largeness, magnitude, quantity; it is common to speak of Brazil as a "giant," a phenomenon, spectacular, outrageously favored, and yet marked by the sluggishness of the greatly outsized. And if the giant is not quite on his feet, he is nevertheless thought of as rising from the thicket of sleep and the jungle of apathy, coming forth on some dawn to seize the waiting riches of the earth. This signaling, promissory vastness is the curse of the Brazilian imagination. Prophecies are like the rustling of great trees in a distant forest. They tell of a fabulous presence, still invisible, scarcely audible, but surely there as possibility in the vastness.

Remember the opening of *Tess of the D'Urbervilles*. The father with his rickety legs, his empty egg basket, his patched hat brim, is addressed on the road as "Sir John" because it has been discovered that he is indeed a lineal representative of the ancient, noble family of the D'Urbervilles and thus he somehow includes what he cannot lay claim to. Brazil is a lineal descendant of Paradise, a remnant of the great garden of natural surfeit,— a sweet, bountiful place sometime to be blessed. In Brazil the person lives surrounded by a mysterious, ineffable plenitude.

He lives in a grand immensity and partakes of it as one partakes of pure spaciousness, of a magical placement in the scheme of nature. Small he may be, but the immensity is genuine. His own emptiness is close to the bone and yet his world is filled with the precious and semiprecious in prodigious quantity, with unknown glitters and granites, with sleeping minerals—silvery-white, ductile. These confer from their deep and gorgeous burial a special destiny. To say that Brazil is the land of dreams is a truth.

Rio Grande, Mato Grosso, Amazonas. Numbers enhance, although there is a dreamy stupefication about them also. Brazil is larger than the continental United States, excluding Alaska, and slightly larger than the bulk of Europe lying east of France. Its borders flow and curve and scallop to Guiana, Uruguay, Argentina, Paraguay, Bolivia, Peru, Colombia, and Venezuela. Out of this encroaching, bordering, nudging sovereignty, life has a peculiar statistical consolation. Where there is isolation, loneliness, and backwardness, where the tangle of existence chokes with the complexity of blood and region, where torpor, negligence, and an old historical lassitude simply and finally confuse—there even the worst may be thought of as an unredeemed promise, not an implacable lack. Delay, not unalterable deprivation, is the worm in the heart of the rose.

Growth, exploitation, coming forth to meet modern possibility—a necessity, impatient, also maddeningly slow. The military rules partly under the banner of growth-mystical and its battle against the living is often represented in the name of growth-practical. The histrionic jungle, the romantic coffee and sugar plantations, the crazy rubber Babylon at Manaus with its ruins and the marble shards of the opera house, these last representing the old tropical slack, and, of course, misfortune: against the authoritarianism of nature, the police and political oppression takes on a private character of merely human vengeance, feeding upon itself insatiably.

A beggar, bereft, a scabby bundle of ancient Brazilian backwardness, a tatter of the rags, an eruption of the sores of underdevelopment; there he sits against an "old" 1920 wall in São Paulo. Without a doubt, he, shrunken as he is, salutes the punctured skyline, salutes the new buildings that from the air have the usual look of some vibrating necropolis of megalomaniac tombs and memorial shafts—all, like our own, enshrouded in a thick, inhuman vapor, the vapor that sustains the alertness of all the world's cities. Around the somnolent beggar the cars, with their attractive, volatile occupants, whir in a thick, migrating stream. Or come to a halt, the barrier created by themselves in multiplicity. And there it is, in the explosion of automobiles and their infinite signification, magic visible, quantity realized, things delivered.

Yes, all will be filled, all will be new, tall, thrusting, dominating, rapid, exhausting, outsized like the large, stalky watercress, the plump, round tasteless tomatoes grown by the inward, enduring will of the Japanese farmers. Everything new is an emanation, sacred; and the "growth" is the inevitable mocking paradox, the challenge and puzzle and menace of almost every useful scrap of perpetual inventiveness. Brazil, beggars and all, has in movement something quick and almost preternaturally "modern" about it, something dashing and sleek and ironical. That is in movement; at rest and for the misbegotten it is old, lethargic, indifferent and casually destructive. The centuries seem to inhabit each moment; the diamonds at Minas, the slave ships, Dom Pedro in his summer palace at Petrópolis, the liberal tradition, the terrorists, the police, Vargas, Kubitschek, the Jesuits. All exist in a continuous present—a consciousness overcrowded and given to fatigue.

It is as it must be. There is no other way and the sun is very strong. In Brazil the presence of a great, green density, come upon like yet another gift to the over-laden, makes the soul yearn to create a gray, smooth highway. Thus Le Corbusier in 1929 saw Rio, radiant, and said, "I have a strong desire, a bit mad perhaps, to attempt here a human adventure—the desire to set up a duality, to create 'the affirmation of man' against or with 'the presence of nature.'" The affirmation was to be a vast motor freeway and why not, since space turns the inspiration to engineering. The glory of Brazil is glory elsewhere, a vast junk heap of Volkswagens, their horns stuck for eternity. The imagination does not contain enough motor cars for the creative possibility of Brazilian spaciousness; indeed all contemporary manufacture, foolish or brilliantly unexpected, would find its happy and fitting rest here in the very up-to-date, end-of-the-century backwardness.

The new world rises from a hole in the ground where once stood a mustard-colored, decorated stucco with its small garden. Now, buildings, offices, hotels with their anxious dimensions that give, no matter, a kind of happiness to practicality and newness. In the swimming pools beautiful butterflies float in their blue-tiled graves. Birds, hammers, the high hum of traffic: the mellifluousness of the tropics.

The endless, blue shore lines. Life under the Great Southern Cross, Cruzeiro do Sul: under the blazing sky or the hanging humidity a resurrection of steel and concrete, a transfiguration of metals, of dollars and yen. And this year, death to students, to radicals and guerrillas, and a fear, very modern, up-to-date, of the teacher, the writer, the priest, the reporter, the political past. The pastoral, romantic, and romanticized world of Gilberto Freyre, with the masters and slaves in a humid commingling, the stately old prints of the family and servants in brilliant dresses and hairbands walking to the plantation chapel—where is that? The land and its murky history are buried under "methods," and Nordic interrogations, and fresh words for the spirit of the times, "decompression," and electric, motorized, screaming initials (DOPS, Department of Public Order and Safety). Words and "equipment" fill a vacancy, the hole in the heart of the Brazilian government. In the torrid air how cold is the claim of development.

I had been here in 1962 and now, 1974, I returned. Indeed it is impossible to forget the peculiarity and beauty of this rich and hungry country. Paradox is the soul of it. Droughts and floods, fertility and barrenness seem to reside in each individual citizen, creating an instability of spirit that is an allurement and a frustration, a mixture that was formerly sometimes thought of as feminine. It was the time of the installation of the new President, Geisel, under the military rule. Latin America's wars are, for the most part, of the internal kind, the kind beyond armistice. Heavy police work that gives the generals time to run the country. *General*, the word itself appears to be a sort of validation, a kind of Ph.D. without which General Perón and General Pinochet might have appeared to be mere citizens presuming.

Geisel, the new President of this land of color—olive, black, mixed, European, Indian, reddish-brown like dried flowers— turned out to be a lunar curiosity thrown down from some wintry, arctic, celestial disturbance. He is thin and colorless, as ice is colorless. A fantastical ice, solid in the heat of the country. No claim to please, astonish, nothing of the cockatoo or macaw. Dark glasses shield the glacial face, as if wishing to filter the tropical light and darken the glow of the chaos of bereft persons, the insects, slums, French fashions, old ports at Bahia and Recife—the brilliant, irredeemable landscape.

Is there symbolism in the whiteness of the leader? He is not, as we would view it, the will of the people, but Will itself. Will set against underdevelopment, against the sheer obstruction everywhere, and so much of it one's fellow beings.

A small card sent out by the family of a young student killed by the police:

> *Consummatus in brevi, explecit*
> *tempora multa*
>
> Tendo vivido pouco, cumpriu a tarefa de una longa existencia. Profundamente sensibilizada, a familia de JOSE CARLOS NOVAIS DA MATA-MACHADO agradece a solidariedade recebida por ocasian da sua morta.
>
> (Having lived little [1946–1973] he accomplished the task of a long existence.)

The pictorial in Brazil consumes the imagination; leaf and scrub, seaside and treacherous inlands long for their apotheosis as word. Otherwise it is as if a great part of the nation lay silent, unrealized. Your own sense of yourself is threatened here and speculative description seizes the mind. A landscape drenched in philosophical questions finds its masterpiece in the great Brazilian prose epic, *Os sertões*, translated into English by Samuel Putnam as *Rebellion in the Backlands*.

A Brazilian newspaper around the turn of the century noted: "There has appeared in the northern backlands an individual who goes by the name of Antonio Conselheiro, and who exerts a great influence over the minds of the lower orders, making use of his mysterious trappings and ascetic habits to impose upon their ignorance and simplicity. He lets his hair grow long, wears a cotton tunic, and eats sparingly, being almost a mummy in aspect."

The appearance of the deranged evangelist, "a crude gnostic," and his gathering about him a settlement of backlands people

in the town of Canudos in the northeast was the occasion for
military campaigns sent out from Bahia in 1896 and 1897 in
order to subdue the supposed threat of the Conselheiro and his
followers to the new Republic. Euclides da Cunha went on the
campaigns as a journalist and what he returned with and published in 1902 is still unsurpassed in Latin American literature.

Cunha is a talent as grand, spacious, entangled with knowledge, curiosity, and bafflement as the country itself. The ragged,
impenetrable Conselheiro is himself a novel, with his tortured
beginnings as Antonio Maciel, his disastrous marriage, and his
transformation as a wandering anchorite, solitary and violently
ascetic in habit. His distorted Catholicism, his odd prophecies
("In 1898 there will be many hats and few heads"), and prediction of the return of the monarchy "with all his army from
the waves of the sea," attracted ragged followers and he made
his way north to Canudos.

The campaigns against the Conselheiro are the occasion for
the book, the center from which Cunha engages Brazil itself
and the nature of its people. Even to his great mind it is a mystery, a *mestizo* mystery of contradictions of blood, of north and
south, backland and coast, soil, temperament, climate, destiny.

In the campaign Cunha is struck by the unknown country,
his own, by the relentless conundrums of race and space, by the
very nature of the forgotten, lost, unnamed—in the sense of
undescribed, uncontemplated—population of the northeast. The
horsemen and cattlemen have lived in a long isolation from
history, lived amid the destroying natural vicissitudes this part
of the Edenic promise can provide. The people of the northeast are strong and weak, superstitious and crafty, backward and
yet a large, "natural," product of peculiar Brazilian history.

As the author sees it, the backland people are under the misfortune of the country's haunting *mestizo* heritage, a racial mixture of African, Indian, and European, cut off from the "opulent

placidity" of the south. They are "atavistic"—and still Brazil itself. He describes the land and the people with a passionate curiosity that is without condescension. Instead there is an obsessive quality to his exploration of psychological and environmental detail. On every page there is a heat of idea, speculation, dramatic observation that tells of a creative mission undertaken, the identity of the nation, and also the creation of a pure and eloquent prose style. Everything interests him, the scrub, the flora and fauna, the temperatures, the posture of the men, the clothes, the way they sit on a horse, the droughts, well-known and always unprepared for, the separation of types within the backlands and their ways.

When the soldiers from Bahia, themselves of the same *mestizo* stock as the backlanders, set out on their campaigns they have no idea where they are going, except that they are to reach a rebellious settlement in a town by the name of Canudos. They have their equipment and no premonition of the guerrilla warfare that will meet them. They go off in their brilliant, somewhat Napoleonic uniforms to encounter the heat of the day and the dampness at night and the horror of the thick scrub. "In the backlands, even prior to the midsummer season, it is impossible for fully equipped men, laden down with their knapsacks and canteens, to do any marching after ten o'clock in the morning."

In the end it took four campaigns and ten months of fighting before the settlement of fifty-two-hundred houses and all of the people, each one, was destroyed. Cunha sees the campaign as "an act of crime and madness," and worse, as the destruction of "the very core of our nationality." It was "the bedrock of our race, which our troops were attacking here, and dynamite was the means precisely suited. It was at once a recognition and a consecration."

The dramatic, unreal, deranged image of the poor Conselheiro prevails over the final charred scene. His corpse, "clothed in his old blue canvas tunic, his face swollen and hideous, the deep-sunken eyes filled with dirt," was "the sole prize, the only spoils the conflict had to offer." At last the corpse was dug up from its shallow trench, decapitated, and "after that they took it to the seaboard, where it was greeted by multitudes with delirious joy."

Euclides da Cunha was a military engineer by profession and by curiosity and learning also a botanist, a geologist, geographer, a social historian and an inspired, inflamed observer. His mind is a thicket of interests and ideas and if some of them, such as "atavistic traits" as the result of racial mixture, come out of the science of the time, he transcends his own categories by humane, radical, obsessive genius. The extraordinary landscape of northern Brazil, the fantastical environment, and the people of the backlands who live in "unconscious servitude" to nature and isolation seem to appear to him as a demand, an intellectual and emotional challenge he must find his energetic art to give word to and to honor.

His "vaqueiros" and "jagunços" of the north are men of a different breed from the "gauchos" of the south, who live under the "friendly" natural abundance of the pampas. The gaucho "does not know the horrors of the drought and those cruel combats with the dry-parched earth . . . the grievous sight of calcined and absolutely impoverished soil, drained dry by the burning suns of the Equator."

This backland epic with its "philosophy" of environment and biologic predisposition is an unrolling landscape of collective psychology, of Brazilian temperament with its ebb of inertia and flow of primitive guerrilla and politically sanctioned violence and disorderly bravery. The book gives the sense of a summing up, a conclusion of a part of history that nevertheless continues in the unpredictability of Brazil, an astonishing country so peculiar that its inclusion in the phrase "Latin-American" never seems entirely appropriate.

Euclides lived to be only forty-three years old. In 1909 he was shot and killed by an army officer. Putnam's introduction says that the assassination is thought to have come about "as the result of a grim domestic tragedy that rendered the victim's life a tormented one." In that he leads back to Antonio Maciel whose wife ran off with a police officer and in so doing created the wandering Conselheiro of the backlands tragedy. Cunha's appearance also, from contemporary accounts, reminds one of the "crude gnostic" on his travels: "An intimate acquaintance tells us of his disdain for clothes, of his face with its prominent cheekbones, his glance now keen and darting and now far away and absorbed, and his hair which fell down over his forehead, all of which made him look altogether like an aborigine, causing him to appear as a stranger in the city, as one who at each moment was conscious of the attraction of the forest."

At the time of his death, Euclides da Cunha was at work on another book about the backlands. Its title was to be "Paradise Lost."

The magnificent Rio landscape of sea and thick, jutting rocks, which Lévi-Strauss thought of as "stumps left at random in the four corners of a toothless mouth." Like *Os sertões*, *Tristes Tropiques* is a classical journey of discovery, a quest for the past and for the realization of self. It is also in many ways a discovery of Brazil as an idea. Speaking of the towns in the state of Paraná Lévi-Strauss writes:

And then there was that strange element in the evolution of so many towns: the drive to the west which so often leaves the eastern part of the towns in poverty and dereliction. It may be merely the expression of that cosmic rhythm which has possessed mankind from the earliest times and springs from the unconscious realization that to move with the sun is positive, and to move against it is negative; the one stands for order, the other for disorder.

Lévi-Strauss left France in 1934 and went to teach at the university in São Paulo and from there to travel into the interior of Brazil in order to pursue his anthropological studies of various Indian tribes. He was ambitious, abstract, learned, in exile, and violently open, as one may speak of a violence of inspiration and energy coming when the mind and spirit meet the object of dedication. This French mind met not only the Indians of the interior but the obstinate, dazed fact of Brazil. And immediately Lévi-Strauss conveys to us that sense of things standing in an almost amorous stillness. Standing still—or when moving somehow arduously turning in a circle that sets the foreign mind on edge, agitates the thought of possibility, of loss and renewal.

Tristes Tropiques, written fifteen years after Lévi-Strauss left Brazil for the last time, has the tone of a memorial. It is a work of anthropology, grandly speculative and imaginative in the encounter with the Caduveo, the Bororo, the Nambikwara. And the anthropology lives like a kernel in the shell of Brazil. The search for metaphor, the weight of doleful contradiction; these tell you exactly where you are.

In the town of Nalike, on the grassy plateau of the Mato Grosso, Lévi-Strauss studies the body painting, leather and pottery designs of the Caduveo Indians. The style of representation —hierarchical, still, symbolic in the manner of playing cards— is of a striking sophistication and inevitably calls forth a sense of "kinship" with primitive styles far away in time and place. These remarkable chapters, so intense in their contemplative beauty, are aspects of scientific investigation—and beyond that always is the presence of an absorbed, French genius, living out, in a hut next to a witch doctor, his exemplary personal history and intellectual voyage.

> Great indeed is the fascination of this culture, whose dream-life was pictured on the faces and bodies of its queens, as if, in making themselves up, they figured a Golden Age they would never know in reality. And yet as they stand naked before us, it is as much the mysteries of that Golden Age as their own bodies that are unveiled.

The Mysteries of the Golden Age. When Lévi-Strauss traveled to Brazil in 1934 and later, fleeing the Nazi occupation in 1941, he found, one might say, in Brazil his genuine autobiographical moment, found it as if it were an object hidden there, perhaps a rock with its ornate inscriptions and elaborate declamations waiting to be translated into personal style. The book is a deciphering of many things. One of them is a magical and profound answering of the descriptive and explicatory demand Brazil has at certain times made upon complex talents like Lévi-Strauss and Euclides da Cunha.

What is created in *Tristes Tropiques* is a work of science, history, and a rational prose poetry, springing out of the multifariousness of the landscape, its baffling adaption or maladaption to the human beings crowding along the coast or surviving in clusters elsewhere. Lévi-Strauss was only twenty-six when he first went to Brazil. The conditions are brilliantly right. He is in a new world and it is ready to be his, to be named, described. The newness, freshness, the exhilaration of the blank pages are like the map of Brazil waiting to be filled. When the passage grates and jars, it is still *material*. Two French exiles in their decaying, sloppy *fazenda* on the edge of the Caduveo region; a glass of maté; the old European avenues of Rio; the town of Goiania: he speculates, observes, re-creates in a waterfall of beautiful images.

It is the brilliance of his writing at this period that is Lévi-Strauss's deepest preparation for his journey through the Amazon basin and the upland jungles. He is pursuing his professional studies, but he is also creating literature. The pause before the actual writing was begun, when he was forty-seven, is a puzzle; somehow he had to become forty-seven before the demand that was the inspiration of his youth presented itself once more. It was stored away, still clear, shining and immediate. Often he quotes from the notes he made on the first trip and they, perfect and intense, seem to have brought back the mood, and the mode also, and to have carried the parts written later along on the same pure, uncluttered flow.

A luminous moment recorded by pocket-lamp as he sat near the fire with the dirty, diseased, miserable men and women of the Nambikwara tribe. He sees these people, lying naked on the bare earth, trying to still their hostility and fearfulness at the end of the day. They are a people "totally unprovided for" and a wave of sympathy flows through him as he sees them cling together, man and woman, in the only support they have against misery and against their "meditative melancholy." The Nambikwara are suddenly transfigured by a pure, benign light:

> In one and all there may be glimpsed a great sweetness of nature, a profound nonchalance, an animal satisfaction as ingenuous as it is charming, and, beneath all this, something that came to be recognized as one of the most moving and authentic manifestations of human tenderness.

Tristes Tropiques is not a record of a life so much as a record of the moment of self-discovery. At times, in a place "few have set eyes on" and among uncharted images and decimated tribes, he will feel the past stab him with thoughts of the French countryside or the music of Chopin. This is the wound of the journey, the cut of one place against another. But there is nothing of love, of family, of his personal history in France. At the same time the work is soaked in passionate remembrance and it does speak of a kind of love—that is, the love that determines the great projects of a great man's youth. It is the classical journey again, and taken at the happy moment. Every step has its drama; all has meaning and the shimmer of creation; the mornings and evenings, the passage from one place to another are fixed in a memorial light.

And it is no wonder that *Tristes Tropiques* begins: "Travels and travelers are two things I loathe . . ." and ends, "Farewell to savages, then, farewell to journeying!" The mood of the journey had been one of youth and yet, because it is Brazil, the composition is a nostalgic one. At the end there is a great sadness. The tropics are *tristes* in themselves and the traveler is *triste*. "Why did he come to such a place? And to what end? What, in point of fact, *is* an anthropological investigation?"

Lévi-Strauss was in his youth, moving swiftly in his first important exploration; and yet what looms out of the dark savannahs is the knowledge that so much has already been lost. Even among the unrecorded, the irrecoverable and the lost are numbing. The wilderness, the swamps, the little encampments on the borders, the overgrown roads that once led to a mining camp; even this, primitive, still, and static, gives off its air of decline, deterioration, displacement. The traveler seldom gets there on time. The New World is rotting at its birth. In the remotest part, there too, a human bond with the past has been shattered. *Tristes Tropiques* tells of the anguish the breakage may bring to a single heart.

Breakage—you think of it when the plane lets you down into the bitter fantasy called Brasilia. This is the saddest city in the world and the main interest of it lies in its being completely unnecessary. It testifies to the Brazilian wish to live without memory and to the fatigue every citizen of Rio and São Paulo must feel at having always to carry with him those alien Brazilian others: the unknowable, accusing kin of the northeast, the backlands, the *favelas*. If you send across miles and miles the stones and steel, carry most of it by airplane, and build a completely new place to stand naked, blind, and blank for your country, you are speaking of the unbearable burden of the past. Brazilians have more than once moved the capitals that stand for collective history; they shifted from Bahia to Rio and now to Brasilia. This new passage, the crossing, was a stark and at the same time manic gesture. It is a sloughing off, thinning out, abandoning, moving on like some restless settler in the veld seeking himself. At last, in Brasilia there is the void.

It is colder, drearier in 1974 than in 1962. Building, building everywhere so that one feels this prodigal people can produce new structures as simply as the national cuisine. In every direction, on the horizon, in the sky, the buildings stand high, neat, blank; and below cruder housing called "superblocks." Everything leads to a highway and there are, strictly speaking, no streets and thus no town or corner life. A soulless place, a prison, a barracks. *There are no streets*, you remind yourself even as you keep looking for them, as if, as a foreigner, you had misunderstood. At every turn there is a roadway, wide, smooth, filled with cars. Nothing to do with the sad tropics, with the heart of history. Still, this city without memory is the dead center. Everything comes from this clean tomb, a city that only can have been conceived in order to be dramatically photographed from an airplane.

So Brasilia has its space, its contours, its placement and design at a removal; that is, in the sky. Down below in the red dust, in the sunshine, it is yet another mysterious dark entrance. The purpose of the new capital, away from the coastal cities, was to open up the country, to make a whole of this very large "little

Portugal." This city, pure idea, coldly dreamed, a modern folly, seems to represent only itself, another contradiction. It could not perhaps be otherwise, for it is still Brazil about which Cunha wrote, "There is nothing like it, when it comes to the play of antitheses."

The Sense of the Present

Guilt

Do you know a brooding Bulstrode? Guilt, central to classical fiction, was the secret of dramatic natures who found themselves greedy for something and, when seizing it or annihilating obstruction, were nevertheless conscious of their usurpation and its violation of others. This "type"—greedy, impatient, violent and as the saying goes, "filled with guilt"—lives in a condition beyond irony, the attitude that sweetens guilt and alters it to absurdity or, most frequently, rotten luck.

The private and serious drama of guilt is not often a useful one for fiction today and its disappearance, following perhaps the disappearance from life, appears as a natural, almost unnoticed relief, like some of the challenging illnesses wiped out by drugs or vaccines. The figures who look out at us on the evening news—embezzlers, crooks, liars, murderers—are indeed furiously inconvenienced by the trap that has sprung on the free expression of will. It seems unfair, their chagrined countenance indicates, that they should be menaced by arithmetical lapses, by their natural, self-protecting gun shots from the window of the getaway car, by insurance policies cashed with impugning haste, by the follies of accomplices. And how rapidly does the startled glance of the accused shift to the suspicious, outraged grimace of the wronged.

The ruin of one's own life as the result of transgression is punishment, but it is not guilt, not even remorse. What sustains the ego in its unhappy meeting with consequence, the meeting that was so felicitous for drama and fiction? The "popular" response to error, crime, bad faith in which our own actions are involved, is paranoia. Bad luck, betrayal, enemies, the shifting sands of the self-interest of accusers, briberies, lies: these indeed enter the mind with blinding rapidity. The culprit is carrying a thousand mitigations in his pocket, whether his delinquency be legal or merely having to do with offenses in personal relations. When he is being judged, he is judging, and not himself, but the tangle of obstructions oppressing him. He rages about in a crowd of others, saying that he is not alone; individuals and abstract society are whoring about, shooting, thieving, and going scot-free. You can't go to heaven on other people's sins, we used to say. Well, why not?

Character

The literature of paranoia is naturally different from the literature of guilt. A wild state of litigious anxiety slides, as if on ice, into the spot held by the ethical. Free-floating, drifting in his absorption and displacement, the paranoid is not a character at all. Most of all he comes to resemble a person with a cerebral stroke and shows peculiar, one-sided losses, selective blocks and impairments, unpredictable gaps.

Nathalie Sarraute said in a lecture that she could not imagine writing a novel about, for instance, a miser, because there is no such thing as a miser. Human beings with their little bundle of traits and their possession of themselves as a synthesis. Yes, they have vanished because they are not what they seemed to be and least of all to themselves, which confuses and undermines the confidence of the observer.

The coquette, the spendthrift, the seducer, the sensitive were points of being, monarchies of self, ruled over by passions and conditions. How smoothly the traits led those who possessed them, led them trotting along the path of their lives, to the end of cause and effect, to transgressions that did not fade but were still there at the last stop. This was known as plot.

When the young man in *The Mayor of Casterbridge* comes into town and decides in his misery to sell his wife and daughter we *know* what is ahead. He will succeed, he will be mayor, and the wife and daughter will return, borne on the wheels of plot, the engine of destiny, and he will be ruined. As he says, in the midst of gathering consequences, "I am to suffer, I perceive."

For us the family could very well vanish into its fate, which is expressed in the phrase, "making a new life." Still, mayors fall, the past is discovered by the opposition and we have our plots—in the conspiratorial sense. Ruin is another matter. It becomes harder and harder to be ruined; for that one must be a dedicated fool. For the well-placed there are always sympathizers. Through support, flattery, and the wonderful plasticity of self-analysis, paranoia enters the wrongdoer's soul and convinces him of his own innocence as if it had been confirmed by the accounting of St. Peter at the gates of Heaven.

Fiction, taking this in, shrugs, and while a shrug is not as satisfactory as ruin in the aesthetic sense, it will have to do. Aesthetics, Kierkegaard said, "is a courteous and sentimental science, which knows of more expedients than a pawnbroker."

Possibilities

Contrivance is offensive to the contemporary novelist and it bears the further strain of being impossible to make use of without full awareness. Awareness turns contrivance into a self-conscious jest. But without it the novelist is hard put to produce what everyone insists on—a novel. It is easy to imagine that all possibilities are open, that it is only the medium and not life itself that destroys the branches one by one. Caprice, fashion, exhaustion, indulgence: these are what the novelist who has not produced a circular action of motive and resolution is accused of. Meanwhile he looks about, squinting, and he sees the self-parodying mirror and this is his present, now, in its clothes, make-up, with its dialogue, library of books read, his words, his memories of old spy stories, films, baseball scores, murders, revolutionaries, of *Don Quixote* to be rewritten, Snow White, and "all of this happened, more or less."

The newspapers are alive with inexplicable follies. Men, safe in important positions, earning huge salaries, *forget* to file income tax forms. What a block-headed, unrealistic contrivance, *out of character*. We see, particularly in persons high in public and political life, the recurrent, bold dissolutions of the very core of themselves as it has been supposedly observed in endless printed repetitions, in biography, in assertion of principle. The puritan drinks too much it turns out, the Christian is a heathen. Even if a number of opinions and habits have attached themselves like moles to the skin of personality, it is not unnatural that our favorite word for character is *image*—"a reproduction of appearances." Since the image is impalpable, one is not obliged to keep faith either with the details or with the gross accumulation of what one is supposed to be.

Spiro Agnew, an almost forgotten, verbose Vice President, with his long donkey face, his arresting alliterations, his tall, broad-shouldered ease in the pulpit, was, in his reign, old fiction. He might have been Mr. Bounderby. "I was born in a ditch, and my mother ran away from me. Do I excuse her for it? Have I ever excused her for it? Not I." Yet, in collapse, Agnew became an unaccountable post-modernist who ceased suddenly to be a character, his own character, and became a man who roams the world without a memory of alliterative abuse, without a voice, born again in middle age as a baby, alien to the "role" that had brought him to our attention in the first place. So there he is somewhere, freely "mutating" like V.—Veronica, Victoria, Venus, VD, "the incursion of inanimate matter into twentieth century life."

Time

The three-act play is no longer in fashion, having given way to the long one-act, occasionally punctuated by an intermission, an intermission that is a convenience for the audience rather than the signal of a diversion in the flow. Impatience plays its part as one of the powers of our existence and no doubt it has much to do with dramatic structure. The celestial arithmetic of three acts turned out to be authoritarian and oppressive to the shooting-star conceptions. More importantly—a three-act play implied a three-act life.

Curtain lines ending the first act with a question, a riddle leading to unexpected turns in act two, act three resolving and returning in some way the call of act one. In the realistic American theater it was the habit to have, in the end, flashes of "understanding" which arose like a perfume out of the soil of the past. Yes, these characters would say, I discover that I have been a selfish dolt and just where I had been most convinced of my nobility and rectitude. The curtain fell.

In life, in domestic conflicts, in matters of wounded feelings, it is so often those who have been acted against who are required to uphold a pretense of form. (I don't mind what you do to me, but it is so awful for the children.) The pedantry, the conservatism, the intransigence of the hurt and the inconvenienced are scarcely to be separated, we feel, from bitterness and frustrated will. Suspicion of motive afflicts the decent as well as the dishonorable.

Resolutions, recognitions, the strands at last tied in a knot? Whose experience can that be faithful to? In contemporary theater, it is usually the popular and commercial work, manipulating the assumed moral and aesthetic traditionalism of the audience, that insists the gun hanging on the wall in act one must indeed go off before the final curtain falls.

The tyranny of the nineteenth-century three-volume novel leaves its wreckage in Gissing's *New Grub Street*. A chapter entitled "The Author and his Wife": the wife anxiously inquires about a work in progress, where are you? what have you done?

Reardon, the burdened novelist, cries out, "Two short chapters of a story I can't go on with. The three volumes lie before me like an interminable desert. Impossible to get through them. The idea is stupidly artificial, and I haven't a living character in it."

The Novel

Perhaps we cannot demand a "novel." The most practical solution seems to be an acceptance of whatever designation the publisher has put into his catalogue. The object in hand, its length not defining beyond a hundred pages, is not an essay, not a short story, not autobiography since we are told so much of it is "made up" and altered from the truth; it is then a novel of some kind. In the reviews of Renata Adler's *Speedboat*, a work of unusual interest, many critics asked whether they should consider the fiction *truly, really* a novel. The book is, in its parts, fastidiously lucid, neatly and openly composed. Its structure is linear and episodic as opposed to a circular development and while this is more and more the rule in fictional practice, traditional readers sometimes question the nature of what they are reading.

In *Speedboat*, the narrator—a word not entirely apt—is a young woman, a sensibility formed in the 1950s and '60s, a lucky eye gazing out from a center of a complicated privilege, looking about with a coolness that transforms itself into style and also into meaning. Space is biography and conflict finally, and going from one place to another is the thread of experience.

The girl takes flying lessons; she lives in a brownstone in New York among others little connected to her except as voices, scenery; she visits the starving Biafrans as a journalist ("We had been told to bring cans of food, jerry cans of gasoline, and a lot of Scotch"); she examines her generation ("Some of us are gray. We all do situps or something to keep fit"); she teaches at City College and worries about language (" 'Literally,' in every single case, meant figuratively; that is, not literally").

For the girl, the past has not set limits and the future is one of wide, restless, interesting "leaps." Not the leaps of lovers (she has lovers, but this is a chaste book), not leaps of divorces, employment liberations, but a sense of the way experience seizes and lets go, leaving incongruities, gaps that remain alive and are valuable as conversation—conversation, the end result of experience. She writes that, "the camel, I had noticed, was passing, with great difficulty, through the eye of the needle . . . First, the velvety nose, then the rest." And how right she is. If the rich can't get into heaven, who can?

To be *interesting*, each page, each paragraph—that is the burden of fiction composed of random events and happenings in a more or less plotless sequence. *Speedboat* is very clear about the measure of events and anecdotes and indeed it does meet the demand for the interesting in a nervous, rapid, remarkably gifted manner. A precocious alertness to incongruity: this one would have to say is the dominating trait of the character of the narrator, the only *character* in the book. Perception, then, does the work of feeling and is also the main action. It stands there alone, displacing even temperament.

For the reader of *Speedboat*, certain things may be lacking, especially a suggestion of turbulence and of disorder more savage than incongruity can accommodate. But even if feeling is not solicited, randomness itself is a carrier of disturbing emotions. In the end perhaps a flow is more painful than a circle, which at least encloses the self in its resolutions, retributions, and decisions.

American Practicalities

Our novelists, sensing the shape of lives around them that do not conform to the finalities of the novelistic, nevertheless are reluctant to alienate, to leave so much of life morally unaccounted for. Novels that are profoundly about illicit fornication have a way of ending on accidents, illness, or death.

In John Updike's *Rabbit, Run*, the young husband is in a restless mood of flight and infidelity; the wife is confused, sore, exhausted, and not sober. The new baby dies in the bath in a powerful scene very near the end of the novel. This is meant as a judgment on poor Harry and Janice. It says that Harry is not supposed to run around and Janice is not supposed to be sitting, drunk, before the television set in the afternoon. In Joseph Heller's *Something Happened*, the hero pays for his disgruntlement, acrimony, and self-absorption by the death of his damaged son. In Francine Gray's *Lovers and Tyrants*, the heroine has a hysterectomy, in what may be thought of as a rebuke to her promiscuity. In *Speedboat*, the girl, perhaps worried that her autonomy is out of line, like an overdrawn expense account, announces that she is going to bear a child. In this way she chooses the impediments of nature to act as a brake on the rushing, restless ego.

Deaths, accidents, illnesses, and babies are a late resurgence of normality or morality (late in the books, that is.) They seem to say that a distraction in the order of things will not go unpunished. It appears that free as we are, determined upon experience as we are, there is a lingering puritanism somewhere, a mechanical accountability that links transgression with loss and grief.

The resolutions are not always convincing, being as they are an afterthought of moral contrivance. The drowning of the baby in *Rabbit, Run* is the most truly prepared for and has the least hinting of an unnecessary, retroactive moral assertion. The unconvincingness of most resolutions is a measure of the practicality, the businesslike accounting at the end of a spree, the drawing back from observed life. The telegram about your mother's death after you have been in bed with your secretary, the automobile accident as you come home from an infidelity: how far all of this is from the indulgent grip on experience that preceded it. The willingness to accept, or to offer for the public, a bleak vision without palliative intrusions is not in the end congenial to the American writer. Perhaps it is that the author steps aside from the scene he has created in such zestful detail to punish not on his own behalf but on behalf of his audience, whom he judges, somewhat patronizingly, as more vindictive than himself.

Banalities

A strict and accurate ear for banalities provides much of the subject matter in the work of Barthelme, Vonnegut, Philip Roth, Renata Adler, and many others. Blood, sex, and banality, as Malraux recently described the "terrible world in which we are living."

Vonnegut:

Toward the end of maneuvers, Billy was given an emergency furlough home because his father was shot dead by a friend while they were out hunting deer. So it goes.

Speedboat:

The girl was blond, shy, and laconic. After two hours of silence, in that sun, she spoke. "When you have a tan," she said, "what have you got?"

From a California newspaper:

The pastor of the New Life Center Church in Bakersfield and a woman member of his congregation were arrested on suspicion of plotting to murder the pastor's invalid wife.

Banalities are not meant as a narrowing of intention. They are quite the opposite. Banalities connect the author with the world around him. They connect the extreme and the whimsical with the common life, with America, with the decade, with the type. They serve, in a sense, as a form of history.

Boredom

Emma Bovary, struggling along with her last lover, Léon— a man whom even romantic love and adventure cannot sever from the anxious calculations of a bourgeois—finds "in adultery all of the banality of marriage." The most moving instance of such boredom in literature is Vronsky's exhaustion with Anna Karenina's love and with his own. It is not so much that he falls out of love as that the conditions of the great passion are a weariness: isolation, anxiety, idleness, the criticism of society. Boredom with love is as powerful as love itself and, psychologically, much more confusing to the spirit. Anna herself falls into one of the masks of boredom with love, obsessive, random jealousy.

Both of the women, Emma and Anna, try to modernize, to politicize the illicit. Anna and Vronsky live in a corrupt, self-indulgent world that retains its pieties about the details of indulgence. At one point Anna pathetically cries out that in living with Vronsky she is at least being "honest." Emma, a naïve provincial, nevertheless understands that her nature inclines her toward the bohemian, the sophistications of the demimonde. She appears with a cigarette in her mouth and can be seen in town "wearing a masculine-styled, tight-fitting waistcoat." Anna's passion is inseparable from her position in society and Emma's passions soon cannot be severed from her debts. Still, in their different ways, they are "new women," and their husbands represent to them an intolerable boredom they do not see themselves destined to endure. They are to be trapped in a further boredom, but of course that lies ahead.

Sex, without society as its landscape, has never been of much interest to fiction. The limitations of the human body are nowhere more clear than in the fantasies of Sade. Nearly all of his "imaginative tableaux" involving more than two persons are physically impossible. In current American fiction, the novels that are most concerned with sex are becoming more traditional in form and imagination each year, and especially those that attempt solemn scenes of gasping and thrusting, the hopeless pursuit of the descriptive language of sensation, without the comic spirit of, for instance, Henry Miller. The body is indeed a poor vehicle for novelty. In many women writers on the current scene, the union of license and literary conventionality is quite noticeable. More and more they suffer from what Colette called the great defect in male voluptuaries: a passion for statistics.

Conservatives

The enclosed, static, oppressive nature of Soviet society makes it possible for Solzhenitsyn to write books that are formally conservative and yet profound and far-reaching in their significance. His fictions concern nothing less than the soul of Soviet Russia itself. The cancer ward is more than itself; it is the diseased state; the prison, the concentration camps are the setting in which history acts upon imagined characters realistically. The resonance of these great works from the cage is greater than we can produce in the openness and freedom of our lives; and altogether different. Totalitarianism is nothing if not a structure.

In *Mr. Sammler's Planet*, a novel that is very American and yet conservative in both form and matter, Bellow needs the voice of one who has not shared the experience of the American last thirty years, one who has not come under the free-wheeling economic conditions here after the War, who in his own life has felt no strain from the sexual revolution, the draft, divorce, television—anything. He has chosen rightly. Mr. Sammler, over seventy, a European, profoundly formed and sure in character and values, another planet. Mr. Sammler is a suitable instrument of refusal: he says, I will not accommodate the New Left students or the nihilism of New York. I will not find the Negro pickpocket in his camel's hair coat, his Dior dark glasses, his French perfume, *merely interesting.*

A novel like Pynchon's *V.* is unthinkable except as the composition of an American saturated in the 1950s and '60s. It is a work that, in its brilliant decomposition, explodes in a time of seemingly endless expanding capitalism. It comes out of our world of glut, reckless consumption, enviable garbage, and disorienting possibility. Life is not a prison. It is an airplane journey and on this journey the self is always disappearing, changing its name, idly landing and departing, spanning the world in hours. Geography is a character and town names have as much meaning as the names on the passenger lists. The novel does not end. It journeys on in a floating coda: "Draw a line from Malta to Lampedusa. Call it a radius. . . ."

In a recent article on the new fiction, Tony Tanner looks upon much of the work as a game, "games trying to break the games which contemporary culture imposes on us at all levels." Entropy, carnival, randomness—the language of the critics of "post-modernist fiction"—seem to bring the novel too close to a poem, to put it under the anxiety of influence and to find it more subject to refinements and tinkerings of craft than a prose work of some length can actually be.

What is honorable in "so it goes" and in the mournful brilliance of Barthelme's stories (" 'Sylvia, do you think this is a good life?' The table held apples, books, long-playing records. She looked up. 'No.' "), in *Speedboat*, in the conundrums of *V.* is the intelligence that questions the shape of life at every point. It is important to concede the honor, the nerve, the ambition—important even if it is hard to believe anyone in the world could be happier reading *Gravity's Rainbow* than reading *Dead Souls*.

English Visitors in America

Englishman has hard eyes. He is great by the back of his head.
Emerson, *Journals*

O Shenandoah, O Niagara. In a text that bristles like the quills on a pestered porcupine, Peter Conrad, a young English critic of music and literature, fellow of Christ Church, Oxford, has written a book called *Imagining America*. It is easy to read, and yet a torture to unravel. This is not due to the absence of footnotes, bibliography, or to the very reduced index—that is the least of it. The most of it is a great fluency of style, a military confidence, an extraordinary range of intimidation that sweeps over the country, America, and a good many English writers, the two in collision being the subject of the book.

Imagining America follows a number of English persons on their journey here: Mrs. Trollope, Dickens, Anthony Trollope, Oscar Wilde, Rupert Brooke, Kipling, H. G. Wells, Stevenson, Lawrence. In the latter part of the book, Conrad "examines," in the surgical sense, the deformities of the three gifted English authors who chose to remain: Auden, Huxley, and Isherwood.

· · ·

Unusual conjectures, connections that move from the text to interpretation with the speed and force of a bullet in transit, dazzle and brilliance that often exceed the fluency of the authors themselves: these uncommon gifts in alliance with a nervy vehemence of tone make *Imagining America* a daunting addition to "Anglo-American Studies." We, it appears, have much to answer for, and they, especially the English writers in exile, have a great deal more.

The putative thesis of the book is not striking and, since the book is very striking, the thesis is only in part a suitable frame. The brief statement of intention at the beginning and end is rather like a bit of brown-paper wrapping that disguises the volatile materials within.

> Before America could be discovered, it had to be imagined . . . Geographically, America was imagined in advance of its discovery as an arboreal paradise, Europe's dream of verdurous luxury. After that discovery, the political founders were its inventors.

The passage of time from the Victorians to the present does not find the country, America, in a condition more gratifying to the senses and the spirit; instead, the visitors themselves "re-imagine" our obscure or glaring deficiencies into amusements, curiosities, or personal escapes. "Americans tolerate and even abet this contradictory European fantasizing about them. Loyal to the ideal pretensions of their society, they're as much prisoners of their millennial self-image as they are of the prejudicial images Europeans continue to inflict upon them." Thus, the scene opens.

The ending, after the clash of text, person, and Conrad's rhetoric, is a forgiving downfall.

> America is ample and generous enough to tolerate all these impositions on it, and various enough to adapt to all these transforma-

tions of it. The moral of this book, like that of America, lies not
in its unity but in its diversity.

This benign accommodation, so general in its application to history, would scarcely be worth the ticket. The book, freely speculative, does not have a moral, but is nevertheless rich in statements with a moralizing tone. It is not easy to separate tone
and statement, paraphrase and text, opinion and illustration.

"At home [England] you are assigned a surrounding world
by the circumstances of your birth; you don't invent a reality
for yourself but inherit one, and exist in a society which prides
itself on having restricted the range of imaginative choices. A
civilized society, according to Matthew Arnold, is one in which
the center prevails, in which metropolitan standards constrain
the regions, and artists club together in a clique at that center."
As for America, it is "centerless, not a claustrophobic, centripetal
society . . . but a chaos of disparate realities." The English
writers, grinding their heels in the dust of Vermont, New York,
New Mexico, California, and so on, are not experiencing a
place fixed by history and tradition. They are caught instead
in a sort of whirl and flow, which they identify and use as they
will. "Lawrence's New Mexico is not the same as Huxley's, nor
is Huxley's California the same as Isherwood's."

Conrad's America, as he extracts it from his literary texts, is
hospitable to interpretation, exploitation, and finally to therapeutic manipulation, but its spacious indefiniteness is not hospitable to literature, and not to the novel in particular. The
problem of the novel appears in the early pages that announce
Peter Conrad's themes and the direction of his thoughts. The
refractory landscape and the people dwelling in it are not agreeable matter for the *English* novelists in their transformation of
experience and idea concerning America—perhaps, perhaps,
that is what Conrad meant. In any case:

The Victorians assume America to be slovenly and backward, unworthy of the novel's social graces and subtleties of observation. Later writers admit the novel's irrelevance to America, but they suggest alternatives. In Kipling's case, the alternative is epic, in Robert Louis Stevenson's it's chivalric romance. . . . In Wells's case as in Huxley's the alternative is science fiction. . . .

"England *prides* itself on having restricted the range of imaginative choices"*—many impediments to agreement here, intensified by the accent of the self-evident. "Victorians *assume* America to be unworthy of the novel's social graces and subtleties of observation. . . ." Mrs. Trollope and Dickens did not find America of the 1830s and 1840s a commendable accumulation of graces and subtleties, but there is no evidence that they considered the creation of Victorian novels, on the English model, a task for the Republic or that they were mindful of the country's unsuitability for fiction.

Mrs. Trollope's *Domestic Manners* may be said to have squeezed the American lemon very profitably. Her book is a masterpiece of novelistic scenes, dialogues, and dramatic conflict between herself and her subject. She is the only writer in *Imagining America* to have discovered herself here. Mrs. Trollope, with her intrepid talents, her great ambition and need, transformed her chagrin and her frazzled nerves into a classic. She, more than any other of the travelers in Conrad's book, confronted America in a gambler-emigrant frame of mind—that is, in a confused mood of hope and panic. Her failed Emporium in Cincinnati shows that for all her "refined taste," she understood schlock and kitsch and was drawn in her commercial dream toward the outsized. (A premonition of the World's Largest Drugstore in Los Angeles that Aldous Huxley is later scolded for tolerating.) The front of the Emporium, facing Third Street,

---

* All italics in quotations from Conrad are mine.

was "taken in part from the Mosque of St. Athanase, in Egypt," and the front facing south was an Egyptian colonnade formed with columns modeled after those "in the temple of Apollinopolis at Etfou, as exhibited in Denon's *Egypt*." The large rotunda was to be topped by a huge Turkish crescent.*

It is true that Dickens' caricature of America in *Martin Chuzzlewit* testifies to the author's loathing of the country, but it does not testify to Conrad's idea of the Victorian novel's "social graces." Instead, the intrusion of the American theme indicates Dickens' anarchic, daring, inventive practice of the possibilities of Victorian fiction.

Anthony Trollope's *North America*, more studious and less journalistic than the other two Victorian accounts, is annoyed by much, but Trollope does not seem as a traveler to be in pursuit of an extension of his novelistic world. He had a tangled view of literature in America and knew something, if not much, about it. Both of the Trollopes were political conservatives. "I do not like them. I do not like their principles, I do not like their opinions," Mrs. Trollope writes about Americans at the end. She lay these vivacious negatives at the door of Equality.

"Later writers *admit* the novel's irrelevance to America . . ." Here the example is Kipling's *Captains Courageous*, which doesn't admit anything since it is not a document by a literary critic but is instead a "worked up" creative act, which grew out of Kipling's cold, litigious years in New England. Conrad's verbs are an elastic—they stretch in order to confine.

Niagara Falls, a phenomenon, is for Conrad an interesting measure of temperament, English, and tourist obligation, American. His chapter on the great resistant cataract is thoroughly

---

* From the introduction by Donald Smalley to *Domestic Manners of the Americans* (Peter Smith, 1949).

original and diverting, but also, as it swims along, *accusing,* not to the waters, but to some of those who made the trip and, worse, to those who did not.

Dickens rendered Niagara in strenuous prose: "What voices spoke from out the thundering water; what faces, faded from the earth, looked out upon me from its gleaming depths; what Heavenly promise glistened in those angel's tears. . . ." Oscar Wilde, observing the honeymooning couples, said: "The sight of the stupendous waterfall must be one of the first if not the keenest disappointments of American married life." H. G. Wells was more interested in the dynamos of the power company than in the Cave of the Winds. Rupert Brooke wearied of the comparative statistics that established the supremacy of the Falls and wrote that the real interest was not to be found there but in "the feeling of colossal power and of unintelligible disaster caused by the plunge of the vast body of water." But this acceptable sentiment, written in 1913, two years before Brooke died in the war, becomes the occasion for Conrad's own leaping: "The eager self-sacrifice of the waters anticipates the reaction of Brooke and his generation to the war, which excited them not because they wanted to defend a cause but because it promised them heroic self-extinction." *Anticipates, excited, promised*—not only the rushed young Brooke sending back his American dispatches, but his entire generation.

Still at Niagara: "Objects in America aren't determined by history or enmeshed by association like those of Europe." For the Victorians Niagara was a "prodigy of nature," but for later writers "imagining the object comes to mean cancelling it out." On it goes:

This is why the neglect of Niagara by the later writers in this book [Auden, Isherwood, and Huxley] is itself significant, because it is a consequence of the imagination's meditative withdrawal from observation. The later subjects of this book don't even bother to practice imaginative distortion of America's physical reality, for they are simply incurious about it.

No matter that Niagara has suffered a drastic falling of its "ratings" and that the incuriosity of sophisticated travelers and American writers is too widespread for "significant" rebuke. In 1914, Bertrand Russell said, "Niagara gave me no emotion"— said "with priggish philosophical rectitude" in Conrad's disposition of the remark.

In the ordering of the chapter there seems to be some sympathy for the sublimity of the accident of nature which America shares with Canada. Conrad seems to prod the visitors to take leave of themselves and offer an appropriate version or vision. Few are sufficient to it: Sarah Bernhardt wants to harness the Falls to her "capricious egotism." No similar unspoiled challenge occurs again, for any of the writers. A "nightmarish" America, of "nonchalant vacancy" and "savagery" and "moral amateurism" lies ahead.

Extraction of Conrad's thought is outstandingly difficult. Nearly every sentence is a thorn of perplexity. First, there is his *saturation* in the texts, an absorbing so thorough that the texts have little life outside his own mind; they are expropriated. Assertions, declarations, an unbalancing use of the present tense: "America . . . promises death and a rending but salutary resurrection." "Huxley lives in hell . . ." and the "awfulness of America is . . ." It is often Conrad's practice to meet a phrase—his quotations are for the most part brief—and to pass swiftly to revisions, rephrasings, bewildering gifts to the originals of his own intensifications. Dickens, arriving in 1842 in Washington, "the head-quarters of tobacco-tinctured saliva," observed the unnaturalness of the city, its formality, its insufficiency as a living town, the ornamental thoroughfares and buildings without people to walk on them or to inhabit them. He thought few would wish to live there, who were not obliged to do so. This scene becomes in Conrad's revision, "These vacant, haunted places, from which people have fled *in fear and loathing.* . . ."

Conrad on Anthony Trollope:

Trollope's longing for a smallness of scale which guards privacy explains his furious resentment of a remark made in Dubuque, alleging that England has no vegetables. The aspersion infuriates Trollope, and he is prompted to a eulogy of his own abundant kitchen garden. He is enraged because the domesticity of England, for him its dearest quality, has been impugned.

Furious, infuriates, enraged have taken wing from Trollope's exclamation mark. "No vegetables in England! I could not restrain myself altogether, and replied by a confession 'that we "raised" no squash.' . . . No vegetables in England!"

On behalf of the Victorian writers Conrad asserts that they found America to be "the vast death-chamber of English individuality," that the country was indifferent to the civilized separation of public and private life and unable to "validate individual existences." During the thirty years that spanned the visits of Mrs. Trollope, Dickens, and the second visit of Anthony Trollope, roughly 1830–1860, *Walden, Moby Dick,* and *Leaves of Grass* had been published. Lincoln was alive and Poe had lived and died.

The "aesthetes," Oscar Wilde and Rupert Brooke, endure in *Imagining America* the bashing and battering endured by the country itself in the writing of the earlier visitors. Brooke's felicitousness and Wilde's epigrammatic genius are cut down by the power-saw of Conrad's moral disapprobation. The curious and singular slide into the defective. Even with Mrs. Trollope and Dickens, little note is taken of the comic expressiveness, the texture of comic aggression, that give light to their dark detestation and make their records alive today.

Wilde's genius, it appears, is a "pederastic precocity" he shares with his kind. No quarter is given to his lasting turns of phrase on America, such as, "The Atlantic is disappointing, the prairie is blotting paper, the Mormon Tabernacle is a soup kettle, and the vastness of America has a fatal influence on adjectives." Conrad finds that Wilde's "wit not only subverts morality, but subjugates America by diminishing it." When Wilde holds forth on American marriage—"the men marry early, the women marry often"—he is "disestablishing marriage." Why should Wilde on his vaudeville tour be guarding American morality and marriage? And what turn of mind insists that we disallow Wilde's "act"? When he arrives, flamboyantly dressed for his part as a vivid and original self-promoter, he is wearing "a bottle green overcoat of otter fur, with a seal skin cap." For this and other requests for his dress-props, he is denounced by Conrad because the fur coat "symbolizes nature sacrificed to art: seals and otters have been flayed merely to adorn his precious body." The truculent language, the supererogatory *precious*, exceed the provocation of Wilde's fur coat.

In St. Joseph, Missouri, Wilde observed souvenir hunters buying up Jesse James's dust-bin, foot-scraper, and door-knocker, "the reserve price being about the income of an English Bishop." He ends the paragraph from a letter: "The Americans are certainly great hero-worshippers, and always take their heroes from the criminal classes." Conrad interprets this as "by implication" an alignment of Wilde himself with the hero as criminal. The innocent observation in the letter becomes "a self-fulfilling prophecy, for his [Wilde's] subsequent career confirmed his heroism by making him officially a member of the criminal classes." The punitive linking of "homosexual misconduct" and murder is one of many gratuitous asides in this work of literary and social criticism, a work of remarkable self-sufficiency, it might be added, since not a single line of other critics is drawn upon or mentioned and the reader, stopped by the many road-blocks of language and thought, is required to search himself for primary and secondary sources if he should wish to make a few before-and-after comparisons.

Rupert Brooke's mild *Letters from America*, written about his journey in 1913, is thrashed by a belligerent exegesis. Certain "pop" aspects of the American scene strike Brooke as suitable moments for a journalistic expenditure of adjective and meta-phor. Automobiles, huge neon signs blinking in the sky, base-ball and cheerleaders, the old grads lined up for a Harvard commencement. ("I wonder if English nerves could stand it. It seems to bring the passage of time so very presently and viv-idly to mind.") On a summer day, Brooke sees a young man driving through the streets in a handsome, expensive motor car and it seems to him that the car is richer than the young man, an observation still of visual and social interest here today, if not to be so tomorrow.

Brooke imagines he might be a young mechanic, taking the car for repair—a decision somewhat "foreign" we might say, knowing the murky economics in America of automobile owner and income. The young driver has "an almost Swinburnian mane of red hair, blowing back in the wind, catching the lights of the day." In the summer heat, he is wearing only a suit of yellow overalls, "so that his arms and shoulders and neck were bare." He is "rather insolently conscious of power," and if per-haps ordinary in real life, behind the wheel he "seemed like a Greek god, in a fantastically modern, yet not unworthy way emblemed and incarnate, or like the spirit of Henley's 'Song of Speed.'"

Conrad decides from this and other passages that Brooke wanted to "undress America." He thinks the description of the young man in the car "conveys the concentration of excitement: Brooke has to notice separately each uncovered area. A divinity of physical delight. . . ." *Delight, excitement,* seem to put Brooke on the street, to say nothing of back at the hotel composing, always in a state of incessant homoerotic dreaming. Even in an "unexcited" passage on American faces: "Handsome people of both sexes are very common; beautiful, and pretty, ones very rare. . . ." To the dots which end the paragraph Conrad gives the name "yearning dots."

Brooke's cheerleader "addresses the multitude through a megaphone with a 'One! Two! Three!' hurls it aside and, with a wild flinging and swinging of his body and arms, conducts ten thousand voices in the Harvard yell. That over, the game proceeds, and the cheer-leader sits quietly waiting for the next moment of peril or triumph."

"Hedonistic abandon"—a phrase Conrad uses about Brooke—applies to his own "pale fire" speculation about the cheerleader, up yelling one minute, mutely down the next: "Brooke considers this contradiction to be 'wonderfully American' because Americans are both agitated and idle, and switch from one state to the other automatically, dispensing with intermediaries, rejoicing equally in the body's dynamism and its inertia, its paroxysms and (as if post-coitally) its repose."

Kipling and the "epical America." It would seem foolhardy to try to outpace Kipling in spiteful utterance about America and yet "atavistic rabble" and "savagery" give the clue to Conrad's efforts. "Epical" in this chapter appears to mean a warring struggle for survival against "punitive nature," and "the minimal human character" determined by weather and the search for a survival technology. What it may indicate about literature is extremely shadowy, since the word "epic" is not meant to jar the brain with *The Odyssey* or *Paradise Lost* but rather to send it back to pre-literate dialect and the specialized language of fishermen and woodsmen.

Robert Louis Stevenson also weaves in and out of Kipling's anti-novelistic America, but he is woefully weak in the chest, soul-sick in the pursuit of his married lady, and suffering from the refinement of his prose style. For Conrad this "chivalric quester" posing in the derelict Silverado mine is just that, a poseur, but then, "so is America, since it is a vacuity onto which each emigrant projects his own fantasy."

Ideas, many in a state of alarming freshness. As you go through Conrad's densely written pages, it is a little like wandering about an arboretum with plaques giving the name and the place of origin of the trees and shrubs. Brought here from China, brought here from India. The English writers have all been elsewhere and have many things, other than America, to think about. Most of them were productive without intermission. In *Imagining America*, it is not precisely the authors, and certainly not the complexity of their *oeuvre*, not even America that are being labeled—no, not exactly. But still they are transplants, for a long or a short time, and onto the tree that is themselves there is a showy grafting of the branches of Conrad's ideas, an ingenious hybridization.

The obsessive, incomparable reflections of D. H. Lawrence on America seem with their jerky, private originality to be beyond paraphrase, all gleaming intuition. Yet when Lawrence uses capital letters in *Studies in America* (THOU SHALT NOT) Conrad is alerted to the grating meeting of mind and country. So, "In corrupting his own language Lawrence was supplying America with a style appropriate to its overbearing crassness."

When we come at last to Huxley, Isherwood, and Auden, the English writers who remained in America, Conrad's language rises with a deplorable heat. The scorching is painful indeed and the critic, like an immigration officer catching aliens whose visas have expired, becomes, in Auden's phrase, "a summary tribunal which in perpetual session sits."

It is as if these extraordinary talents had arrived empty of learning, experience, temperament and were blank pages waiting to be scrawled upon by New York tenements, the sun, American boys, drugs, drive-ins, "hymns and movies and Irving Berlin." Huxley and Isherwood landed as unthinking guided missiles, driven by an awful, deserved destiny, in California. (Suffer any wrong that can be done you rather than come down there.) These three Englishmen are not only to be grounded in America, but each is to be defined by the particularity of New York or California. Places have almost a genetic fatality. They guide the helpless writer as if he and the city were identical twins, separated at birth, but doomed to be hit at last with twin cancers and uniformly faltering heart beats. For Auden, the "numbered grids" of New York's streets "encouraged his punctilious ritualism," his attraction to regular meter and a liking for crossword puzzles.

Perhaps no country can deserve the grace that fell upon California with Huxley, Stravinsky, Schoenberg, and Thomas Mann; or the beneficence to the East Coast of Auden, Hannah Arendt, Nabokov, and I. A. Richards. But the subject matter, the landscape, the magical rendering of American follies and symbolic meanings do not make Nabokov's American novels "American." The strength, the majesty of the creation of self, style, idiosyncrasy—the very claim of art and their individual practice of it the exiles brought with them to America. They are not, like the prairies, blotting paper to soak up the inchoate ink stains of Los Angeles and New York.

Aldous Huxley appears from his letters, his books, his exhausting curiosity, his roots in his family, his large and unexpected learning to be a genuine and valuable person of great innocence and gullibility. Above all, he strikes one as incorruptible. Part of the incorruptibility lies in his removal from class snobbery, and in the austerity of his personal life and habit. Asceticism in him unites with a peculiar experimentalism that had in it an eager supply of hopefulness; the hopefulness of the Bates Method as a way of alleviating his tragic near-blindness, or the hope of a relief from "intolerable self-hood" by way of mescaline.

The mechanistic direction of Huxley's urge to transcendence is characteristic. He seems to have been overwhelmed by the mystery of brain, body, and temperament, and he inevitably saw in Sheldon's classification of body types a clue to the individual struggling with his obdurate self under the doom of height and distribution of weight.

When he first sits down to take mescaline, in the company of his English friend, Dr. Humphrey Osmond, he has a tape recorder beside him, *to see what it does*. His early (1954) and dismaying eulogy of mind-altering drugs, *The Doors of Perception*, is a sad book, telling of happy, rather orderly visions. It is completely out of touch with drug culture and the uses to which his friendly Mind at Large might be put. For himself, in the course of ten years, his "sessions" are estimated to be about a dozen. In the last three years of his life he went through, without complaint, a medically sensible struggle with cancer.

Huxley is one of the oddest figures in English literature: brilliant, credulous, something of a wizard. He is not Californian. Both of his wives were European and his true friends were Englishmen like Dr. Osmond and—how to name his opaque qualities—Gerald Heard. Huxley's world is the library, that first of all, and a sort of libertarian hope for the laboratory. Huxley's curiosity was general rather than intimate and as a wanderer he was tolerant of the vulgar and outrageous, of the drugstore, the drive-in marriage bureau, the most hideous cemetery, and always, it appears, abstracted, not measuring his worth or even his convenience.

Conrad is rancorous on Huxley, clobbering him for abiding some time in a rented house with a naked-lady lamp and a full-size Fay Wray in the paws of King Kong; berating him for stoicism when a fire burned down another house containing his library and files; degrading his concern for overpopulation, treating him as a fool, the object of a ludicrous condescension.

"Drugged" appears as a Conrad adjective again and again. "Huxley *prefers* his chemical heaven to the drab world." The last line in the chapter on this unusual man is: "At last, without noticing it, Huxley became a drugged subject of his brave new world."

Christopher Isherwood is "blithely self-indulgent and self-forgetful, and therefore suits hedonistic California, which licenses Isherwood's peculiar manner of self-deprecating narcissism." That these qualities, even if they were an accurate description, would need a state, a climate to "license" them simply cannot be thought about with any reasonableness. Isherwood is said to have only one subject, himself, and then is told that "he doesn't know himself." This arises as a way of discrediting Isherwood's artistic good fortune in discovering the rightness for him of first-person narration, the rightness of *Goodbye to Berlin, Mr. Norris,* and *Prater Violet,* works of art able to stand with the best of the last forty years. It appears to Conrad that Isherwood may write novels but he is not a novelist because his own "nonentity obliges him to write novels about a character who is not a character." Many curious prunings of the tree of art are suggested by Conrad, and Huxley, in a California slump, is rebuked for admiration of Joyce and Lawrence,

Boulez and Pollock. Isherwood, in his narrations, has "cancelled himself out" by "treating himself as discourteously and dismissively as if he were someone else."

In *A Single Man*, the central character dies at the end, a very common plot device that has more convenience in fiction than in life. The "blacking out" of George is extraordinarily well done, although there is some worry about point of view in a death that is not seen from the bedside but from the dying heart and fading brain itself. To Conrad this fictional death draws its meaning from geography, not from nature. It signifies that "the choice of America is not the choice of life, but the choice of self-extinction."

Sometimes in this critical work, the intimacy of rejection is so warm that we feel that the author must have had private viewings of the persons. Isherwood, present tense, sometimes "looks tired, lined, and shriveled, like an ancient monk, but when he laughs he regains the face of an adolescent, with a shy smile and sparkling eyes." The agreeable concession of smile and eyes is not, however, entirely a compliment since Isherwood is thought to be impossibly working against time and trapped in the belief that "youthful form is recoverable."

No scruple deters Peter Conrad in the swift execution of W. H. Auden. He slices on, in his practiced, glinting way, gathering authority where he finds it, in yesterday's garbage pail, in policemanlike sifting of texts, in the scene of the crime, New York City, in bad associates, cash in the drawers. Poems are evidence and he investigates them in the sense that a handwriting expert investigates a ransom note. The question throughout *Imagining America* is nearly always the question of evidence, the challenging circumstantial kind, inessential, but rich with adversary hintings. The book is about writers but no sentiment clings to the fact of accomplishment. Irascibility, Conrad's, lies on the pages like some hidden code, impossible to decipher. How far will he go? Ah, don't ask, as we say.

Thus: "The United States offers a sleek affluent new life: Auden and Isherwood in 1938 were ravished by the luxury of New York, dizzied by their own celebrity, teased by the availability of athletic sexual partners, and sustained in a state of euphoria by daily doses of Benzedrine and Seconal; no wonder they hastened back in 1939 for more of the same." Auden, on the one hand, is a "shrewd businessman" out for "top fees," and, on the other, a miserable, rootless derelict. The drastic inflation of the riches to be gained from writing poetry, reviews, from giving readings and lectures was shared perhaps by Auden himself and is a testament to the outstanding modesty of his commercial ambitions.

One of the American texts by Auden, examined by Conrad in a sweeping interpretation suggested perhaps by the theme, is *Paul Bunyan*. This is an unimportant, throw-away libretto for music by Benjamin Britten, written in 1940, soon after Auden's arrival in America. The text was never reprinted by Auden and exists now in a 1975 publication by Faber, offered when the work had its second performance in England that year. This jazzy working of a folk legend is propitious for Conrad because Paul Bunyan cuts down trees, clears the forests of the West to make way for towns and settlements. Moral judgments of the most extreme kind can fall on Auden who is, as if in some kind of retribution, flattened under Bunyan's murdered trees.

> Let the architect with his sober plan
> Build a residence for the average
> man;
> And garden birds bat not an eye
> When locomotives whistle by . . .

Conrad: "Milton's justification of the fall is a metaphysical leap of faith. . . . Auden's justification is more complacently economic. The fall is fortunate not because it immortalizes the soul but because it enriches the body."

When Auden says, in his celebrated phrase, that poetry makes nothing happen, we are advised to see this as an admission that "poetry is artificial, formulaic, inconsequential." In *New Year Letter* the circumstantial evidence of the setting is looked upon as impugning. The poet is on Long Island, at the house of a friend who is in exile from Poland; they are listening to Buxtehude. Conrad's interpretation would have it that Auden and his friends are no longer citizens, being exiles, and are outside the moral conditions imposed by nationality and roots. "Having ceased to be subjects of political authority, they now constitute a voluntary group convened in and by art." But in what sense are they not subject to authority, if only the authority of the Long Island police force?

"Lay your sleeping head, my love, human on my faithless arm," a beautiful poem in the classical English lyric mode, is intolerably chastised in a governessy aside of great foolishness. Conrad writes: "Personal ties in America remain breezily casual, never becoming familial as they do in England, where everyone seems to be related if not by birth then by the homogenizing institutions of school, college club, or adultery." *Or adultery*, a happy afterthought for sequestered England, represented in Conrad's comparative clauses as a smug little group of atoms, homogenized and pasteurized like milk in a bottle.

Auden's house in Kirchstetten, Austria ("Thanksgiving for a Habitat"), by dividing up its space for work, guests, cooking, etc., becomes far from home but another New York, "not a public place but a catacomb of separate privacies . . . an arbitrary selection from a global crowd of displaced persons." This "compartmentalization of his territory," Conrad imagines to derive from the philosophical reflections of Hannah Arendt who had "decamped [*sic*] from Germany during Hitler's persecution of the Jews." By way of *The Human Condition*, which contains a chapter on public and private space, Hannah Arendt is somehow felt to be in connection with Auden's New York and its "grid" and with the arrangement of the house in Austria because of its allocation of space for various uses.

This is a travesty of Hannah Arendt's thought. If there is any value in her analysis of alienation, it is the value of an analysis of modern life and modern man, and would be as true of Conrad himself in England as of Auden in New York and Austria.

About the person, Auden, Conrad sinks into a galling hysteria, abusive and in repetition somehow savoring of its own adjectival inventiveness. Auden's New York apartment was "a cave of defilement." This rootless, friendless caricature delighted in "domestic ordure" and "the squalor of the nursery." He is "pickled and prematurely aged" and "looked forward to senility and did his best to advance it, behaving like an ungovernable, finicky baby, organizing his regime around regular mealtimes and early nights . . ."

Auden's eccentricities were harmless and he had the good fortune to be predictable, which relieved his conduct of unexpected rushes of paranoia, violence, and pettiness. If he knocked off from a dinner party at nine, his example was not of sufficient tyranny to drag anyone else along with him. His mind, his loneliness, his ability to love, his uncompetitive sweetness of character survived his ragged bedroom slippers and egg-spotted tie. And his genius, the high seriousness of his life, survived his death. He died of a sudden heart attack in a hotel in Vienna, dispatched in Conrad's requiem ending of his chapter with "callous, merciful American efficiency." Why callous, why merciful, why American?

In a memorial volume, edited by Stephen Spender, one of

About the Author

ELIZABETH HARDWICK is the author of two previous collections of literary essays, *A View of My Own* and *Seduction and Betrayal* (Nominated for the National Book Awards). Her novels are *The Ghostly Lover, The Simple Truth* and *Sleepless Nights* (Nominated for the National Book Critics Circle Award). She has received, among other honors, the George Jean Nathan Award for dramatic criticism, and is a member of the American Academy and Institute. A professor at the Columbia Graduate School of the Arts, she lives in New York City.